RIDING JAMES
KIRKWOOD'S PONY

WILLIAM RUSSO

To order additional copies of this book, contact:
Xlibris Corporation
1-888-795-4274
www.Xlibris.com
Orders@Xlibris.com
39715

CONTENTS

ACKNOWLEDGEMENTS

Let me thank Jan Merlin, a Renaissance Man of the first rank, Emmy winner for writing as well as stage and screen star. No one has been a better friend, mentor, collaborator, and editor over the years. I have come to rely upon him and treasure him every day.

Many others have helped me with this work, especially Robert Wagner, Jack Hannibal, and James Leo Herlihy, who shared their cherished memories of Jim with me. Several interviews with Kirkwood biographer Sean Egan confirmed much of my information.

Let me send my appreciation to my colleagues at Curry College who have been so supportive of my writing and helped me in many small but essential ways: Professors Nick Krach, Gabrielle Regney, Phil Lamb, John Riccio, Gail Shank, Judy Kennedy, Linda Jarvis-Randall, Roberta Kosberg, and Paula Cabral. The students in my classes in 'American Classics' and 'Film and Novel' during 2006 were helpful sounding boards for the literature and film of *There Must Be a Pony*. I appreciate the sabbatical granted to me by Curry College, which gave me time enough to realize this work.

My research 'assistants' all contributed a piece to this book: Barbara Merlin, Joshua Janson, Benjamin Maguire, Priscilla Pope, Frank Stemen, Jose Diaz, William Cate, and Nancy Kelly.

Without the valuable contributions of the Howard Gottlieb Special Collection at Boston University, this book would not be possible. I also need to send appreciation to the Margaret Herrick Library of the Academy of Motion Picture Arts in Beverly Hills for their remarkable collection of movie history. The availability of newspaper accounts from decades past has been made possible by online services like NewspaperArchive.com, and that gave me a breadth of original tabloid accounts of Jimmy Kirkwood's nightmare in 1936. Photographs are courtesy of Wire Service, the author's collection, from James Kirkwood.

Most of all, thanks for your love and friendship to Jim . . . .

PREFACE

—From Ben's suicide note in *There Must Be a Pony.*

"You always liked to hear stories so I'll tell you one more. Shall I start out once-upon-a-time? Yes. Because you represent all the once-upon-a-times I might have had.

"Sooo, once upon a time a psychiatrist had twin sons age eight. One was an incurable pessimist—the other was an incurable optimist. Their father became alarmed and decided to try an experiment. Christmas Eve, he filled the pessimist's room with everything a boy could wish for; and he filled the optimist's room with horse manure. Early the next morning he went to observe their reactions.

"The pessimist sat among the toys, books, clothes, sporting goods—just sat there—eyeing the presents suspiciously, trying to figure out what the catch was. His father sighed and walked toward the other boy's room.

"When he peeked in the door he saw him standing waist high in the middle of all the manure, shoveling it up in the air over his shoulder and laughing—as you would say, Cosmo—like a fiend! "Son," the father said, "what's the matter with you? What are you so happy about?" The boy turned, still laughing, and replied, "Gee, Dad, I figure with all this horse shit—there must be a pony!"

"So, Josh, don't do as I did—do as I say. Hunt for the pony I couldn't quite locate. And even if you never find him—you'll live Life looking. It's more fun that way."

Pictured here are bottom to top: Mrs. Victoria Russell; Lila Lee; Jimmy Kirkwood; Ruth Morris; Gouverneur Morris. In 1936 newspapers made them the central cast in a sordid death story about a young man who made their friendship. James Kirkwood later turned the story into a novel, a play, a radio drama, a short story, a staged reading, and at last a television movie. "My work is my life," said Jim of his memories as The Body Finder.

CHAPTER ONE

PONY BOY

"I think the best way to win friends and influence people is to find a dead body in your back yard!"

So concluded Josh, the fictitious narrator of *There Must Be a Pony*. The words came from James Kirkwood who, like his counterpart Josh, just happened upon a dead body in his back yard and, inevitably, it changed his life.

Jim Kirkwood once mused, "This all reminds me of my initial reaction to the statement, 'The Show Must Go On' . . . Why?"

Box office traditionally requires there be no way to cancel, to abort, or to subvert the inevitable performance. If you wish to sell books, if you want to reach wide audiences, and if you have a public with expectation, you need to be as flamboyant as a movie star, as dynamic as a seasoned stage performer, as shrewd as the best copy writer of sound bytes. Most writers fail to accomplish this on a Book Tour.

Jimmy amazed me; he was all of these components, and more. He knew how to handle people, how to carry himself, and at first I thought he snapped it on and off as if using a switch, but I was to learn he never acted the role of James Kirkwood. He presented exactly who he was. "My bag is so full of human frailties, how can I be objective? Not that I feel mauled by life—but is has certainly had its fingers on me . . ."

The Book Tour was a full day's work, multiplied by a month, stretching for twenty hours, without break; the Boston itinerary started at 9am, shortly after he flew into town. Every city had its morning talk/news program, and he was scheduled to hit one within minutes of arriving. He'd meet the press, too, in a series of quick interviews, culminating with the big one—lunch with the *Boston Globe's* top drama critic. He'd catch a few winks of sleep before having supper with me, and together we'd carry on the rest of the publicity stops in Boston. I had a list of destinations. During our drive I'd have him all to myself. Midnight talk radio was followed by an early, early morning talk show on television. Hours later he'd fly off to the University of Virginia. "Oh, I can get by for a day or so on two hours of sleep, which I will do before we go out to dinner."

Arriving at the Copley Plaza, I rang up Jim's room, and he was perky, telling me to come right up. At the door to 327 I rapped twice and prepared to compose myself to look nonchalant. Before I put on a placid expression, the door was yanked open. Immediately I was sucked into the James Kirkwood vortex. He was as high-powered as his most manic character. Dressed in a short, rose-colored robe of silk, Kirkwood was tanned (all that Key West sunshine), trim and fit, with close-cropped facial hair. He looked like a man of forty; it would be seven more years before I learned his real age.

"Oh, I am too early for you," I apologized.

"No, no, I'm running late. I was just about to take a shower. But let me call Room Service first. We need a drink." He was in rare form that night, and he teased me relentlessly about my selection of "a sissy drink." I had blurted out, "How about a Sombrero?" Aghast, he made a face as I described its ingredients. Relating the drink to room service, he commiserated, "No, I never had one either." He headed for the bathroom, chattering about the rejuvenation the shower would provide.

He was more than unique, I thought, contemplating this ebullient man who was to be approached in East Hampton a few years later by one of my students who declared enthusiastically, "I had Dr. Russo!" To which Jim blandly answered, "Yeah, so did I."

I asked if he had booked his planned trip to Europe.

"I'm going to Venice next week, nyaaah," and he stuck out his tongue before closing the bathroom door. He decided to vacation there for a few days and earned his passage back to the States by lecturing on the cruise ship to New York. Jim was never one to spend money gratuitously, despite having the biggest hit on Broadway with its weekly residuals in four figures.

For me the spell came years earlier when I first read *Good Times/Bad Times*. Little did I know when the work became one of my favorite novels that I'd soon fall into the orbit of its author. A freelance writer, I interviewed him—and we hit it off. When I chose to teach his works in my literature courses, I always used his stories. They were highlights of my courses for years.

During conversations he told me how much he disliked going on book tours alone. One involved twenty-six cities, and he apparently went alone. It puzzled me that there was no assistant or friend to go with him. I always thought he wanted me to offer to go along as his amanuensis, though my responsibilities as a college professor conflicted with his tours. If only they had been in summer, or if only I had a sabbatical . . . now, after decades, I kick myself for not dropping those responsibilities to attend to his needs and travel with him. Today, to jump at a thirteen-city book tour with the author of *A Chorus Line* seems a Disney adventure. Years ago my stodgy sense of duty would not allow me the liberty. However, during his 1981 tour for *Hit Me with a Rainbow,* I took a break, and wanting to help, I offered my service. He readily accepted. If nothing else, I wanted to see why he could not find a travel companion for these tours.

During the most active part of his literary career, James Kirkwood displayed a gallery-pleasing bravado. Just as an actor in performance might savor each line to be delivered, Kirkwood never meant to write a boring passage. "I mean, about the only thing I haven't done yet is kill someone. And every now and then I get the feeling."

James Kirkwood turned his novels into "shimmering nightclub performances in prose," as had been attributed to the writer whose literary voice most influenced him, J.D. Salinger. The authorial voice in Salinger's *Franny and Zooey* calls his writing a "prose home movie." All Kirkwood's work came from his personal experiences, outrageous and glamorous, the vivid recollections of the son of silent movie stars. His impetus came from visceral experiences of finding dead bodies everywhere. There were at least five that he openly discussed with me—or anyone who'd listen: involving three suicides and a couple of heart attacks. It was a fluid bunch, more or less, different people in each telling, dying in different manners. After a while I began to think a few of these souls were murder victims.

Jim may have pandered to the adolescent whims he depicted, works geared to the young at heart. All his narrators remained young men, if not teenage boys. Without Salinger, there could likely be no James Kirkwood. After all, *Catcher in the Rye* made its appearance at the height of the Cold War in 1951—and all Salinger's major work was completed during that decade, all done before Kirkwood embarked on his series of novels. Jim's first novel, *There Must Be a Pony,* came out in 1960. Voices in print of Salinger and Kirkwood are eerie echoes of one another. Neither man completed a college degree, and each treated writing as a true vocation in which they worked tirelessly. They were never part of the established circle of serious writers in American literature, but rather cult figures.

Kirkwood's background proved him one of the first to be obsessively controlling in his biographical and public persona. Jumping feet first into the era of the book tour, partaking in a media blitz, and attuned to the publishing market, Jim didn't need some publicity hack scrambling to make his writing career flourish. He automatically did what was necessary to keep his name and his novels before the public and in the minds of Hollywood producers.

Jim was part of a comedy team (listed on his author profiles as Kirkwood and Goodman) and performed at the trendiest clubs of the 1940s and 1950s in New York and Los Angeles. Being the son of movie stars, he gained easy entry into show business and acted on stage, in films, and for television. He thought his life was a series of incidents in which he put on "a happy face when each foot of the 21 feet of my intestines is tying itself into a separate knot worthy of an Eagle Scout." He once lamented to me, "I've never been anyone's good luck charm."

Adept at handling publicity tours, he neutralized the media by playing to the most sensational aspects. He learned press control by watching his celebrity parents fend off the early forerunners of the *paparazzi* in Hollywood and received his own baptismal by doing 300 television shows. A guest on PBS talk shows, like Dick Cavett's classic talkfest, he also hosted his own series on Mutual Broadcast Radio. He spoke often and regularly at college, where he answered every question, especially the most private, with deft sharpness and humor. He was coy and charming, an elixir to audiences. I knew the surge of energy that came from his powerful catnip personality.

If traumatic adolescent experiences are the stuff of contemporary American film and literature, Kirkwood epitomized the psychological damage. Jim claimed to have attended at various times between twelve and eighteen different schools in Los Angeles, New England, and Middle America. His mother's flighty travails threaded him through private schools, public schools, Catholic schools, and military academies.

His stories and characters have a kinship to Hollywood and vaudeville; the Kirkwood tales create a world populated with show people. Often main characters wind up institutionalized. In the early Salinger stories. Jimmy saw the parallels to his own life when *The Catcher in the Rye* debuted. "Omigod, I thought. If I ever wrote, I'd sound just like that. Holden's voice struck me right off as a variation of my own." A meeting with Jim Kirkwood resembled an opportunity to meet the adult Holden Caulfield.

After he went into the bathroom, I resisted an irrational temptation to go through the pockets of his pants or to rifle his wallet for clues about the man. Serious literary critics dismissed him, and though no other contemporary writer succeeded in as many genre, Kirkwood was perceived as a pop writer making a good deal of money by being off-the-wall. How did he find time for all his creative projects—and still appear to be a photo-op *People Magazine* Glitterati? Booze and drugs burned out so many writers in similar social stratum. Evidently Kirkwood nurtured strong virtues, like self-discipline and dedication, beneath the surface.

He came to Boston on a long-ago promotional tour for his latest work, published by Delacourt, called *Hit Me with a Rainbow*. As Kirkwood described it to me, "It's the first time I've done a love story, sort of an adventure-love story. It's about a young man's first affair and an older woman's last affair. And they have it together under certain stressful circumstances because they are pursued by her insane ex-lover who has Mafia connections."

Typical of the author, his work dealt with couples kept apart by death, insanity, and the Cosmic Joker (appearing in this work under the pseudonym of the Booking Agent). "And the woman in *Rainbow* is an actress who is a combination of Ava Gardner and Lauren Bacall, one of those very mellow ladies who've been around for a long time, who knows exactly what she wants and exactly how to get it. And there's some humor in the novel. I won't divulge any more because that kind of ruins it for the reader."

Inspiration for *Rainbow* came years earlier when Kirkwood had met the provocative movie star, Ava Gardner. Referring to his encounter as a "flirtation," Jim related to me how he and Gardner seemed to feel some chemical attraction, as evident through their mutual eye contact. His latest book was a work he contemplated since he first started writing.

The hot shower calmed him down, and he donned blue jeans and blue shirt, making a casual request. "It will probably bore you, but I need you to cue me on some lines." He put on his stockings and spoke of the lecture the next day. I couldn't understand how he didn't know the text already, but perhaps he just needed a refresher. "I'd like to go over several speeches from *A Chorus Line*," which explained why the script was casually opened on the bed.

Perching comfortably one of the twin beds, he took a pen to the script. "I told Michael Bennett to change this," and in his scrawling penmanship altered a line where the character of Bobby spoke about setting "his brother's toys" on fire to simply setting "his brother" on fire. "This is funnier, don't you think?" Kirkwood marked off the scene.

Kirkwood's lectures at colleges lasted about ninety minutes, although once, when he was particularly wound up, he spoke for three hours. He usually read from each of his major works and reviews, with some humor, referred to his deranged childhood. When we finished rehearsing the vignettes, I asked him why he selected these two. "Oh, one's light; the other's heavy."

He insisted strongly that the writing of his Pulitzer Prize winning musical drama was not a rehash of tapes of interviews with dancers, a common myth supported to this day by non-original cast members of *A Chorus Line* road shows whenever contacted by local papers. Jim was peeved by the endless repetition of this contention. "I didn't listen to any tapes. I wrote the book with Nick Dante." He added, "That was a lovely collaboration. We got on very well. Many, many times when you work with a bunch of collaborators, it's like Vietnam. It can be a real Tong War. But, I think because we'd all been performers we felt such an empathy for chorus dancers competing for a job—and because we all had been up on that line auditioning ourselves, we felt close to it. So, we invested a lot of our own lives and past experiences in that show."

Trying to make a reservation at a Beacon Hill restaurant was a major frustration, as we sat in his suite at Boston's Copley Plaza. The phone line at the bistro was constantly busy. Jim became so agitated that he threatened, "I'm tempted to call the Fire Department and report the kitchen's on fire."

Once at the restaurant, as we waited for dinner to be served, Jim's hyper-drive was evident as he toyed with the place setting. He had a perpetual kinetic energy. At the time we were dining, he had just finished a screenplay, *Witch Story,* another effort that never was produced on film. His time was in general focus lately too on a new major musical murder mystery he was writing, titled *Murder at the Vanities.* It was to feature Phyllis Diller among others, and he labored on it for a long time—to no avail. Not even the writer of *A Chorus Line* could find backers for an expensive risk like *Vanities.*

His writing process was simple. Jim wrote every morning, especially when he was home in East Hampton in the four-bedroom house on the water, which he'd bought in 1971. Its upstairs contained a suite, bedroom, and sitting room, study, with "a window on the world." There was no special chair or other idiosyncrasy other than standing up as he typed, but once he began to write in this spot, words flowed in torrents. His homes in Key West and in Manhattan did not afford him the same reasonable work hours, owing to his social life and its demands.

Though he first conceived writing a novel about his adventures as a boy in Hollywood around the time of Salinger's novel, Jim began to dally with his first novel, *There Must Be a Pony* during the mid-1950s. His narrator was a fifteen-year old boy, son of a has-been movie star ("If you want to know the whole truth—it just about kills me to go over the whole thing.") The character was Jimmy Kirkwood himself. Young Josh's voice was a shameless copy of Holden; the use of "truth" and "just about kills me" were standard refrains from the Salinger novel.

In contrast, Kirkwood took these motifs to places where Holden never went, and Salinger never considered. They were the places in his own heart, a location he knew because he lived there with his mother and father, bona fide movie stars, social friends of Chaplin, Valentino, Swanson, and all the other figures from Sunset Boulevard and Beverly Hills, the gentry from the Dream Factory of Hollywood in the Golden Age.

Living in a parallel universe in Salinger's writings truly became obvious to Jim Kirkwood in 1957 with the publication of the story version of "Zooey" in the *New Yorker.* Had J.D. Salinger met Kirkwood, studied him, done research on his life? Jim's own writing was taking shape when he returned to the West Coast that year. "I didn't like that book as much. It was too introspective, and I didn't see any similarities between Salinger's work and me."

So he said, but the similarities were unavoidable. Differences with Salinger were greater, on the whole. Salinger's imaginary characters wrote for Hollywood, whereas Kirkwood lived the fiction. No other writer labored so long and in so many different forms on one story. Jimmy envisioned *There Must be a Pony* in the form of short story, novel, stage play, radio script, and motion picture scenario. Only author Ira Levin was as successful in every genre of literature. Few writers would be so compulsive about a story.

In Salinger's literary world, a member of the Glass family, Zooey was a child of show business who in 1955 worked as a television actor on a soap opera. That year, in New York, Jim Kirkwood worked as the son of *Valiant Lady*, a popular daytime drama. His 1970 novella, *P.S., Your Cat is Dead*, featured a main character named Jimmy Zoole who came across like Zooey Glass in dissipation. Zooey and Zoole have similar speech patterns, and the tone is a duplication of those other Kirkwood narrators. Jimmy Zoole's theatrical credits are James Kirkwood's. J.D.Salinger may have been playing a cosmic joke on Jim, but the ironic favor was returned.

Sympathy came easily for characters trying to make sense out of a loved one's suicide. For the Glass family, the crux of the tale is the death of Seymour, the guru of the clan. Josh in *There Must Be a Pony* must comprehend the loss of Ben, his mother's boyfriend, to a mysterious suicide.

In July of 1980 Salinger gave a rare interview, his third in 35 years, and said: "There's no more to Holden Caulfield." According to the *Boston Globe*, the reclusive and silent author spoke with finality: "Holden is only a frozen moment in time." Twenty years after Salinger's prep school classic was published, Jim Kirkwood was asked about Peter Kilburn, his own major character, and the man who gave scores of interviews revealed, "Peter is living in New York City. He's a writer, and he's well-adjusted and has a relatively happy adulthood." If only Salinger knew . . . Considering the problems that beset these two adolescents, each author's perception of their literary *Dopplegangers* is both predictable and unsatisfying.

Kirkwood's work also stressed a drawback in personal development that arose from parents who were ill equipped to manage their own lives, let alone guide a child. The character of Josh in *There Must be a Pony* has an unnamed and unseen father. Holden Caulfield suffered the label of a "sad, little screwed-up hero," by one critic; in Kirkwood's *Good Times/Bad Times*, Peter Kilburn expresses his compassion for the "screwed-up people of the world." In Kirkwood's counterpart novel Peter's mother was dead, and his father was a weak-willed alcoholic. Jim Kirkwood always compounded the problem of fathers by making them absent, perverse, cruel, or best not discussed.

The crisis was precipitated by Peter's discovery of his best friend's dead body. Each of his characters, as he said, must "face rudeness in the extreme from almost everyone . . . learn how to control envy, rage, ambition; preferably live in an apartment without a terrace so on those occasions when the thought, 'Jump!' hits you, you will at least have to travel to the apartment of a friend or the George Washington Bridge, by which time the urge would have diminished by the sight of a friend, a nice doggie, or a beautiful sunset."

Kirkwood followed the Salinger pattern of developing protagonists who must deal with the death of a brother, or surrogate brother. Holden's emotional problems revolved around the death of his brother Allie. He broke all the windows in the garage after it happened. The Glass family was torn apart by the suicide of Seymour, especially for Buddy Glass. In three major Kirkwood novels, characters faced the death of their foil and friend. Josh was devastated by the suicide of Ben. Peter Kilburn snapped over the death of Jordan, his prep school *aide de camp*. Eddie, in *Some Kind of Hero*, dealt with the demise of his POW roommate who died of dysentery. The void left by the death of these brother figures often proved an impossible burden.

Like Salinger, Jim Kirkwood began with an attempt to write short stories. He could not find publishers for them and felt the form was too restrictive for the nature of his stories. So, he went in another direction. He tried his hand at playwriting and novel writing. With his ear and his innate theatrical instinct, he found through scenes and dialogues a way to present dramatic situations. Because of his family ties, Kirkwood found it easy to collaborate with directors, actors, set designers, and co-authors, for he'd grown up surrounded by them. As the short story forum faded in the 1950s, Kirkwood moved creatively into both novels and plays, switching between the two regularly. Kirkwood's greatest success came in 1974 with the production of *A Chorus Line*.

In Jim's first long effort, based on the death of his mother's lover, the narrator was a precocious teenager who discussed the "He-Man Myth," at the beginning of his confessional story. "I can't stand to hear a grown up call a kid a sissy". Josh angrily decries the intolerance of gay people or cross-dressers, which is a daring element in a book at the end of the 1950s. The most sympathetic character in the story was a screenwriter named Merwin who told the gas station attendant to check his oil, clean the windshield, and "fluff up the tires, sweetie."

The next book exposed Kirkwood's tenure at Brewster Academy in Wolfeboro, New Hampshire, where he had a rocky time with the headmaster. This story, entitled *Good Times/Bad Times*, was far more daring than his first one. When Peter Kilburn stood accused by the Headmaster of having a love affair with another boy at the school, deadly results were inevitable. With a nod to Somerset Maugham's short story, "Rain," Peter claimed to be the object of the headmaster's lust and killed the school administrator while defending himself against sexual attack—or was it just a calculated lie?

Another contentious point between us was his novel *Good Times/Bad Times*. Our discussions distressed him, as I had a problem with the alibi story of the narrator, Peter, whom everyone usually believed, trusted, and liked. "You just don't believe Peter, do you?" I always admitted to liking Peter enormously, but had an issue with his veracity. This exasperated him, and he took to calling me the "goddam DA."

Again and again, he insisted that Peter didn't have a clue that his best friend, Jordan, was writing a book about him. No, Kirkwood did not know in which historical country one could find Sodom and Gomorrah (a big motif in the novel). When I told him the Cities of the Plain were in the present day country of Jordan "on the banks of the Dead Sea." He smiled, "Oh, yes, those banks of the Dead Sea." It was no accident that the major character influencing Peter was named Jordan.

Jimmy repeated the refrain whenever I inquired, saying Peter did not intentionally murder Mr. Hoyt; no, Kirkwood (who was Peter) did not kill his headmaster ("though heaven knows I wanted to"). Yes, the novel was basically true; yes, Jordan ("his name was Ted") really existed. After a while, he paced around the room when talking about this murder case. Usually at this point I knew I had a tiger by the tail. He muttered one of his ominous statements: "One of these days I am going to disembowel you on the Boston Common." Or, he made off the cuff comments like, "Hiring a mob hit man isn't as expensive as you think."

In 1972 the kinky cult story, *P.S. Your Cat Is Dead*, came tearing out of Jimmy's literary closet as both novel and play. The concept of catching a burglar and tying him up, torturing him, hardly seemed a funny topic, but gave Kirkwood his opportunity for dark humor. Within a few years he chose to use the Vietnam Prisoners of War concept for *Some Kind of Hero*, about two soldiers who must deal with their incarceration by Viet Cong and a situational sexual dilemma.

Next to *A Chorus Line*, Kirkwood's biggest success was *P.S. Your Cat is Dead*, a strange novella and play wherein a has-been actor captured a burglar in his apartment, imprisoning him over New Year's Eve. Critic Clive Barnes once stated that *Cat* was not the play to bring your old maiden aunt to see. Steve Guttenberg produced, directed, and starred, in an updated and transplanted version, set in Los Angeles, losing its original flavor.

During the 1970s and 1980s Jim toyed with the idea of directing a movie version himself. "With a small, independent company, I could do this myself," he said years before the notion of indie films caught on. "Once you've written the screenplay, you lose all control." All his novels went through film packaging and few survived in any recognizable form. He often traced the problem to producer egos. I commented that he seemed irritated by this, and he looked around for something to throw at me. "Irritated! He asks if I am irritated!"

19

The fourth of his major novels confirmed his heroes were always young, though reaching beyond adolescence. He still required the first-person narrative, a highly introspective confessional. He often said, "Life is subjective." Though his characters were not criminals, they populated an ambiguous netherworld where crime and correctness were thinly separated. He seemed to reach for the idea that every human committed sexual crimes, deviation being mentioned in every variation in *Some Kind of Hero*.

By the time *Hit Me with a Rainbow* was written, not his first choice for a title, Kirkwood knew he had to do an objective narrative. If I had pressed him on any point, it was this. His least successful novel depicted the relationship of a young man and an older theatrical star. Was it the autobiographical story of himself and Tallulah Bankhead, or his mother and one of her lovers?

People in Kirkwood's tales were always at the mercy of outer forces, crushing and powerful influences, often up against immoveable institutions or irresistible systems. Social power tended to convolute relationships and to frustrate protagonists in story after story—whether about police and legal systems, education, the circus of theatre and show business, or military-industrial complex. Those who were sensitive or "screwed-up" stood upon the precipice for emotional breakdown.

Rigidity or uniformity also undermined the lives of Kirkwood's characters. In one novel, Gilford Academy (his version of a notable New Hampshire prep school he attended briefly) was called "The Institution for the Criminally Young," and in another novel the U.S. Army denied benefits for the flimsiest reasons to returning veterans while red tape choked the heroes of the Vietnam War.

Kirkwood's most ironic depiction of social crisis was in the little-known play, *UTBU (Unhealthy to be Unpleasant)*, about a secret organization that dispatched people who were not nice to their fellow citizens. The acronym identified a secret murder-for-hire society. The play parodied corporate American concepts, justified to humanitarian ends. Jim's premise was that an organization existed in which one could hire someone to "bump off" anyone whose behavior was unpleasant.

Jim's novels and plays always ended upon an optimistic note. Each protagonist came to grips with his vivid life and uncertain path. Like a devotee and nephew of Auntie Mame (for Kirkwood played Patrick Dennis on stage, opposite the one and only Rosalind Russell), Jim's life and his characters exemplified a man who savored his identity and demanded that he be paid a tidbit of respect. A magical power enervated Kirkwood's literary world. His narrators were always charming and charmers. As credited the fabled Pied Piper, the ability to truly enchant belonged to Kirkwood . . . and now my time had come to pay homage to the Piper whom I loved and followed and to examine the reasons he learned to play so well.

Pictured is James Kirkwood (c. 1984) after his book tour for Hit Me With a Rainbow. He gave William Russo this picture as a keepsake.

With the approach of midnight, I sped along the city's one-way street maze to take Jim to the radio station. There are still about four hours of interviews ahead. I gave him a synopsis of the well-known Boston radio personality on whose show he was to appear. He only half-listened. Since they had been heavily promoting Kirkwood's appearance on the morning shows, I asked him if he knew Jess Cain, the big-time morning radio host of the 1970s and 1980s in Boston. Jim frowned, "Should I?" No, I supposed not, but informed him of Cain's patter that hinted they were old bosom friends.

When we entered the radio station, the place was deserted, except for an on-duty guard who spoke no English. Jim and I wandered into a maze of empty studios, dark offices, and storage areas where our steps echoed eerily. At long last a heavy-set, shoddily dressed man with thick glasses and wearing an oversized brown hairpiece greeted us. This was Norm Nathan, one of the most beloved of Boston's radio personalities for decades. With the show's host came a younger shadow, possibly an intern. At first the intern mistook me for Kirkwood. Correcting him, their visiting celebrity was undaunted and turned up his energy level a notch or two. As they chatted amiably, Norm commented, "Jess Cain always speaks of you, Jim. He remembers you from the nightclub days with Lee Goodman."

Something clicked in Kirkwood's mind, and he shot me a glance without missing a beat. "Be sure to give Jess all my best!"

Mr. Nathan also apologized for not reading the book Kirkwood was ostensibly there to discuss. The talk show's callow intern added something about not being able to find it in the bookstores. Jim was gracious, for it happened everywhere, saying, "Don't worry. It doesn't matter."

When the "ON AIR" sign flashed red, the author and the radio host raised their voices a decibel, chatting self-consciously. It was evident immediately that this was a performance, and each was quite good. The host was relaxed, knowledgeable about his subject, and listened to his guest. Kirkwood responded in kind, and anecdotes flowed freely, pleasantly.

Kirkwood repeated a story about an early trip to Boston in 1965 where his play *UTBU* had its out-of-town try-out. One of the staunchest critics was the Dean of Boston theatre people, legendary Eliot Norton. "It's about an organization of people who go around blowing up not-nice people. It was a farce/comedy. There was a man in the play who dispensed these music boxes that blew up. Eliot Norton didn't like it at all. He said, 'The bomb should be placed next to Mr. Kirkwood's typewriter.' So, the night after the review, we all appeared on Norton's TV show. I had the prop man make me up a little time bomb/music box. And I gave it to him on air. He was very cool about it. It was ticking—but didn't have a charge in it—" He added, "naturally." I wondered whether Eliot Norton should have been greatly worried, "live and ON AIR."

Jim revealed some of his usual personality quirks: "I think people who grow old most graciously keep the child in them alive . . ."

"Many people in the arts keep youth alive because painting, poetry, novel writing, acting, are all make-believe . . . ."

"Writing a book is to give people entertainment . . ."

"I think not being totally sane is not all that bad . . . I tend to get a little more deranged the older I get. I tend to nurture it. It helps me in my work."

"I once held up a store with a squirt gun."

When Norm Nathan led Jim into a discussion of critics, I cringed. Did he have any idea where this might lead? Jim immediately pounced on the touchy subject, railing about a reviewer who lambasted an earlier book. "It was an overkill review. So I wanted, of course, to *throttle* him." (Said with unusual élan), "But we know we cannot go around killing people because they will put us in jail and we have to write books about being in jail—and everyone's done that."

This sent Jim off into another tale. "I went to the offices of *Variety*. And I decided to take out an obituary on the critic. They asked what kind of obituary ad I would like. I told them, 'Something big. Tasteful, if anything' I asked for something with a big black border that lights up in the dark, telling them money is no matter. The ad said: '*In Memoriam* to Raymond Sokolov, never to be forgotten for his literary criticism. Signed, James Kirkwood.' It caused a kind of scandal in New York. Everyone said, 'How dare you do that?' As a result, I think the *New York Times* is out to get me."

Listening to these comments, I cringed, hoping Jim would not continue in this vein. When the interview was over, the talk host—a seasoned vet of on air blabber—conceded he had met the Olympic star of media madness. "God, that was the quickest hour I have ever done," Norm Nathan told the author. Kirkwood had been marvelous. No phone calls tonight, as we were on a tight schedule for a live late-night television show next at one of Boston's top three television stations. At the elevator I paused to remark on the Nathan interview's high quality. Kirkwood was pacing in a frenzy of energy, and he overwhelmed me with his powerful aura. He was like a man in a bloodlust.

Kirkwood consulted his tour itinerary list again. "Needham." When I looked at his large handwriting done in blue flair pen, I could not decipher it. It was quite a ride on the highway. "Why do they always put them so far outside the city?" He wondered as we drove in a downpour. The night was now foggy and the road was slick. When we were told by the guard to park far from the entrance for some inexplicable reason, Kirkwood grew livid. We were already running late. At the door two young interns greeted us and asked why we parked so far away. These college kids were allegedly producers and ushered us into the "Green Room"—a darkly lit place where uninviting donuts and coffee littered a table.

"Hurry," Someone whispered at us. Kirkwood checked his fly and was off. All the agitation was so unnecessary. The show is on commercial break, and Kirkwood shook hands with the host. He was some former radio morning host who now wanted to hit the big time: television. He was totally unprepared, did not listen to his guest's responses. Two oddball callers were taken and that was it.

The producer, surprised that Kirkwood was witty and awake, apologized for the brevity of the interview at 2am. "Maybe a half-hour next time," to which Jim answered, "Yeah, sure." On the ride back to Boston, Kirkwood vented his pique. The trip expended so much energy for ten minutes television time at nearly 3am. Heavy rain continued to slow our return to the Copley Plaza, and Jim went into a sneezing fit.

We were to rest at the hotel till dawn, and a cold drizzle greeted our rush to the lobby from the parking garage. It was April 22, 1981. In nine years to the day, Jim would pass away. How foolish of me, thinking now, to tell him the 1980s would be his decade. I was reminded of our gloomy weather of the conditions of a time when a body was discovered by Kirkwood's literary alter ego on the other Coast, on the other side of his life. Of course, the subject of his first novel came up.

If he tired of speaking about the murder or death and what happened to Reid, I was never aware of it. I told him that the most vivid moment for me in Josh's sad life, as written in *There Must be a Pony*, was the time after discovering Ben's dead body. "Hiding in the bathroom with the pet monkey and the dog and the bird in the cage—it brought the horror of seeing such a thing to life for me. It was so vivid. I can't imagine finding someone you loved so dearly in that horrible state. You must have had so many nightmares about it."

Jim Kirkwood looked off distantly, perhaps seeing his own vision of that long-ago day in 1936. What was he remembering? He seemed oddly detached too, "Yes, that really happened. I was so scared. I had nightmares about it for years after that."

For a long time afterward, I wondered how such an experience might turn a bright twelve-year old boy into a spellbinding storyteller . . .

CHAPTER TWO

WHO DONE IT?

Writing a book about finding a dead body did not exorcise Jim's demon. Hiding the crime in plain sight made perfect sense for him. Novel, play, and movie: what better way to codify the crime with a spin? James Kirkwood was the master of the confessional genre of literature, but what exactly was he confessing in his fiction? And why?

Twenty years after the incidents comprising *There Must be a Pony*, the 32 year-old actor turned writer, always obsessing over the incident, he penned a fictionalization of his boyhood adventure. Then, he scripted a play as well. For the next twenty-five years he returned to the story and pushed to see his spin of a lesser Hollywood mystery put on film. Not as well known as other 1930s' scandals, the story haunted Jimmy, long after he turned into a Pulitzer Prize-winning playwright and film writer.

As Jim approached the pinnacle of his life, the Reid Russell/*Pony* story became his hallmark. He said, "Acknowledgment must also be aired that for ages I planned rigging the game so that objectivity would be the victor. But I would be faking; and if *I* knew I was faking, I could not help conveying that to others. I would as soon level at the start and have someone see my subjectivity head on, rather than see *through* my feigned objectivity." He made the truth of his boyhood trauma open to debate.

Caught in a sequined cesspool of murder, scandal, and outrages of the corrupt Hollywood in the 1930s, James Kirkwood managed to create a minor sideshow of violence and folly at Manhattan Beach, a curio to be studied. Kirkwood's novel and play, and television movie, were subject to as much distortion and misinterpretation as the real occurrence.

Had Kirkwood placed some clues into his own version that spoke the truth of the Russell case? His novel reeked of contradiction, puzzlement, rationalization, and blatant lies. After all, the boy in the middle of the case became a man who wrote fiction. His mentors and adult role models were actors, writers, and pixilated people.

Seventy years after Reid Russell's mysterious death, this retrospection of the case tries to uncover what has been lost, buried, and hidden by a few conspirators. They may be facing eternal punishment ruthlessly meted out by a Cosmic Joker with no governor on his actions . . . Little Jimmy Kirkwood played with variations on a killing like a man with Obsessive Compulsive Disorder. In the end he was plagued by his excessive permutations, though giving everyone else a chance to find the elusive pony hiding in a pile of manure between Art and Truth.

Jim wrote about his mother and the Manhattan Beach incident as a work of fiction, both for a play and novel. He could as easily have expressed it as a true report for the District Attorney. Elements of the case inspired and stalked him. Baffled press and exasperated police may not have accurately reflected the occasion; their attempt was done with more dispassion than the assorted tenants at the 1126 Second Street address could muster.

But Jimmy saw it differently from others.

First, let's look at the "official" statements, at facts culled by press and hard-nosed policemen decades ago.

According to the Jan Dennis chronicle of the beach community, *A Walk Beside the Sea: a History of Manhattan Beach*, the blazing white stucco house where the mysterious death occurred was a new construction. Described in varying accounts as palatial or a mansion, in its era it was considered a luxurious and spacious home for the well-to-do. Today it would be another large, pleasant upper-middle class residence, and nothing out of the ordinary. Built to rent or lease, and owned by Myron Wells in 1933, it was somewhat of an anomaly as a rich estate during the heyday of the Great Depression, but well within the yardstick of lifestyle for affluent Hollywood suburbs.

It was called a "cottage", much as mansions in Newport, Rhode Island, were considered summer homes. Manhattan Beach, like Newport, was a resort playground for many movie stars and the Hollywood community during the Silent Era. The Wells structure was a two-story house, extending over a ground-level rear floor, which made the backside three stories high. Twin balconies marked the upper two levels at the back, allowing tenants a panoramic overview of ample grounds behind the building

Manhattan Beach was extremely rural in the early Thirties, featuring expanses of empty land beyond the paving of Sepulveda Boulevard. This produced one of the first building booms that occurred regularly in the resort town. The community spawned the budding surfer movement, and its attractive youthful proponents congregated like tanning seal groups on the beach nearby. By August of 1936, Hermosa Beach and Manhattan Beach hosted a forty-mile aquaplane race from Catalina Island to the towns with piers loaded with fishing enthusiasts and summer residents.

For a few years after construction, the Myron Wells place stood empty, lacking renters having wherewithal to lease it. The lands east of Sepulveda Boulevard, where the house was built, consisted of small tracts, mostly owned by Asian farmers. The Great Depression took its toll on the properties, dooming them to foreclosure. The tilled acres in 1936 gradually subdivided into real estate lots with rows of bungalow homes altering the landscape. When second-rate novelist Gouverneur Morris and his wife, fresh from their world travels, sought a suitable place to display their souvenir-laden cargo worthy of Charles Foster Kane, they were thrilled by its size and style; it was perfect.

The house cost a staggering $4000 to build and Morris could easily afford the rent. With rooms to spare, he created a trophy room, a game room, den, study, and assorted guest rooms. His eccentric decor included a gun collection, memorabilia from his residence in Tahiti and his African trips, a grand piano, and numerous pets . . . a cockatoo, a Brazilian monkey, plus a pack of congenial dogs of varying pedigree and sizes.

The extensive back yard, its perimeter surrounded by tall screening eucalyptus with slender leaves smelling like cat pee and sweetened by its orange groves, featured a barbecue area nearly 150 yards from the house beyond a rambling lawn. Near at hand, inviting ease, an iron assembly supported a charming garden swing with a wide slatted wooden love seat, pillowed and covered over with jaunty striped green and white canvas matching the canopy above. Best of all, there was the constant fresh sea air blowing in from beaches along the Pacific coastline.

The estate epitomized upper-crust bohemian luxury, occupied by a namesake great grandson of a Founding Father of the United States and signer of the Declaration of Independence. Gouverneur Morris was the essence of Yankee arrogance and elegance for his time. Many may have considered him a pompous prig. Like any "Son of the American Revolution," card-carrying Mayflower-style member of the elite in America, Morris strove to live the comfortable life of a distinguished novelist. After graduating from Yale at the turn of the century, he wrote dull novels achieving a moderate popularity. He was the forerunner of the pipe-smoking, tweed jacket writer, living a stereotyped life in Hollywood, churning out screenplays for silent and sound movies.

Though no innovator, Morris was hardly a hack or populist. His prose and plot lines were contrived in a manner reminiscent of Booth Tarkington, but not quite staid enough to be shunned by Hollywood. The studios thought of him an example of high-class writing. Pretense made his reputation among those who chose to elevate Hollywood potboilers to the level of quality. His stories passed as adventures, tales eviscerated of all excitement.

A few studios considered him a prestige figure, and one film company toyed with the notion of making Morris a celebrity more important than the stars. The public wouldn't be gulled that far. By 1936 he was grist for gossip columnists and his best days as a writer were past. Not a man to avoid limelight or scandal, his messy divorce from his first wife left him married to his one-time secretary, the petite and often thought beautiful brunette, Ruth Wightman. Their marriage in Mexico in 1923, not recognized by the United States, forced them to re-marry a year later for the benefit of California legalities.

A colorful character, she'd often made headlines in the Twenties with her daring fashions. She was one of the first women to wear men's shorts while playing tennis and shocked people by wearing a skimpy white dress on the court, baring her thighs. She encouraged press coverage with her decision to bring a pet monkey with her whenever the couple traveled. Among her publicity-oriented activities was earning a pilot's license, only the second woman in the nation's history to do so. Whether meant to be frivolous or decadent, the activities of Gouverneur Morris and his wife were held up as representative of carefree spirits in the grinding years of the Great Depression.

An odd assortment of people soon swept into the hospitality bosom of the Morris ménage. Ruth Morris, enabled by her husband's writing contacts in movies, gathered friends from the colony of stars. Among her closest friends was the aging ingénue named Lila Lee, born Augusta Appel.

The starlet reported her age falsely on a regular basis. She claimed the earliest films of her career, made in 1917 with Chaplin, Swanson, and DeMille, were done when she was fourteen or fifteen. The lies used then were made to give her a legal majority. She was said to have begun movies at seventeen. "And she was big-chested for her age," was a remark often made by her son, fueling the lies. Kirkwood Senior also joined the act, shaving upwards of eight to ten years off his age. It's a practice indulged in by present day actors and actresses, some fearing loss of work for being too old, and others fearing to be uninsurable for films after reaching 65. Many of today's veteran stars, faces and bodies retouched by plastic surgery, are ten years older or more than the age their public is given.

A performer since childhood, Lila Lee was widely known as Cuddles since she was three years old. "If I wanted to get her goat, all I had to do was call her Cuddles, and flames would come out of her nostrils," Jim laughed at how he could manipulate his mother at will. She was allegedly only seven-years-old when David Belasco found her crying behind stage after a performance, and he promised to make her a star. Lila's first film was in 1918, and by the early 1920s she was a girlish silent film star opposite Rudolph Valentino in *Blood and Sand*, and thought to be the successor to Gloria Swanson, so groomed by Paramount and Cecil B. DeMille. By the time the talkies came into play, she was ready to appear opposite Lon Chaney, Spencer Tracy, and William Powell.

Though frequently escorted by Charlie Chaplin around town, the vivacious actress entered into a shaky marriage in the mid-twenties with silent film star, handsome James Kirkwood, but bore him a son, James, Jr. For misbehavior on a set and/or in public, Lila found herself dismissed from a picture by Columbia's Harry Cohn in late 1931.

Long-time friend and vigilant ally, columnist Louella Parsons reported that all Lila needed was "a good role for her comeback." Lila kept the right network of associates, and early in 1932, the actress checked into a hospital in Arizona for treatment. Whether it was rumored bouts with alcohol, or the official tuberculosis sending Miss Lee to the desert for the cure of a dry climate, Louella dubbed her struggle a "brave fight."

The actress was released into the compassionate custody of Gouverneur and Ruth Morris, who took her on a trip to Tahiti to help her recover. It was not until May of 1932 that she was back in the Hollywood scramble, divorced by Kirkwood Senior, who used her mental condition as grounds for his action. Her eight year-old son, Jimmy Lee Kirkwood, was sent to live temporarily with Peggy, Lila's sister, in Ohio.

Miss Lee was thereafter seen in the company of successful businessmen and tycoons outside the film industry, nevertheless attempting a comeback in talking pictures. Her "health" was a codeword in the trade papers for failure to complete movies, or to get starring roles. Approaching her fortieth birthday, a string of broken love affairs and two divorces behind her (she ended a second marriage to a stockbroker in 1934), the innovative talking pictures and age took its toll on Lila. Seeking a favorable image, she resumed custody of her pre-adolescent and precocious son in 1935. She still had influence in the industry; Louella Parsons, always friendly, could be depended upon to give her a plug in her columns. Playing roles that paid little, she grew desperate; she was open to any suggestion to better her life.

Ruth Morris, accustomed to permitting friends to have extensive stays at her roomy house, devised a perfect solution for her dearest celebrity confidante. The actress and her son were invited to be long-term houseguests. Lila promptly packed bag and baggage and left her Rancho Del Monte residence in the wine country of Monterey to join the other inhabitants of the beach house.

At almost mid-year in 1936, Gouverneur Morris hit the tabloid news for the first time that season. He received a summons to appear in court to explain why he had not paid a judgment of $687 that was awarded against him by a Monterey company. To the judge, Morris made the incredible statement that he was penniless, having been overdrawn by $2.30 in his bank account. The assertion so amazed the court that Morris was ordered to bring his bankbooks to court the next day to explain this.

To the press on the steps outside the courthouse, Gouverneur Morris gave an impromptu briefing in which he told reporters, "I received $5500 for my writing in the last six months." He cried poor. "But that all went for living expenses for eight persons I am forced to support."

Neither the court nor the press insisted on learning the identities of those the novelist was coerced into funding. By then, his household consisted of himself, his wife, Miss Lila Lee, her son Jimmy, a maid, the Morris secretary, and a gardener. Who was the eighth person Morris was "forced" to support? Was it a frequent twenty-eight years old visitor to the Morris estate? Reid Russell was a handsome, personable car salesman, who courted Miss Lee and served as Fourth at bridge with Ruth Morris and her husband. Practically an informal resident, he also closely befriended Lila's lonely little boy.

The occupiers of the Second Street house were to encounter the police next on September 25. On that damp, gloomy day, twelve-year old Jimmy had a keen knowledge of the comings and goings of the household. Knowing the house would be empty when he returned late from tennis practice at school that afternoon, he sauntered into the huge back garden. Heavy cooling mists rolling in from the ocean were frequent occurrences, and he walked through a pale swirling darkness . . . imagining hidden creatures lurking in the movements of the fog . . . an ideal setting to be confronted by a monster.

Jimmy made his way cautiously from the main house across the mysterious sloping grounds towards the barbecue pit and the lawn swing, hearing the ever-present soft rumble of wind-borne surf and flinching from the muffled cry of an unseen solitary seagull soaring overhead. He bumped against the wooden platform base of the swing. According to his own text, he reached out . . . to touch a still figure lying askew on the canvas-covered love seat. Leaning closer, he discerned its blood-spattered rigid face, glassy eyes staring into his; a turbulence of ants jostled one another everywhere on Reid Russell's head and cheeks. The gruesome sight was traumatizing; the more so for the lad being by himself, yet he was riveted by it. After a spine-tingling delay, the chill of a thicker blanketing fog engulfed him, and he fled back to the house.

Ordinarily home at this hour, his mother was away filming *Two Wise Maids*, a comedy with Allison Skipworth, at one of the Poverty Row studios, Republic Pictures; Lila's scant roles were small in major company films, but large in cheaper ones. Jimmy wanted badly to tell his mother about the thing in the back yard before anyone called the police. Trembling, he hid in the hallway lavatory to await the return of an adult to the house.

An hour or so later, Ruth Morris was first to come home. Enormously relieved to speak at last, Jimmy tried to convince her that Reid was lying dead upon the swing. She was skeptical, believing the boy to be playing a joke. Dragging her out to a balcony, he had her peer into the mist. She saw nothing and told him to behave himself. He offered to escort her to the site, but she refused. They went back inside and the boy explained he'd found the body when he came home from school. Ruth chose to disregard him, then ordered him to keep to his room till his mother came home.

Ruth didn't bother to mention anything about his prank when the maid returned. She assumed Tony, the gardener, was somewhere about, and said nothing when her husband and his secretary got home. As Lila was working late at Republic, Jimmy had no recourse but to pester Mrs. Morris further. He pointed out that Reid's automobile had been parked down the street, unattended for a day or more, and no one had seen him around anywhere.

At long last, Lila Lee arrived in slightly unsteady condition. Upon listening to her agitated son, she became hysterical. Ruth calmed her, saying she'd take care of things. Exasperated and beginning to believe the boy, Ruth notified the police, almost twelve hours after Jimmy had seen the body. Unsure of what to tell them, Mrs. Morris gave police a dissembling yarn about the boy and herself discovering Russell's body when they stepped onto a balcony and saw it at a distance. She also stated she was too afraid to go down to the grove.

After they were called, the police raced out to search the back yard in Manhattan Beach; a clutch of newspaper reporters hot on their heels. The obscuring mists of the previous night were gone; the California morning sun was in full charge when the police approached the deceased man. They noted an automatic .32 caliber pistol grasped in his right hand; a bullet had blasted through his right temple.

Officer Percy Jones pried a lead slug from the wood of the swing, and dropped it accidentally. The grass had not been mowed and it was proving impossible to find. But according to those on the scene, this was evidently a suicide; an inquest was a remote possibility, and deemed unnecessary. As the police discontinued their half-hearted search of the area, the body was carted off under the authority of a new, green coroner.

Jimmy and a classmate, Howard Jones, son of the clumsy policeman, avidly spied from a distance as the remaining police and the Morris gardener combed through surrounding grass and shrubbery without success. After the officials left the scene, the two boys went boldly down to the morbid place. Gaining access from the street to do as they pleased, the press fell upon them for information.

The young duo fielded most questions, though Jimmy played detective throughout, making his own intense search and study. A photograph, staged by the press, was taken of Jimmy and Howard. Published photos showed them smiling broadly as they watched the gardener, Mr. Anthony Mumolo, rake the scene of an unrecognized crime. At least one newspaper was to contend Reid Russell had been found face down on the swing seat.

It would not be the last time Jimmy Kirkwood misled the press by slipping them disinformation, something he took glee in doing.

During the next days and months, the Morris household suffered repeated interviews by detectives. It was acknowledged Mr. Russell had been a guest of

Mr. and Mrs. Morris during several nights each week. The haughty mystery author claimed the unemployed car salesman, known to him a few months, was "like a member of the family." He was tolerated because he provided Miss Lila Lee with steady companionship and joined them for dinners, bridge games, and was generally considered entertaining company. Miss Lee and her little boy, he observed, were residing with the Morris couple as semi-permanent houseguests. Mr. Russell, being involved with the actress, was inclined to spend many hours at the Second Street address. To be useful, he occasionally ran errands for the household.

On the previous Thursday, just before the suicide discovery, "Guvvie," as Ruth called him, asked Reid to take some manuscripts to Los Angeles, which he cheerfully did. Ruth also told police that the young man was "terribly depressed" over losing his job as "a motorcar salesman." She could not explain how a cheerful Reid was simultaneously depressed, though he performed his assigned task without fail. She insisted, "He was in good spirits when he left at 2:30 that Thursday afternoon."

Other members of the household claimed the young man had been morose and threatening suicide for days. Guvvie opined Reid was disconsolate over losing his job the week previous to the tragedy. The writer recalled that Reid inquired about the plot of his new book, which dealt with a suicide. Mrs. Morris embellished that by stating Reid said he was going to jump off the Manhattan Beach pier, but no one regarded his comments as genuine or desperate. Later in the day of those interviews, Mrs. Russell, Reid's mother, confirmed to police that her son owned a gun, kept in the bureau drawer at his home at 1059 Manhattan Place. She had seen the weapon there a week before and thought it looked a mite rusty, because Reid often carried it in his car when he went on long trips.

On September 29, Gouverneur Morris made use of his patrician good manners. He put the full scope of his modest writing ability to bear: he composed a sympathy letter to Mrs. Victoria Russell. At least that's what he called it. Whatever Morris intended by his note to the widow of an army officer, she did not take kindly to the words in the aftermath of her grown child's recent demise:

"Your boy had my affection and I think I had his. I like young things and I encouraged him to come down here when he could because the house and grounds are charming and he liked them, and because we are easy going people who like to be liked and like back. Why he came here to end his troubles, I cannot know. He was always so courteous and considerate. But surely he was old enough to know he was letting people who had been kind to him in for a lot of slander, scandal, suspicion, and God knows what."

When the police released more text, it was calculated to show the true character of the arrogant novelist. The letter further informed Mrs. Russell of her son's last days as their houseguest and of his close friendship with the Morris family. If he meant to offer comfort to a grief-stricken mother, Gouverneur Morris showed little understanding or sympathy:

"He had promised to go straight home to you. Instead he comes back here and makes a lot of grief and ghastly trouble for us. The grief we would have felt in any case. But we have done nothing to deserve the notoriety and the endless blunderings and stupid intrusions upon our privacy by the police and the press."

The writer's *noblesse oblige* attitude alienated Reid's mother. She stewed over her son's abrupt death at the hands of people who seemed not to care about him. She was impelled to start sorting through the facts of the case and, for the next month, could not make the facts tally up to suicide. She was so distraught and mentally unstable that Victoria Russell's sister arrived from Yuma, Arizona, to help her through the crisis.

Not long after the official Manhattan Beach Police Department preliminary ruling of suicide in the Reid Russell was published, Mrs. Victoria Russell grew increasingly dissatisfied with the treatment accorded her son. In early November she filed an astounding police complaint. In it she contended she received an anonymous warning, via telephone, to "lay off" pressing for an investigation into her son's death. Who had called? Or knew she was in contact with the police? She was more determined to pursue the mystery. She reported that a series of "frantic" phone calls from an unknown woman to her apartment in the days before her son's death proved to her that an angry and possessive lover was looking for Reid.

In addition to contacting the police, Mrs. Russell retained an attorney to act as her liaison in her quest for justice. On November 10, the lawyers, Stanley Visel and Martin Ryan, released their client's story to the press. The counselor, Stanley Visel, stated Reid's mother learned her son had been carrying on a romance with a wealthy married woman, and that "a number of strange happenings and coincidences" convinced her he did not commit suicide. Visel demanded a "thorough investigation."

Attentive newshounds merrily published hints of a clandestine romance, not specifically identified for the public. Their racy innuendo immediately put two women under the spotlight and brought on further police attention to the assumed suicide case.

For six weeks, the Manhattan Beach police gave short shrift to the gun in Reid's hand; they were not concerned that Russell's mother insisted there was $19.50 missing from his pocket, nor with a missing bullet and its spent cartridge. The coroner ruled Reid Russell had been dead about twenty-four hours before the body was seen, and had no idea Jimmy Kirkwood found him twelve hours earlier than reported by Mrs. Morris. The Manhattan Beach police chafed a bit over the timing of the discovery of Russell's body, since the gardener and other members of the household may have passed within a few feet of the barbecue and swing during that period, yet never saw the dead man . . . and that too was shrugged off as possible.

Media criticism caused Captain Clyde Plummer of the Los Angeles District Attorney's office to take over the investigation, supplanting and replacing the local police department. Plummer's opening statements indicated he'd re-examine all available evidence at the request of the deceased's mother, who suspected foul play. In his confidential talks with Mrs. Russell, Plummer learned two women were pursuing the victim; one was tall and phoned him frequently. Mrs. Russell called the second woman her son's "sweetheart."

The captain also stated no love letters were found at Reid's apartment, nor had his mother located any among her son's effects. Mrs. Victoria Russell had a staunch ally in Plummer. Glorying in the publicity, he declared he was keeping an open mind: he and his staff had formed no theories about the incident. "We are making a new investigation. We intend to question everyone connected with the case. The fact that we take statements from them does not in any way indicate that we believe these may be suspects in the case because we have no suspects. We merely are making another investigation."

Pursued by demanding reporters, Captain Plummer reluctantly disclosed he had identified a "mystery witness" to the intimate details of Reid's life. He described this male person as "a closest chum and confidant, not only in ordinary matters but in affairs of the heart." The mystery name was withheld. The young man allegedly lived in San Bernardino, drifting about and never in any fixed location.

During this period, reporters questioned Lila Lee wherever they could catch her. Describing Reid as a "Fourth at bridge" whom she met after he sold Gouverneur Morris a car, she denied rumors the unemployed car salesman had been "interested" in her. Detectives under Plummer's supervision visited the Morris home wishing to talk with Jimmy Kirkwood, but could not "officially" speak to him since his mother was at work, filming. Morris and his wife being present, they agreed to appear voluntarily at the District Attorney's office to give sworn statements concerning the death of Mr. Reid Russell.

The re-opening of the case brought out "new" details, substantiating Mrs. Russell's concerns. According to the report of the coroner the previous month, the bullet that killed Reid went through his head from right to left; there was a tear in the canvas seat back cover, possibly made by the bullet, but no bloodstains were seen at that spot. The bullet that rent the canvas may not have been the same slug at all. In another of many reports released, Captain Plummer said a small clot of blood and a tiny sliver of bone was listed as having stuck to one of the wide canvas flaps of the garden furniture, but at some distance from where the dead man's head lay.

The press tagged the garden love seat: "The Swing of Doom."

Guvvie and Ruth Morris showed up at Captain Plummer's office as promised, accompanied by Lila Lee. Though they came to assist with his inquiry, they could not have been as co-operative as he hoped since their presence resulted from extreme pressure by the dead man's mother. As if to illustrate the strain of this visit, within fifteen minutes of questioning, Ruth Morris had to leave Plummer's office.

Claiming nervous indigestion, she went to the Ladies Room with Lila. Accompanied by one of the female staff, the security guard waited outside the facility. Ruth returned with both in a few minutes to continue providing answers. The novelist's wife then stunned the District Attorney's staff with a bland announcement that she had found a suicide note from Reid in her jewel box a few days after his death. Ruth Morris said, that in it, Russell wrote: "I told you I would do it and now you see."

Asked why she hadn't mentioned the note when police were at her home or called his office about it, she gave a matter-of-fact reply. Mrs. Morris said Russell's missive was folded, not addressed, and upon reading it, "I thought it would be a mistake bringing up that note. It was so terrible and depressed. I thought it would be best to destroy the note. I lit a match and set it on fire and held it in my fingers and then put it into an ashtray." She added, "Singularly enough, the one person who was inclined to take him (Reid) seriously was little Jimmy Kirkwood. And it was Jimmy, who on the afternoon we found the body, called my attention to the fact that Reid's car had been parked at the foot of the hill leading up to our home all day, but that Reid was mysteriously missing."

Gouverneur took a protective stand behind them as Lila Lee and Plummer sat on either side of Ruth Morris. Lila Lee confirmed the testimony of Mrs. Morris. She saw Mrs. Morris with the Russell note and watched her burn it. "Her hand was trembling," Capt. Plummer quoted the actress as revealing. "I asked her what was the matter . . . 'Oh my god,' she said, 'It's a note from Russell' . . . I asked her what it said and she said it told about how he was going to commit suicide. Then she struck a match and burned the note." She gave a vague account of the note's contents.

When Ruth revealed the contents of the suicide note, it must have been a blow to Lila. That Reid left a brief letter to Mrs. Morris on her dresser in her bedroom, and none to his paramour, devastated the actress more deeply about Russell. His sudden death was without explanation, and he left no note for Jimmy. Lila's son soured and expressed a deep anger with a man he'd admired and trusted.

The fuller version of the brief farewell seemed incongruous with its original disclosure: "Dear Ruth, You thought I would not do it, but now you know. This has been the happiest vacation I have had in a long time. Thanks a lot for everything. I hope you don't think I didn't keep my chin up. Goodbye, Reid."

Ruth insisted that, discouraged by unemployment, Russell had threatened to kill himself in her presence. She then surprised Plummer with an anecdote having details of a "suicide bet" she made with John Grana, proprietor of the Guy Tano Italian Restaurant, where Russell, Mr. and Mrs. Morris, Lila Lee and her son, Jimmy, ate dinner frequently. "Reid had been talking about killing himself because he lost his job as a motor car salesman. More for a joke than anything else, I wagered $10 that he would. Reid told me, after he had heard the bet had been made, that he guessed he'd have to commit suicide so I'd win the money."

According to historian Ms. Jan Dennis, in her account of the incident, John Grana informed Plummer that he recalled Russell's demeanor was melancholy during the week preceding the shooting, and several times expressed a suicidal intent. Grana had been marketing a new salad dressing at his restaurant, and Mrs. Morris quoted Reid as being amusing about it and declaring, "I will go into a club and ask for Guy Tano Salad Dressing and, if they haven't got any, I will say that's terrible and go out and jump off the pier. Then the publicity will come out." Mrs. Morris gave Grana two-to-one odds on the chance that Russell would jump. Russell himself told Grana to accept the wager.

Lila Lee backed up the story that Russell frequently showed a morbid streak in discussing his possible death. "In fact, he talked about it incessantly. I had a long talk with him in the kitchen a week before he died and he told me he was in trouble with the automobile company that employed him, involving money, and he threatened then to commit suicide."

Ruth recalled that on the night of Sept. 20th Russell had not kept a social engagement at the Morris house. "This was most unusual for he was extremely polite and thoughtful. He knew we had counted on him to make a Fourth at bridge with Gouverneur, Lila Lee and myself." Mrs. Morris said Russell telephoned her the next day and apologized, but did not explain his failure to keep the engagement. "I was very formal with him in the phone conversation because the editor of *Collier's Magazine* was our guest that day, and I did not care to be as informal as I usually was in talking with Reid. He came to our house on Tuesday and spent that night and Wednesday night with us. He was talking about suicide."

Step by step, Mrs. Morris recited the happenings of the week, beginning with Sunday, Sept 20 when Russell failed to make a foursome at the bridge table. Monday night, she said, "We played some cards after dinner and Reid seemed very morose and very worried. That was the night he made the statement that he was going to end it all. We laughed it off, thinking that he wasn't really serious about it. He told us about leaving his job and about a man going to garnish his money for a bill he owed." She said Russell stayed Tuesday night at the Morris home because he suddenly said he didn't feel like going home that night.

Reid stayed over again Wednesday night, and on Thursday he went into town with manuscripts to mail for her husband. "As he left he said, 'Well, if I have to die . . .' I didn't quite understand the remark, but I passed it off and let it go." The women also blithely revealed Russell, generally thought to be a bachelor, once or twice casually mentioned a divorced wife and son in Texas, but never discussed the details of his marriage. He was, nevertheless, planning to bring his mother to the Morris estate to meet his new friends.

When these bizarre interviews concluded, Captain Clyde Plummer informed the press new information had arisen from discussions with Mr. Morris, Mrs. Ruth Morris, and Lila Lee. Plummer complimented all for their patience and cooperation, yet, the police captain said the matter did not rest there: "For one thing I want to know how it was possible for that body to have lain there in the lawn swing for hours without being seen by the caretaker or any other persons around the Morris house." Taking leave of reporters, he offhandedly remarked that a reference made about Reid Russell's ex-wife during his inquiry was of no importance to the case.

In full cry, the press posse galloped off on the Texas trail to locate the intriguing new lead. Mrs. Lorraine Crockett Russell was then living in El Paso, expecting them. Though she had not seen Reid since their divorce eight years earlier, she believed he was capable of suicide. "He was the moody type who brooded a great deal and would be likely to take his life if he became too despondent. I believe he shot himself." Russell's former wife also understood Reid's mother and her anguish, but was piqued: "Reid's mother is doing us all an injustice by bringing up our marriage. I know, however, that it is hard for her to believe her son would take his life. I was divorced from Reid in 1929 and did not see him after the divorce, so naturally I know nothing of any love affairs in which he might have been involved."

In 1936 on the grounds of the house at 1126 Second Street, Manhattan Beach, the body of Reid Russell was discovered on a garden swing with a bullet hole in his head, setting in motion an investigation never fully solved and inspiring a boy to become a writer. Pictured are Ruth Morris, Lila Lee, Gouverneur Morris (standing), and Captain Clyde Plummer.

To this point, only one of the key witnesses had been overlooked. Captain Plummer accepted the explanation that twelve year-old Jimmy was emotionally disturbed by the episode, knew little, and the police captain understood the normal desire of Lila Lee to protect her son from the glare of the publicity. This changed to some extent, however, when word filtered back to Plummer that Jimmy talked freely to schoolmates about the body, showed off the crime scene to friends, and finally gave an interview to the *Los Angeles Examiner*. The son of Lila Lee could be ignored no longer.

The boy was bragging in school that he found the body before anyone else. He also chatted about how he'd seen Reid's car by the old barn on the estate, though Russell himself was nowhere around, and this made him suspect something was wrong. Jimmy befriended a *Los Angeles Examiner* reporter, to whom he gave information, and the newspaper was printing scoops before the police knew of them. Other witnesses began to tell the press versions different from those given in official reports by the police. *The Examiner*, much to the embarrassment of the District Attorney's office, headlined that Jimmy Kirkwood was the first one to discover the body, and then brought it to the attention of Mrs. Morris, who telephoned the police. Plummer announced he'd question young Kirkwood immediately about the issue.

The boy rattled the ongoing investigation with his observations, and police believed he knew more. He asserted boldly to Plummer and his uniformed team how he and his friend witnessed a policeman pry a bullet out of a wooden slat of the swing, fumbling it into long grass during the first investigation seven weeks ago. When Plummer checked on this, Officer Jones of the Manhattan Police force confirmed the veracity of the tale, explaining the impossibility of finding the items in the overgrown terrain. They speculated that the bullet and its spent cartridge might have wound up in the pockets of either of the boys.

Jimmy was then photographed in a smiling picture, arm-in-arm with Ruth Morris and Lila Lee on the way to the Hall of Justice for another deposition. The threesome appeared to be on a lark, rather than giving testimony concerning the death of a friend.

Jimmy told me photos like those brought him his first offers to appear in movies, which his mother refused to allow him to do until he was older. He considered his acting career as having begun at Reid's death. The press photographed Jimmy and his friend Howard grinning at the death scene. When Jimmy gave tours of the garden area to local kids for cash, he acted out the role of Reid Russell and plopped down onto the swing to illustrate his death throes. He regarded those "performances" as his first acting jobs, complete with pay.

Jimmy Lee Kirkwood's continuing comments to the press in November brought Captain Plummer's squad swooping down to the Second Street address.

With them was Everett Davis, Special Investigator from the D.A.'s office, who was having detectives search the grounds and the house itself for "a trace of that bullet." Amid a clatter of feet upstairs and down, closet doors and drawers yanked open and shut, Davis explained to Guvvy that the chunk of lead would allow him to conclude whether the bullet was fired from the gun found in the dead man's hand. He said its trajectory, as indicated by the rip in the canvas on the lawn swing, did not conform to a description Ruth Morris gave, during her visit to the Hall of Justice, of the position in which the body had lain.

An expanded force now available, the District Attorney's men could be spared to question all the neighbors. Several claimed to have heard a muffled sound like a gunshot the night before discovery of Russell's death; others stated they thought an explosive noise came from within the Morris house. As expected, Gouverneur Morris became exasperated when advised of it. He flatly denied any shot had been fired inside his home at the time of Russell's death. He couldn't deny his trophy room was filled with collectible weapons, rifles and pistols, and resented hearsay suspicion

Guvvie was told how Plummer and Davis planned to fire a test pistol into a bucket of sand or earth to trace the slug's course, using a .32 caliber gun similar to the pistol held by Reid Russell. For reasons unspoken, the police would do the shooting test in the back yard of the Morris home. They expected to observe where the shell and bullet of the test shot went. An automatic weapon, Davis said, should have thrown a shell only a few feet, and the bullet would have spent its force going through his head and fallen somewhere near the body. If this led at once to the missing bullet, it would indicate that the salesman was shot elsewhere, and his body carried to the back yard. The novelist thought it an excellent premise and joined the officials to look at the scene.

Crossing the garden, they were confounded to see the lawn chair no longer standing near the barbecue pit. It was gone. The absence of the key component of their investigation sent Captain Plummer into overdrive. Men were dispatched to scour the beach district for the canvas-covered swing.

They were delayed, but not defeated.

In the ensuing interim, Captain Plummer quizzed Antonio 'Tony' Mumolo at length. The gardener had worked in the area throughout that tumultuous week in September, but assured Plummer he hadn't seen Russell's dead body. The maid brought the groundskeeper a daily pitcher of ice water, as was her habit, and she saw nothing either. An ocean fog rolled in almost each afternoon, and he'd drive her to the local store in his pickup to fetch needed items. No, they hadn't paid any particular attention to the swing or barbecue; familiar objects like that are fixtures to be ignored. "It is very strange," opined Plummer, "that no one found the body until the following day." He demanded to know what happened to the swing.

Tony innocently replied it was in the possession of a friend of his. He revealed that Miss Lee had ordered the swing to be taken away, as it was an ugly reminder—and perhaps, too, she was annoyed with learning of Jimmy's playing games with neighborhood children at the swing. Tony had given it to a friend. Plummer and Davis were fit to be tied. It was likely the rowdy children could have found clues and destroyed them without understanding their significance. Though the site had been rendered useless so far as clues were concerned, they had to make do with what they could learn there.

Once the wayward swing was restored to the garden, they were able to proceed. Standing on the identical spot where Russell's body was found, Plummer aimed a .32 at a dirt-filled bushel basket. He shot twice, and his assistants combed the grass for ejected shells. They quickly found both of them. Buried in the basket were the two expended bullets, and although the target represented the approximate solidity of a human head, the projectiles did not pass through and exit, as the fatal slug had done. Captain Plummer said he still had doubts following the test.

Morris and his wife, and Jimmy and his mother remained inside the house while the officials staged their macabre test. Their frayed nerves were likely put over the edge by the gunshots. The imperious novelist reached the end of his tether; Guvvie would no longer tolerate having his credibility questioned by persistent police hoping to manufacture a homicide out of a simple case of suicide.

Maintaining he and Mrs. Morris suffered rude impositions by everyone tramping through their home and garden, Guvvie described himself as "completely exhausted" by the ordeal. The couple decided to leave by plane for a Fort Miller ranch belonging to a friend, Charles Green. After informing the authorities of their intention, Guvvie and Ruth hurriedly abandoned their home for a few days of rest. When landing at the Fresno Municipal Airport, Mr. Green was there to meet them. Ruth was amazed to see clamoring reporters already bunched beside him, and she shouted back at them, "It's an out and out suicide!" before being spirited away to the ranch.

Thus, Gouverneur and Mrs. Morris bid adieu to the investigation, leaving Lila Lee and her son to cope with the unpleasantness at the Second Street house.

Captain Plummer reacted badly to the cavalier attitude within the Morris house. "Circumstances still make it difficult for us to believe Russell's death was suicide," lamented the biased officer. He added: "We have been unable to establish any motive to indicate a murder. If Russell shot himself while lying in the swing, it should be an easy matter to find the shell ejected from the automatic. It could not have fallen more than two or three feet from the body and should have been found easily in the matted grass about the swing. Another significant thing is that Russell's arms were folded across his breast when his body was found and one hand was clutching the gun in a position not likely to have been maintained had he shot himself through the head."

As of November 17, the accumulating evidence could be used to support a murder theory as easily as that of suicide. Captain Plummer entertained facts supporting either theory in regard to the young salesman's death. Foremost, Reid Russell may not have been shot at the lawn swing where his body was found. It lay unnoticed for twenty-four hours, during which the entire garden was generally visible from the house balconies.

Plummer admitted no motive had been established for murder, while he'd heard testimony about despondency, which indicated reason for suicide. He asserted that Mrs. Morris, Lila Lee and her son, Jimmy Kirkwood, heard Russell at various times threaten to end his life, owing to the fact he was unemployed and his funds were steadily diminishing. On the other hand, Russell's mother continued to insist her son was slain, reasoning it involved two women in Reid's love life: his sweetheart and a second woman who, she said, pursued him.

To confirm his worst suspicions, Plummer turned over the exhibit pistol to a ballistics expert. Should he discover it unused for several months, the detective said he'd order Russell's body exhumed to determine what caliber bullet killed him. Investigator Everett Davis took it upon himself to depict how a man might have shot himself through the head while lying in the swing. Contorting himself in a reenactment, he showed it would have been virtually impossible to do so and still be able to fold his arms across his chest, as was the body's posture *in situ*.

Contacted for an opinion, County assistant autopsy surgeon, Frank Webb, contradicted Davis, declaring the shot that killed Reid Russell must have taken place at the swing. He based his belief on a large amount of blood beneath the head when the body was examined on the site. Evidence supporting suicide was seen during the *post mortem*. The condition of the brain, having "exploded," as one officer put it, indicated the shot had been fired against the skin. Coroner Frank Nance noted powder burns inside the scalp of the deceased, which tend to support a suicide. Issuing a routine report, the Manhattan Beach police advised the case be closed.

Internecine dissension made the investigation by the Los Angeles Sheriff's department appear conducted by buffoons, or by those engaging in a cover-up of shenanigans of the well-to-do within the movie industry.

The New York Times trumpeted news of the inter-departmental squabbling among the Los Angeles police force, and ended with: "Captain Clyde Plummer said tonight that the pistol discovered in the lap of Reid Russell when his body was found in the yard of Gouverneur Morris Manhattan Beach home on Sep. 25 appeared not to have been fired recently."

As promised, Captain Clyde Plummer sought a court order on November 18th for exhumation of the body of Reid Russell, basing his decision upon the report from E.C. Crossman, ballistics expert, whose study of the pistol found in Russell's hand did not establish when it was last fired. Mr. Crossman could not testify to a recent usage.

Before the week was over, District Attorney Buron Fitts personally entered the case. People in the highest circles of Los Angeles and Hollywood began to worry. Plummer was stepping on the wrong toes, and those discomfited had reacted. Fitts gained the reputation in his ten years as D.A. of accommodating the highest bidder when it counted. Denounced for his corruption, detailed in books like *The Fixers,* Buron Fitts was a World War I veteran, a limping war hero enjoying the dole of the major studios. Put into office in 1928, he was secure so long as he was useful to filmdom's powerful moguls.

If Captain Clyde Plummer nurtured greater ambitions, this case was a godsend. Garnering daily national headlines bearing salacious hints about the Manhattan Beach suicide, he upstaged his fitful boss in his most outlandish news conference to date when he announced Reid Russell was the victim of a romantic entanglement.

The investigation turned from one about an unemployed auto salesman, protégé of a celebrity novelist, into that of a boyish gigolo for the women of the Morris household. Victoria Russell's son now looked like an opportunist, bringing on his own fate. "This is a love-slaying and not a suicide," insisted Plummer. "We have eliminated the suicide theory. As far the love-slaying theory, all I can say now is that I have information to support it."

Plummer planned to recall the likeliest of suspects from their self-imposed seclusion at their friend's ranch. The obstreperous Morris did not deal well with authority, and he was about to be baited. At Fort Miller, his wife held a derisive press conference to ridicule the notion of murder. Ruth laughed off the "love theory" and insisted Russell slew himself because of "worry over financial troubles."

On November 19th, the Los Angeles press reported the District Attorney's pique about the Reid Russell case. Fitts refused to grant an exhumation order, despite press accounts attempting to link Russell's death to another in the area. The D.A. needed to confer with his staff before agreeing to disinter the victim, declaring: "I believe too much emphasis has been placed on the murder theory."

A news follow-up printed that Burton Fitts called Captain Plummer, his chief investigator, "on the carpet" for what was described as "too much publicity" in the reinvestigation of the death of Reid Russell. The prosecutor objected to Plummer's abandonment of the original suicide theory for one of a "love murder." Though D.A. Fitts was hardly sensitive to lurid headlines; apparently someone or something struck a nerve.

Clyde Plummer fought back, insisting further study of the corpse was needed to prove Russell was not a suicide as first believed. Saying scientific evidence indicated the rusty automatic in the dead man's fingers had not been fired for more than a year, the detective offered two other lines of thought: chemical experts were studying splotches on the swing pillows were the body was found to see if they were human blood, and he was searching for "a love crazed woman" connected with the tragedy.

Captain Plummer received belated information about Russell's activities before his death had surfaced. Lt. Harry Hansen said he happened to attend crowded party Russell gave the week before the used car salesman was found dead. Over a frequently filled glass, Russell told the off-duty detective he was about to obtain a $300 per month job, connected with smuggling of arms and munitions either to Mexico or China. Hansen thought it was a pipe dream.

Another attendee, buxom Frances Patten, described as a radio artist, submitted her view of the lavish shindig. According to Miss Patten, champagne flowed freely. She called Russell a jovial host, who spent money with generous extravagance. The party-girl quoted Reid as claiming he was well on the road to "a large fortune." The police team wondered how unemployed Russell managed to engage in "spectacular revelry" in Los Angeles in the "gayest hot spots."

Though the story seemed "fantastic," Captain Plummer argued with D.A. Fitts about its credibility. They discussed expanding the inquiry into the financial affairs of the dead salesman. A subpoena was issued for bank accounts of an important figure, and they was examined the first of the week. A heavy withdrawal of funds was regarded as unusual, yet failed to yield proof of murder. Public support for Plummer's demand for an exhumation order overwhelmed anything Buron Fitts attempted to derail the idea. The following day, Reid's body was removed from his grave under a court order obtained through the District Attorney's office.

Reid's exhumed corpse was re-examined. Autopsy Surgeon Frank Webb and an assistant measured the wound. It was 10 millimeters wide, establishing that the weapon used was a .32 caliber, the type found in Russell's hand. Powder burns inside the scalp and at the entrance wound were present, and the trajectory of the bullet indicated the gun was held exactly horizontal against the temple.

Reid Russell was again determined to have died of a self-inflicted .32 caliber gunshot. Although the assistant surgeon speculated such a wound might also result from a shot by a .45 or .38 caliber gun, his remark made little impression. The new autopsy summary offered nothing to differ with the first finding. "My original report of suicide still stands," gloated Frank Webb, and despite the hullabaloo, the case was not considered a homicide.

A mysterious element intruded. One telltale bruise marred Russell's right temple. An abrasion like that occurs when a weapon is slammed with "terrific force" against a head, so it led Detective Lieutenant Harry Hansen to suggest the gun may have been jammed against the victim's temple to simulate suicide.

Headlines heralded the death: "Murder in Disguise" and surmised the killer was fiendishly clever, trying to mask his assassination of the young man.

After two days above ground, the body was re-interred at Calvary Cemetery in the suit Reid's mother provided for his funeral. What happened to what he wore at the time he was fatally shot on September 25th? The Manhattan Beach undertaker, who prepared the body for each burial, did not recall what became of the soiled clothes. They were certainly not in the possession of the youth's mother. The coroner didn't have them. And neither the sheriff nor the District Attorney's office could give an accounting. "We'd like to find the clothing," said Clyde Plummer doggedly, "to check it for possible blood stains or other evidence which might even determine whether Russell killed himself or was murdered."

Plummer sent police to the Second Street house to scour the grounds anew for hidden, buried, or misplaced clothing. During their dedicated hunt for new clues, they dug up a set of unrelated garments buried on an estate adjoining the Morris place. These bore suspicious dark stains; estimations of their condition indicated they were buried several weeks past. Police refused to comment further on a rumor that central figures in the investigation might be recalled for questioning and possibly placed under arrest.

The comedy of errors was corrected on November 22nd, when the stained apparel of Mr. Reid Russell was located in the responsible mortuary, after all. Officer Everett Davis announced that the mortuary undertaker had conducted a successful search. "The clothing has never disappeared. It has been in the undertaker's possession since shortly after the body was discovered. We now have it in our possession and will subject it to a rigid examination for corresponding bloodstains over the weekend."

On the 24th of November, Guvvie received a summons to return to Manhattan Beach. Followed by a gaggle of press chasing the novelist and his young wife to their airplane, Morris stayed in character, spitting out vituperative comments. Accusing investigators of "asininity" in their handling of the Reid Russell suicide, Gouverneur Morris and his wife, Ruth Morris, took a private plane ride from Fort Miller ranch. The famous writer declared that, if necessary, he'd take legal action against the D.A.'s office to end the "business of making a public show of me." Met at the airport by their attorney, C.P. Von Herzen, the Morris couple drove to Manhattan Beach, where Captain Clyde Plummer waited with his questions. They repeated their mantra, uttered since the first days of the body's discovery: Reid Russell committed suicide. The usually garrulous Mrs. Morris became taciturn under the orders of her attorney.

A week before Christmas, with publicity cooling, the case of Reid Russell reached its whimpering conclusion. An announcement issued from the District Attorney's office that Buron Fitts "finally accepted" that suicide caused the death of the used car salesman. Unanswered questions would never be officially explained. A chemist's unequivocal report terminated the inquiry, confirming bloodstains on the clothing and garden swing, substantiated the beliefs of Gouverneur Morris, his wife, and other witnesses. Captain Plummer was silenced by a flurry of potential job offers, and Lila Lee and Jimmy departed Manhattan Beach to be with the Morris couple at the Fort Miller ranch briefly, avoiding more publicity.

While public interest waned and gradually ended . . . Jim Kirkwood's obsession with the violence at Second Street had only begun.

For the next fifty years James Kirkwood would write multiple versions of his experience, revise his novel, his screenplay, and his stage play of the Reid Russell mystery, re-assessing the facts and his understanding of what happened. Only in his future versions would the public learn this was hardly the end of the story. Kirkwood would return again to Manhattan Beach in a shocking coda to the truth of his role in the death of Reid.

Those productive years went badly for others. During the first week of March, 1937, D.A. Buron Fitts was shot by unknown assailants while driving home from his office. He survived the attack, but the mystery of who did it and why was never solved. On August 8th of the same year, Lila Lee appeared at Buckeye Lake Pier Ballroom in New Jersey as one of the featured personalities in the *Hollywood Hit Parade* revue. The program featured the music of Jackie Coogan and his Trocadero Club orchestra. Lee, a New Yorker, originally made her theatrical debut as a member of the Gus Edwards School Days unit in vaudeville, and beamed coyly when saying it felt as if returning home. Thus began a series of aborted comebacks as her career petered out.

Captain Clyde Plummer was named Warden of Folsom Prison in a controversial appointment, on November 22, 1937, and began innovations at prison. His appointment was thought to be strictly political, arranged through pressure from Gov. Frank Merriam of California, and it effectively removed Plummer as a potential candidate for District Attorney of Los Angeles County, which he'd intended to do.

In April of 1939, his wife distraught and behaving strangely, Gouverneur Morris moved to Coolidge, New Mexico. Thereafter, Ruth Morris, whose behavior was more irrational with each passing day, was admitted to the Alameda Sanitorium in New Mexico. There on April 19, after two weeks of hospitalization, she committed suicide by taking an overdose of sleeping pills. The matter was kept out of the newspapers, except to note she was the second woman in the United

States to be licensed to fly an airplane. She was also referred to as the so-called "second woman" in Reid Russell's life on Second Street.

In May of 1939, a few weeks after his wife's death, Gouverneur Morris was injured in New Mexico. Alone in his car, he drove off the road near Bluewater, suffering cuts and bruises; witnesses reported the accident as inexplicable. Morris gave his home as Carmel, California, though he lived in Coolidge, New Mexico, for the rest of his life. His writing career and public life ended abruptly. He died of a massive coronary in 1953.

In November of 1940, after several terms in office and much controversy, Buron was defeated in his run for District Attorney. He lost in a landslide. The headline in the *Los Angeles Times* spoke volumes: "Biggest Upset in History of DA's Office!!!" Thus began a lifetime eclipse from the limelight for the man.

CHAPTER THREE

A NOVEL MYSTERY

In 1978 Kirkwood went West for the Los Angeles premiere of his Pulitzer Prize musical drama, *A Chorus Line*, at the Schubert Theater in the Century City section of Los Angeles. Alone one day in his temporary residence at Oakwood Apartments, he took time to rent a car in order to travel down to Manhattan Beach secretly with the intention of visiting the former Morris house where he first met Reid Russell.

Disoriented by the changes of forty years, confused due to unfamiliar street signs and numerous dwellings he'd never seen before, he became lost and drove back to his rented digs, convinced the old scene of the crime had been torn down, lost forever to history. He had tried his best to locate the house off Sepulveda, fearing the worst. It was there still, hidden from him, being smaller and more insignificant than the mansion he remembered.

"My God, why couldn't I find it? I was dying to go there just for the memories." A boyhood trauma site of decades past eluded him. The scripts he created about Reid Russell's death had never satisfied him. He wanted to see it again, live it again, just one more time. It was not to be.

A burgeoning population had over-developed the Pacific Coast and prevented Jim from finding the estate of his nightmares.

Though in Kirkwood's own voice, his first-person novel was basically true and autobiographical; any reader of the story needed to realize it was created as a work of imagination, in fact an alibi, not a docudrama. Jim changed certain facts, altering the truth for dramatic purposes, and compressed situations and timetables. Within his plot constructions and foundations can be found impressions and details that tie in with old official press and police reports.

In some instances he provided background information the press could not access. The mood of the besieged household, including his mother, the onslaught of the press mania, the ambiance of the classmates at his school, the emotional impact of the crime upon himself, was recalled and catalogued in his book, *There*

Must Be a Pony. He neatly omitted much of what took place; some of what he left out of his narrative and explanations may have arisen from not knowing what happened, or was an effort to protect people. However horrific the *Pony* tale was, his guarded reality was skillfully interwoven with his fictional approach, often substituting a red herring to keep us from the painful truth

Kirkwood was a classic witness, with all the advantages and disadvantages memory causes. His endless re-telling of the tale permanently clouded the facts. He led his pony to the water trough so often it never wanted to drink. By careful selection of details, Jim created an unsettling annotation about the scandal. His creativity of sifting facts with fiction from novel to play to film within the framework of the official documentation of the case was literary chess.

Some changes were monumental on the surface. The character of Merwin, a Hollywood screenwriter with an effeminate streak and nasty wit, was really a combination of pretentious Gouverneur Morris and of his wife Ruth, which added a belligerent demeanor and resilient toughness. With Victoria Russell still alive, Jim changed Reid's mother into an older, well-to-do wife, sprinkled with elements borrowed from Ruth Morris. Somewhere in the mix of his novel there remained the essence of truth because, as he said, "It's harder to dissemble to a friend."

Kirkwood's depiction of his *Doppleganger*, Josh, was of a fifteen-year-old, going on sixteen when the affairs of re-christened Manhattan Beach, now fictional Paraiso Beach, occurred. (In reality, young Jimmy had only turned twelve a month before the death of Reid Russell.) For four weeks of that summer (the plot date of the year was updated another twenty), Josh was delighted because at long last, his mother had a boyfriend who was not abusive to her, or insensitive and hateful to Jimmy.

"You should see the men she falls in love with," Josh states about Rita, explaining the nastiness of her former husbands. "They might look all right on the outside, but on the inside they're each one more rotten than the next." If Josh seems a precocious fifteen, Jimmy had himself seemed far older for twelve. He was in many ways like a little old man. Jimmy's attitude, if not size (spurting up to almost six feet at age twelve), often led people to think the twelve year old was fifteen.

Two incidents became highlights in flashback moments during the novel. First was the explanation of Rita's ill-fated, short-term marriage to an untrustworthy man whom Josh disliked. Kirkwood has Merwin tell Josh that his mother's honeymoon with her well-to-do man came to a devastating end when a woman showed up at the door, claiming to be his current and abiding wife. It seems the gentleman married Rita before divorcing his other spouse. Rita quickly ends this marriage.

Anecdotes in the novel explained sealed records in Lila Lee's second divorce, which was done less to protect her son, Jimmy, than to protect the three children of the other wife by her erstwhile husband, wealthy stockbroker John Peine. Lila Lee left him in mid-May of 1935, after their first six weeks of wedded bliss upon learning he was a bigamist. She drove to Reno to establish residence, reaching there "in a day or so." In Los Angeles, her lawyer, C.P. Von Herzen, explained carefully that the actress and Mr. Peine were temperamentally unsuited to each other, but they remained good friends despite their differences.

In Nevada, Lila required a Reno attorney. Von Herzen recommended divorce expert, H.C. Rawlings, to represent her. A brief trial under Judge Clark J. Guild allowed divorce on grounds of cruelty after Lila's complaint was heard. The judge was sympathetic to her situation. No testimony was released to press; particulars of divorce were sealed from the public, ostensibly to protect minor children. Newshounds didn't expand upon the pathetic scandal.

The public learned only that she married Peine in Harrison, New York, on Dec. 8, 1934, and formally received her divorce on July 2nd, 1935. Lila, who'd been living as Mrs. Lila Lee Peine, once more resumed her former film name. Lila Lee commented wryly to the press, "The honeymoon is over when you go into divorce court." Her Los Angeles lawyer added, "Miss Lee long planned this necessary legal action." She and husband Peine separated weeks after the marriage, owing to issues of "incompatibility," which was Von Herzen's bland term for the duplicitous nature of Lila's husband.

Jimmy wrote the second key incident into the narrative, mentioning it in the novel's chronology rather than the play. This damaging item hinted his mother was dangerous and capable of violence. The substance of the anecdote used in the manuscript had its confirmation in a news account about Lila Lee during that first week of July in 1935.

Celebrating the Fourth and her renewed freedom, Lila attended a beach party in Santa Cruz with John Beach of New York. They were among guests at the exclusive Pasa Tiempo Country Club, operated by Marion Hollins. Lee blushed when questioned regarding rumors of a secret marriage to Beach, following her quickie divorce from Peine in Nevada two days earlier. Beach was described as Miss Lee's latest wealthy escort, and they played hide and seek with the entourage of press pursuing them.

As part of their evasive games, the two lovers cancelled reservations on a steamer bound for San Francisco, via Sacramento, leaving reporters standing on the dock while they jumped into an automobile to speed away. They were soon linked in Carson City columns as a romantic item. Lila Lee continued her madcap movie star behavior for the remainder of 1935. It took sobering news from her sister, Peggy, that their father had died after Thanksgiving, to pry her from adventures on the West Coast, and to resume care of her son.

In the fictional account, that second incident is mirrored in Rita's engagement to Cedric, another ostensibly "rotten" rich playboy, which ends with Rita aiming a .22 pistol at him, chasing him into a bathroom, where the terrified man locks himself in. Her motive for the threat is attributed to his infidelity. He's able to get to the police, where he exposes this facet of Rita's character, which will enforce their suspicion that she's capable of shooting her next paramour, Ben Nichols, if sufficiently angered. Like Lila, three years earlier, Rita is then institutionalized in a hospital for alcoholism or mental problems. Jim Kirkwood named the rich boyfriend, Cedric Morris, which may be a variation on the name of Gouverneur Morris, their host at Manhattan Beach.

In the first novelization of his life, Jim translated several instances of his experiences with Lila Lee's numerous beaux. Josh, like young Kirkwood, has mixed feelings about the various men attracted to his mother. At first Josh doesn't like Lee Hertzig, a high-powered attorney who has an interest in Rita. The actress considers the youthful balding attorney as a companion who can provide her with both financial aid and legal cover. To all purposes, they are a couple, of sorts.

The lawyer boyfriend is apathetic toward Josh and ridicules his shyness and lack of aggressiveness, calling the boy by the name he most loathes, "sissy." Hertzig is meant to be Beverly Hills lawyer, C.P von Herzen, later president of the Los Angeles Lions Club, one of the most active and popular leading citizens of the city. Herzen's benign looks, that of a CPA rather than an attorney, hid a hard-nosed, successful defense lawyer, adept at any criminal case involving a celebrity.

Jimmy regularly eavesdropped on his mother and her chats with Ruth Morris. The fault Lila mostly disliked about Jimmy was that he behaved like a "sissy," the same word that irritates Josh. Kirkwood said the bane of his childhood in Hollywood was to be exposed "to a lot of weird stuff" in the motion picture business and in theater. As a teenager, he learned one lesson about sexual attraction: "I mean if there's a *bona fide* homosexual within a thousand miles, you can bet he'll find me and make a pass." He complained he was stuck with a sensitive face.

Pre-adolescent Josh is limned as timid and shy. That dominates Rita's conversation, indiscreetly discussing his situation with Merwin, which Josh overhears. Rita laments the femininity of her son, referring to him as "not a regular boy." A more likely term used by Lila was "poof" or "fag", or another more common vernacular of the Thirties. In one of the updates Josh is called "gay," but that label was not common usage in Hollywood back then.

Out of anger at his mother's expressed feelings, Josh dumps a bottle of perfume down the bathroom drain instead of presenting it to her as planned. His affectionate attempts are quickly rebuffed, and his adolescent emotions ride a rollercoaster of insecurity. Merwin is written as a 1960 homosexual, a shockingly assured gay man. Josh depicts him as one of few friends to both himself and his mother, but someone who comes into his life only periodically, and always to cheer him up. Kirkwood's metaphor for Merwin was "a certain tropical bird—a cockatoo or a cockateel."

Like Guvvie Morris, Merwin is small, thin, fragile . . . with a beaklike nose and "bright blue eyes that blink just like a bird's." In other ways, Merwin and Guvvie took their fashion sense from the Fred Astaire look of the 1930s, "a kind of English-Italian cut to sort of pinched waist . . ." Josh's conclusion about Merwin is that he's "kind of sexless. I don't think he ever 'does it' with anybody. He's more an observer and commentator."

Though Jim dubbed Manhattan Beach as Moorish-sounding Paraiso Beach, it's the identical locale with a resort mentality. As for the Morris house, Kirkwood recalled it as "a great place: an enormous Spanish-type house about a mile back from the beach, with about three acres running downhill behind it, a barbecue pit, orange and lemon groves, a barn and a hothouse, and just about everything you could imagine. And tall eucalyptus trees and high hedges all around the place so it was completely isolated."

Because of a ground floor game room extending into the low backyard, the rear of the residence appeared to be three flights high. Kirkwood described "great verandas and decks jutting from each storey on the back side of the house." Owing to the quickly sloping grounds, the vista from the upper balcony rose high above the tree line, making for a spectacular view on clear days. Over the game room was a movie-set style living room, fitting in with early California ambiance. Jim noted its "beamed ceiling and white walls and a lot of tiled floor and scatter rugs." He liked the big hearth because the tiles on the floor "made the room about as cold as a public toilet."

Off the living room was another room with a Morris flavor: the trophy room, Jim called it. "He had all kinds of antique guns and pistols and swords and keys to a lot of castles and palaces in Europe." This character in Jim's novel is the image of Guvvie, a rabid collector of historical items, as might be expected by a man whose great-grandfather was a Revolutionary War hero. On the level below, in the game room, soundproofing truly isolates it from the rest of the house. He describes how the game room is "fixed up terrifically, but I don't think there's anything as miserable as a terrific game room when there aren't a lot of people in it playing games." Among available amusements are slot machines that loomed like sentinels along the walls.

On Josh's birthday, August 22nd, at the height of the tourist season, the narrator's mother takes him for dinner "at the pier." Manhattan Beach's famous pier of the era extended far into the Pacific Ocean and terminated with its landmark octagonal pavilion; Josh states he spent time playing miniature golf at another nearby recreational spot. Jim likely referred to one of the popular amusements in the town: "The World," as it was called, which gave players an eighteen-hole miniature golf course on Center Street, which harbored a plethora of nearby small restaurants. The attraction centered on the colorful flags at each hole in the little course, representing a different nation of the world with corresponding features and symbolic models (miniature Eiffel Tower, Tower of Pisa, *etc.*).

Jimmy, like his image Josh, seldom lived with his mother for long stretches, owing to her career's deterioration and general health problems, brought on by her hectic celebrity life. He had not seen her between 1932 and Christmas of 1935, until they moved to the Los Angeles area and accepted the hospitality of Ruth and Gouverneur Morris. That stay at Manhattan Beach was one of the longest times he spent with Lila uninterrupted. Manhattan Beach was a year round resort: it was not unusual for it to be filled during summers with 25,000 bathers, fishing expeditions, and sun worshippers.

Entertainments for visitors to help locals with their businesses became a paramount idea. In this way the community became less and less of a retreat for the rich of Hollywood and more of a demographically diverse town. There was no movie theatre in town in 1936, (La Mar would open in a few years), and recreation was supplied by the relatively simple pastimes of any resort community. Beachside amusement parks were basically designed to keep tourists enthralled.

As narrator, Josh lets the reader know he is hardly reckless, and playing Chinese checkers is about daring as he can be. Josh and his mother often visit the pier's amusements, and on one occasion the boy is challenged to get aboard a contraption that whirled suspended seat-swings around a pole. The "ride" repels him, yet he's bullied into taking a seat on the thing. Being strapped into one of the scary wide swings, he glances warily at a man taking the seat beside him, a complete stranger who tries to put him at ease with an assuring smile. At first, Josh does a double-take, thinking he's sitting next to Cary Grant, who in 1936 was thirty-two years old, and was at the start of a monumental movie career, having done *Gunga Din, Sylvia Scarlett,* and *I'm No Angel,* hardly the most famous of his motion pictures. By 1960, when Kirkwood wrote the updated series of these episodes, his reference to Grant indicated the most popular star of the generation.

Turning sick during the giddy ride, as the spinning seat tumbles round and round, the boy vomits on the man at his side. Dismayed, the boy and Rita are amazed because the victim of this accident does not fall into a temper, but is remarkably civil, despite having Lobster Newburg heaved on him. Hurrying to one of the nearby restaurants abutting the pier, likely, the Silver Spray or a long-gone greasy spoon along Manhattan Boulevard, he cleans himself up. There, the boy and his contrite mother meet the man again and thank Ben Nichols for his forbearance. (Kirkwood leaves out the interesting aside that Cary Grant bore a startling resemblance to his own father, James Kirkwood Sr., the imperious leading man of silent pictures in the Twenties.) The new-met trio instantly bond and become fast friends.

For rest of the night at the amusement pier, they go everywhere together, including the funhouse. They throw baseballs at wooden milk bottles and wind up going to the beach house, where they play blackjack until 2 a.m. Josh is taken by Ben's subtle and twinkling demeanor. To Rita's questioning, Ben tells them a few mundane specifics about his background, and recognizes the notorious movie actress. His startling resemblance to Cary Grant intrigues Rita, who always wanted to work with or meet the greater star, and never did.

Photographs of Reid Russell show him to be a suitable catch: tall, dark, and handsome, also easily mistaken for Cary Grant. The trend in films then, far more so than today, always featured the same upstanding type as the hero. At twenty-eight, he had a lanky athleticism and a relaxed manner. He certainly appealed to the youngster as a role model. He became instrumental in helping the boy reveal his talents as a tennis player, and to take out his aggressions on the clay courts.

Reid Russell became Ben Nichols in Kirkwood's jigsaw version of events. In press accounts, Russell was often referred to as a boy, though he was twenty-eight. Kirkwood's literary description of the man who became Rita's boyfriend is limited, yet much was applicable to Russell. Unlike Reid, who was nearly ten years younger than Lila Lee, Ben is written as a year older than Rita. Whereas Ben is from New York, and works in advertising (at least that's what he tells his new two friends), Reid hailed from Pico Heights in the Los Angeles area, and was an unemployed used car salesman, born in Virginia, the son of a deceased military officer who traveled extensively.

Josh and his mother are not in the least concerned why such a handsome, charming man as Ben comes alone to the pier. It never occurs to either he might have been stalking them. In the novel, Ben becomes Rita's lover immediately after their first meeting; Josh hears him snoring lightly in the guest room the following morning.

Kirkwood's unshaken notion was that the meeting was utterly coincidental. Having been hit by the contents of the Jimmy's upset stomach, Reid Russell could not have planned a more opportune introduction to Lila Lee. Reid was never publicly called anyone's lover. Contemporary press accounts carefully listed him as a friend of the Morris couple. It was Reid's mother who declared he was having an affair with an unidentified married woman. As Lila was divorced and Ruth still married, this led to speculation about them. The press left open whether the unidentified woman was Ruth Morris or Lila Lee or both. Kirkwood, in his book, and in countless interviews of the decades to follow, never minced words on this point: Reid/Ben was his mother's lover. He never characterized his mother's relationship to Ruth.

Similar to Reid Russell, Ben Nichols ingratiates himself into the household and nuclear family unit of Josh and Rita. Part of his charm and ability is making himself indispensable to Rita. He plays mentor to her son. Josh, like Jimmy, sees himself as "some little, furry, woodland creature that was scared of its own shadow." Kirkwood described how his relationship with Reid turned himself into a bubbling extrovert and how his tie to the man contributed greatly to coming out of his shell. "We must have talked for hours," claims the usually taciturn Josh. "My own personal horizon started to clear up" on that day of meeting Ben. "He told me to start speaking up about what came into my mind."

As for the impact of Reid Russell upon young Jimmy, Kirkwood asserted, "And you know something—I haven't stopped sounding off since, except for periods of shock caused by some catastrophe or other."

Of all the people in the house at Second Street, Jimmy was the only intense observer of whatever took place. He was the one with curiosity and awareness, as Ruth Morris informed both police and press. The boy was the one who noticed everything. And so it remained in the plotline Kirkwood wrote. It is Josh who learns that Ben Nichols is calm and easy-going on the surface, but there are darker and more hidden demons below the surface. The narrator of the novel observes how inconsistencies in Ben's personality emerge over time. He tells, for example, how Ben dislikes "drunk women," but imbibes freely himself.

According to Josh, Ben often "froze up. He didn't make a scene or anything. He just turned into a sheet of steel and didn't utter a word the whole rest of the evening." The boy points out how the man isn't a lightweight in his own drinking habits, though Josh insists that Ben maintains an even mood when he drinks alcohol. What he sees is that "every once in a while he'd get very quiet for maybe ten or fifteen minutes." It's the sad look in the man's eyes that most bothers Josh: "a sad perplexed look." Ben can shake off this minor catatonia after a while and continue on as if nothing has happened.

Another disturbing characteristic Josh duly describes is Ben's tendency toward nightmares. His crying out loudly in the night often awakens the youngster in the next room. He can't understand why Ben has nightmares. Josh can't possibly imagine what Ben dreams about "that would upset him like that."

Ben increasingly talks in generalities about business troubles. (In the summer of 1936, Reid was jobless and depressed. He lost his job as a used car salesman, and was looking for possible ways to make a great deal of money fast.) Josh mentions that Ben seems upset and depressed over his future. He snaps at Rita and Josh over lost accounts. "I mean, do we have to talk about it? I came here to get away from it for a while."

As the boy grows closer to Ben, Josh gives various examples of how Ben's humor and style appeal to him. After meeting one of Rita's more catty friends, Ben answers her matter-of-factly when asked his profession. Ben says, "Fornicologist." His response tickles Josh.

Beneath the comment may have hidden Ben's deeper resentments and attitudes. Though Josh is amused, it indicates that there is in Ben's nature (but was more in that of Reid Russell) the inclination of a paid escort. For Ben, allegedly a high-powered and mature ad agency executive, this is not as funny or apt as it would apply to Reid's unemployment as a motorcar salesman. We learn Ben may have married his older wife because she held the purse strings, but at the time of the quoted remark, it is witty in isolation.

One of the rare photographs of Reid Russell, aged 27, ex-used car salesman, and self-proclaimed "Fornicologist," was found with a bullet fired through his head. His mother, Victoria Russell, believed he was murdered, and Clyde Plummer of the Los Angeles police agreed with her.

Talking about marriage cools a tense relationship between Rita and Ben. He provides a variety of excuses about how to proceed with her plans; all result in delays. Rita's past bad experiences with men make this hesitancy worry her. The idyllic days of the carefree trio ends soon enough. When Rita and Josh prepare to visit some of her friends, Ben declines to accompany them. He has his own destination to follow, but makes a great to-do of saying farewell to them. As they drive off in their car, the boy looks back to see Ben's arms flop to his sides after waving goodbye. It's the last time he sees Ben alive.

Late the next night, Josh is awakened at home by the sound of arguing voices. Though his usual habit is to investigate everything that happens in the house, he claims not to have interest in this and goes back to sleep. In the morning Rita seems preoccupied with memorizing lines from a script, and Josh goes off to school. When the boy returns that afternoon, his tennis match with a Hermosa Beach school cancelled owing to coastal fog, Josh is alone with the household pets. Modeling them after those belonging to Mr. and Mrs. Morris, Kirkwood enumerated the menagerie of the Second Street house: several dogs, a Brazilian weeper monkey, and a parrot.

Squinting at enveloping mists, Josh lets the dogs have a free run in the yard. While standing on the tiled veranda outside the game room, he barely discerns the terraced grounds where a path leads through a grove of citrus trees to another lawn area, in which the barbecue and a croquet course are located. There are some trees and a small cottage where the gardener used to live when he was full-time. Either side of the property has low white fencing, or a stonewall encircling the estate. The dogs come running back shivering, with their tails between their legs.

The Pekinese faces the fog and starts yapping madly. Curious, Josh begins a slow ambling walk into the misty area. The anxious barking and whimpering of the animal makes him reluctant to proceed. "Halfway down through the grove I stopped. I can't forget the sensation right then. I had the most terrific impulse to turn around and run back—not to the house—but right on by it to the driveway, out to Calle Vista, then up to Sepulveda Boulevard and away!"

As he proceeds toward the lawn swing, he sees a foot on the ground. Lying under the green and white striped awning of the lawn swing is Ben, looking disheveled. On closer inspection, Josh sees the man's face, a tint of blue showing on the cheeks where his beard has grown a bit. The boy leans closer to the face of the man to determine if there's warmth or breath. He feels neither. A sense of shock weighs upon the boy, and the trauma of finding his friend dead will imbed an indelible memory. "My senses seemed to be more alert than ever before."

As part of the boy's curious behavior, Kirkwood indicated that Josh couldn't tell whether he imagines or merely performs some irregular actions. He tries to rearrange the dead body, to make it more comfortable, and he wipes a stream of ants from the bloody head wound. Removing a handkerchief from the dead man's sports-coat pocket, he brushes ants from Ben's cheek and mouth. Josh cannot estimate how long he remains kneeling before the dead body, staring at it in complete awe and amazement. "I wanted him to blink his eyes and look over at me and tell me it was a joke."

The weapon appears to be one from the gunroom collection.

Josh plucks it from the ground. It's a "funny-looking, European style gun, so old I was surprised it had fired at all. I just held it a while; then I put it down" next to the leg of the victim. The unquestioned conclusion Josh draws is that Ben killed himself.

Racing back to the house, he suffers a delayed reaction. "I got so scared." Alone in the house, the boy gathers all the animals with him into the hall lavatory, a tight space, and keeps them with him. In Kirkwood's fictionalized account, because Rita is at the studio filming a movie, Josh calls Merwin, who must drive miles to reach the house. Over the telephone, Josh informs Merwin that Ben shot himself.

In preliminary police reports, Ruth alleges she has made the discovery of the body. Her testimony was that Jimmy informed her the next morning of his own sighting. From the veranda, she looked through binoculars towards the barbecue pit where Jimmy insisted Reid Russell was dead. Ruth Morris contacted Lila by phone and insisted that Lila must return to Manhattan Beach right away, without saying why. Listening to the conversation, the boy wondered if his mother already knew about the death of her boyfriend. He could not understand how she might know already. Kirkwood was then told that his mother was frantic because she had been trying to call Reid and could not reach him anywhere.

At some point Jimmy and his witness went down to the body again. Ruth said it was the next morning. Jimmy, as Josh did in the novel, placed that toward dusk. They confirmed the death, but the boy wanted to remain with the body, not leave him alone. Ruth (and Merwin) wanted to hurry away to the house. After all, they were awaiting the return of the boy's mother and had to break the news to her. At this point the decision was made to withhold information from the police until the boy's mother was present.

Here was the great inconsistency the police could not fathom.

Why was it that no one went down to the barbecue area until the next morning? Did Jimmy tell adults what happened immediately, or did he wait? Or was he alone all night with the animals and had no adult supervision? If so, where were the adults? Neither the novel, nor the police record, can answer this. Jim danced around this point in our conversations.

Throughout the novel, Josh is spy, eavesdropper, busybody, and constant audience to all that happens. Like many quiet youngsters whose life center on adults, having few friends and close peers, he spends his time keeping tabs on those older folk around him. It is Josh who knows the police botch the investigation. He observes the body before anyone else. When he goes down to the scene with the policemen and studies the treatment of Ben's body, he answers more questions about where the gun was. The Manhattan Beach police captain is named Roy Clymer, whereas the real one was Clyde Plummer.

Josh repeatedly returns to the death scene, and tags after Roy Clymer. Though his mother is against it, the officer denies it's a problem. In all likelihood, the officer believes the boy has something to say about the case, but not willing to say it in front of the household. What the police don't understand is how dedicated the lad is to protecting his mother, if not himself. Josh simply lies to questioners about whatever he saw and heard the last night Ben visited.

Fictional Josh never poses for press photographs at the site of the death and insists he is far more upset than pictures which show young Jimmy at the time. In newspaper account photos, the grinning face of young Kirkwood watches the gardener raking clear the area, indicating his fascination with the incident. Captain Plummer became infuriated when he learned the upshot of this photograph: Gardener Tony Mumolo had been told to make a bonfire of the piled leaves from the site. It gave police the extra job of sifting through ashes in search of a lead slug six weeks later.

Kirkwood wrote how Josh receives hysterical, drunken, and increasingly nasty phone calls from a woman who accuses his mother of killing Ben, killing "my Baby." Do we assume they came from Ben's wife? The question remains unanswered if the calls came from Reid's mother to Jimmy. Was Reid's mother a well-known alcoholic? Or was it based upon Lila calling Reid's mother when in her cups?

In official accounts of the real situation, the series of phone calls went to Reid Russell's mother from a distracted and jealous lover. Conversations in Kirkwood's manuscript attributed to a wife sound much more like the desperation of a mother—or were they transposed calls made by Kirkwood's mother in the days before Reid was found dead? In the novel, Ben's wife is considerably older than her husband. Mrs. Victoria Russell was fifty at the time her son, Reid, was twenty-eight.

The woman calling Josh does not identify herself and is increasingly unstable and drunk. When finally she shows up at the house, Josh watches her toss a brick at a door, demanding to see Rita. When the older woman smashes a window, the police are summoned. "You has-been, you killed my baby," she cries out and collapses. Police take her away.

Victoria Russell demanded a police inquiry into her son's death six weeks after the official ruling of suicide in September. In Kirkwood's book this occurs within a few days of the death of Ben. The woman in question makes an indelible impression on Josh. Kirkwood never gives this woman a first name. She remains either Mrs. Nichols or the Widow Nichols, more sarcastically. Her obsession with the death of the young visitor to the beach house is a parallel to the interest Reid Russell's mother showed, for Mrs. Victoria Russell was a widow about the same age as given for Ben's older wife.

Unspoken in press accounts was the likelihood that Mrs. Russell's complaint about the police investigation arose after she was picked up in a drunken state, taunting the residents of the Morris house to come outside. Altering incidents and roles of an older woman from mother to older wife indicate Kirkwood's concern in 1960 that Victoria Russell, still alive, might take the issue to a lawsuit. He fictionalized reality for his storyline. Mrs. Russell had gone publicly silent on the issue, finally accepting her son's death as inexplicable, probably never accepting it as suicide.

About the gun, Josh talks freely: "I picked it up," he admits, to see if it was one of the private collection kept in the glass case of the game room. In the evening after the body was removed, Merwin calls Ben "an inconsiderate son of a bitch," which echoes comments made by Gouverneur Morris to the press and to Russell's mother about how insensitive Reid Russell was by his self-destructive action.

Like many summer residents, especially when there was no cook or maid on duty at the Morris place, its residents dined at one of the many seaside restaurants. A variety of places could be found along Manhattan Beach Avenue. In his book, Kirkwood describes an Italian restaurant run by an immigrant family—Mama, Papa, and the three Paganelli children. It closely matches the famous Ercole Restaurant, founded in the 1920s by Joey Ercole, who hailed from Italy and started a soda fountain with his wife Blanche, but expanded to a full-fledged and famous dining experience, complete with cocktail lounge.

During the 1930s the small restaurant contained small tables, a fountain with stools and a few wooden booths against the walls. It was, by then, a family business with wife and children pitching in to perform the daily operations. According to Jimmy Kirkwood, the Ercole owners, Joe and Blanche Ercole were warm and supportive people, and in this, the Paganelli family was modeled after them.

Mama Ercole extended an invitation to the Morris house residents to come dine after hours on that awful night, because she was certain none of them had eaten since finding Reid's body. "The way they took us in you'd have thought we'd been trapped down one of those mine shafts for at least a year." Kirkwood thought everyone shared the same need to escape the premises after the police left with the body . . .

From the Ercole family came about something of Reid's last hours on the fatal evening. Fairly tight, he'd been drinking at their bar. He mentioned that his friends went elsewhere to dinner that night, and he may have been referring to John Grana's restaurant, the Guy Tano. Mr. Russell was not his usual jovial self, observed Joey Ercole worriedly, adding that Mr. Russell made a phone call and soon left. The Morris group concluded Reid drove to the Second Street house, left his car on the street, walked down the long way to the barbecue pit area on the lower lawn, and shot himself there.

In the story version, Josh doesn't react to the death as one expects of a child in a morbid situation. He's surprised and irritated at how the older people hover about him and want to protect him; the changed treatment by his fellow students at Manhattan Beach schools amazes him. Students often ignored him as a transient new kid on the block, but suddenly grant him an inspiring respect. He becomes a celebrity on a par with his mother and father, is asked ghoulish and unpleasant questions about the dead man and the relationship to his mother. In many ways this notoriety delights him. Mickey Emerson, a character Jimmy Kirkwood played on the television show, *Valiant Lady,* makes an appearance now as one of Josh's classmates, among the worst of the insensitive culprits, asking inane questions and making cruel comments.

Chased by reporters and ambushed by paparazzi, Josh is made uncomfortable by the added attention. This is unlike Jimmy, who posed proudly for reporters. Josh does make frequent and interesting statements to the press, and often inflames the situation with revelations about police incompetence. Some of his motivation stems from the deep anger he expresses at the death of Ben. In Josh's words, "His death started me on the road" to becoming an extrovert.

Reid Russell frequently told Jimmy stories that could not be checked or verified; in the book, Ben withholds an equal amount of information from Josh. For example, Reid informed Jimmy and Lila that he was married once to a rich Texas woman (which Kirkwood turned into a fact in his plot). Both Ben and Reid were gamblers, owing considerable sums of money, which they could not pay back. When the floodgates open and the information about Ben (Reid) flows through, Josh is overwhelmed by what he doesn't know about the man he loves. Josh comments, "You had to hate Ben—as much as you could." It seemed every day brought knowledge of "another of his crummy vices."

James Kirkwood spoke of Russell bitterly: "I found him in our back yard with a bullet in his head." Decades after his death, he was not sympathetic to Reid in the slightest. "If you're going to kill yourself, you should go off somewhere by yourself, instead of doing it that close to people you supposedly love."

Jim confessed how much he still hated Reid Russell, and his nightmares never abated. "Even to this day," he saw the bloody wound on the man's head and a parade of ants marching in and out of the bullet hole. That picture "will sometimes flash in front of me just as I'm about to drop off to sleep."

In his autobiographical novel, Kirkwood never mentioned selling tickets to the murder site on Halloween, or profiting from the death and giving the creeps to local children with morbid curiosity. One can only speculate about exaggerations or truths Kirkwood added to his guided tours of the spookiest spot at Second Street. Jimmy's enterprising behavior undercut the carefully constructed trauma that fictional Josh allegedly suffers, but the newspaper images of Jimmy enjoying the attention at the scene of Reid's death was unmistakable . . . and alarmed his mother. It led her to demand the lawn chair be removed from the property. Her reaction, and that of her son, was far more indicative of a twelve year-old boy's actions than what a fifteen or sixteen year old might do.

Because of that, Kirkwood omitted this from his story's text. Circumstances altered that in years to come. The boys in Kirkwood's story became written much younger than high school, and far more immature. Josh's sidekick, Sid Traylor, resembles Howard Jones, pictured in national newspapers with Jim at the mysterious suicide scene. Jimmy's friend happened to be the son of the friendly officer who first declared the case was not a homicide. One could have surmised Officer Jones to be in collusion with the Morris couple, and Van Herzon thought so too. There are several such references to the police officer in the novel.

Josh, in parallel to Jimmy, finds himself pulled out of school by police for questioning. When he sees his mother's friend, crime lawyer Lee Hertzig at work, Josh starts to admire the man, and how he goes over his testimony with him The lawyer and his mother are worried about Josh and want to influence his answers. As a witness, Josh impresses Hertzig and wins accolades, which shows he can be dependable. Rita suggests a lawyer be with her son constantly, but Hertzig says it looks bad if a kid needs legal protection, and he rejects the notion as bad strategy. Unspoken, however, is whether Rita fears that Josh is guilty of much more and needs protection for a graver reason.

Josh quotes Hertzig as saying: "if that sonovabitch only left a note." The gravity of the situation hits Josh when he realizes his lawyer fears a possible grand jury call-up. Hertzig also does not want to keep the boy off the scene, the activity of which Josh/Kirkwood likes to observe. The lawyer may have seen Josh's insights as valuable to the case. Hertzig has noted how the investigation by Clymer and coroner has been botched. This triggers some pleasure, too, in Josh.

During the worst of the investigation for Jimmy Kirkwood and Lila, they were repeatedly questioned by the detectives of the District Attorney's office for inconsistencies in their stories. However, it was Ruth Morris who took the brunt of the heat, causing her to collapse at one Hall of Justice meeting. Early in the book version, Rita is put through the wringer explaining about Ben for one and a half hours. Though Rita is extremely anxious about her son getting subjected to a similar onslaught, Hertzig insists that Josh must face it alone. They have to trust he could deal with it. Hertzig, though never stating it openly, sees some inner strength in Josh, and feels confidant.

Despite newspaper accounts to the contrary, Jim claimed that Josh never heard Ben/Reid talk of suicide. The man was called depressed and distant; Jimmy was cited in press accounts as one who testified to Reid's suicidal talk. Jimmy and his alter ego were easy targets for an embarrassed police captain, but he had to be handled carefully because the boy's testimony was worse than a loaded gun. The pluck of the young witness became one of the sidebar stories of the case.

When studio executives took an interest in Jim, Rita's agent parlayed the machinations into a film career for the boy. He was offered a role in a movie. Lila was against it, and Jim was furious at this lost opportunity. In differing accounts, however, he revealed that within a year or two, he was on stage with his mother in one of her New York plays, filling in during his Christmas vacation from school.

During the case of Reid Russell, Buron Fitts, the reigning District Attorney during the 1930s, remained unnamed in the book, though he stated to Jimmy Kirkwood: "I'm an old admirer of your mother's, young man." Fitts was a corrupt official in the pocket of the studios. Every major studio was listed among his campaign contributors. He covered up more than one Hollywood scandal and let a few others leak when he deemed it to his own advantage. Since he responded to higher authority, he was under pressure in all likelihood from the old guard friends of Gouverneur Morris and his equally patrician wife.

Friends of silent film star Lila Lee could not be underestimated, and no doubt brought pressure to bear on the District Attorney, who had two recent major scandals under his aegis: the mob-related killing of Thelma Todd and the strange death of Jean Harlow's husband. In the glaring spotlight of those glamorous cases, something like Russell's death was a minor note.

Von Herzen didn't want his clients walking into a courtroom, and therefore neither does Lee Hertzig. The legal whiz is adamant that the worst-case scenario would be a convening of a Grand Jury. Under threat of this development, Josh hates Ben even more for the torment being heaped upon his mother. It's obvious the two criminal lawyers, fictional and real, feared the ramifications that come from groups of ill-informed citizens who'd feel sympathy for the wife of an Army veteran pleading justice for her son. This was not a winnable situation. It had to be ended quickly.

On Dec. 12, 1936, Fitts dismissed the Russell case based on "blood tests" allegedly performed on the lawn swing pillows and Reid's clothing. However sensational, in spite of many unanswered questions the matter fell from the press scrutiny and public interest.

In Josh's version, it turned out differently. Under an unresolved cloud, Guvvie and Ruth Morris went with Lila and son to a ranch about two hours away to avoid press and publicity. Charles Green's Fort Miller Ranch was truly secluded in the 1930s. Named Andy Midge in the book, Green allowed Jimmy to have his own bunkhouse, a small cottage, and Jim rode to school in Friant on a horse.

The ranch was along the highway on the route to Bakersfield. Its view was of a mesa, a table mountain prominent in the valley. Most of the buildings on the ranch complex were made of wooden beams and adobe. The complex included small private residential cabins, a barn, shelters, stables, an office, a smokehouse, and such. There was the standard bunkhouse for the hands. Kirkwood saw it as a small community where Hereford cattle and horses were raised. The nearest civilized businesses were a country store and gas station several miles away.

In Kirkwood's fictional account, the disposition of the case results from a more secretive act. The onus of saving Rita and, to a degree himself, from a life of guilt, both psychological and legal, causes Josh to come to the rescue. In the book, he recognizes a key insight into Ben a few weeks after his death. Kirkwood's insight may have come as early as Christmas, 1936, at which time Jimmy was living in Friant on the Green ranch, but could have extended any time to the end of the school year in June of 1937, when he returned to Elyria, Ohio.

Josh is so distressed over Ben's death that he can't stop thinking about him. He finally plays a "What If" game with himself. He at once realizes he has overlooked one of the most significant aspects of his stay at Manhattan Beach. There he hid money and other things in a loose newel post on the staircase. He shared this information with Ben, who occasionally used it to secrete notes and other personal communications for the boy. It now dawns on Josh that, if there were suicide notes, the loose newel post would be where Ben placed them.

Having no car, Josh decides to go to Manhattan Beach. He hails a cab for part of the two-hour journey and hitchhikes the rest of the way. This can be a big adventure at fifteen, but if Jim Kirkwood did it at twelve, it was highly risky and amazing. Josh leaves in the middle of the night, expecting he'd return to Fort Miller and the Green ranch around dawn, without being missed. Josh speculates that if no notes are within the hidden spot, it could well mean his mother murdered Ben.

Making this long, dangerous journey at night, the boy arrives at the Manhattan Beach house and finds it locked up and, so far as he knows, deserted. Without any hesitation, he breaks into the house and turns on the lights. The only fear he experiences is of the ghost of the dead man being around any corner. He goes to the loosened newel post immediately, unscrews it and looks inside: There are two notes from Ben. Just as before, when he discovered the body, Josh never considers the notes to be other than suicide letters—one to his mother and one addressed to him.

Farewell notes may be left in only one-third of all attempted or successful suicides. Most psychological studies on the subject have recorded the severe, and sometimes devastating effects such notes have upon survivors. Many times the suicide victim penned the notes to serve as an apology or as an attempt to ease the pain or responsibility of those the deceased has left behind. A note may be an attempt to bring closure to relationships and situations, supplying a reason for the death. Less often, the victim will sum up his or her life, his or her problems. These final missives have taken the form of anecdotes, poems, or stories that provide a metaphor for the death; in worst-case scenarios, the intent is an act of revenge to add to the guilt of survivors.

In the majority of cases, psychologists have speculated, when notes are not left, it is because the despondency of the victim led to feelings of worthlessness, or rendered the act pointless in their minds. Some victims believed nothing could explain the act and made no attempt to provide an explanation for an uncaring world. In sympathetic cases, suicides didn't wish to increase the guilt or grief of survivors that such a note might cause.

Ben left one short note and one long one. To Rita, he offered an apology for the failure of his life and professed his love. The longer note to Josh was far more complex, taking the form of an instructive anecdote. The moral of his tale for Josh was: "Don't do as I did—do as I say." These notes could have been interpreted as goodbye letters provided by a man planning on leaving (but not dying), or giving a farewell without an expectation of death.

According to Josh, the police want the letters authenticated. Josh calls Lee Hertzig at 4am that very morning to inform him of his discovery. And the boy insists the letters are not meant for the press, but only used to exonerate anyone of the charge of murder. He knows Hertzig can convince D.A. Buron Fitts to accept the verity of these exhibits. All concerned will then have the opportunity to escape the case's chokehold.

When pressed, Jim Kirkwood insisted the letters were not typed. "They were handwritten. No one in that situation has time or cares to type them, and they were not dated." In the true case of Reid Russell, the author acknowledged that Russell left three notes. Two stuffed into the newel post and one in the jewel box of Ruth Morris in her bedroom. The two found by the boy happened *after* the case had been closed and dropped by the District Attorney. Had Jimmy discovered the notes before mid-December, it would explain the abrupt dropping of the case by the D.A. For Jimmy, the main value of the notes was to relieve the anguish of his mother, Lila.

In late May or early June in the story's chronology, Mrs. Nichols—the erstwhile wife of Ben—commits suicide. Since Mrs. Russell—the mother of Reid—lived for 30 more years in Pico Heights, California, and Ruth Morris committed suicide in April of 1939, it seems the death Jim referred to was that of Mrs. Morris. Within the closed circle of Hollywood friends, the matter of Ruth's demise was discreetly avoided. Motive for her suicide went unreported and ignored by the newspapers.

Well, what did Kirkwood make of this? In his book this death occurs, but it's that of Ben's little-understood wife. Jim carefully tiptoed around this sad situation, mirroring the media. Kirkwood described Ben's wife as Ethel Heisler whose father was an entrepreneur who made tons of money, millions. She married the younger man and kept him away from all women. She also was an alcoholic, in an out of sanitariums.

All of these pertained as much to Ruth Morris as they did to the fictional wife of Ben—and not at all to the ex-wife of Reid. The bizarre car crash Gouverneur

Morris suffered several weeks after his wife's death could be interpreted as a suicide attempt too. Whatever so pushed these two to the brink? Was it the discovery of notes, allegedly from Reid Russell, located by Jimmy Kirkwood in the newel post?

Josh made this extraordinary statement after the hullabaloo over the so-called suicide letters, "You'd have thought I'd written the notes, not found them." Of all the weird statements issued by the boy, this one smacked of the deepest secrets of the heart. Jim Kirkwood went into deep psychological analysis to help deal with these unresolved horrors.

While still residing at Manhattan Beach, Josh relates how he often goes down to the scene of the death. It's like a pilgrimage for the benefit of his memory. He never wants to forget it and all the resonance of those days. He will relive the incidents again and again over the next fifty years. There in the distant yard of the Manhattan Beach estate, the hammock is long gone, and traces of the brutal suicide have vanished, too. Josh does find patches of ground where the grass has died. These little spots mark where the lawn chair once sat. Josh stared at this area.

In a coda to the story, Josh reveals how he remains at Fort Miller ranch all that summer while his mother gets institutionalized for mental instability. By September Josh returns to Eliston, Ohio, to live with his mother's sister.

In the real world, Jimmy was sent that year to Elyria, Ohio, to live with Lila's sister, Peggy. He tried to visit the spot of Reid's death again in 1978, but lost his bearings.

Chapter Four

THE BODY FINDER

"Life was offbeat from the beginning."

James Kirkwood mastered the art of the comedic understatement, but he was less kind about the years of being dismissed by his parents, taken in by an aunt, and shunted off to sundry schools. "My childhood was not happy, but my adulthood has been." When we discussed the subject of Lila Lee and James Kirkwood, Sr., he described his relationship with his parents as "strange."

Jim might have been shocked and/or inspired by finding one dead body. For the adolescent, it was merely the forerunner of more during his formative years. "I discovered five dead bodies while in my teens (not all stacked together in a clump, mind; separately, three of them suicides) . . . and I attended seventeen schools. Thank God, that stopped. Not school. The bodies. There's something definitely weird about being known as the Body Finder." He recalled that everyone joked when he was a boy in Elyria, "Don't let Jimmy go out hiking. He'll find another one!" Sure enough, he went out for a walk in the woods near a lake and found a dead body. It was uncanny.

Though he often jumbled chronologies deliberately, Jim Kirkwood knew and seldom revealed that his mother's dead lover was not the first of the bodies he encountered. The year before, while living with his Aunt Peggy in Ohio, he liked playing Chinese checkers with his grandfather, Charles Appel. In this instance, the old man asked for a cup of tea. When Jimmy returned to the room with the teacups, he discovered his sixty-eight year-old grandfather had expired. A modified version of the discovery appears in a flashback scene in *P.S. Your Cat is Dead,* and in this fiction the victim was named Ben, as also identified in the *Pony* story.

After Peggy phoned to inform her sister of their family tragedy, Lila flew to Ohio. On December 1st, greeting her at the airport her eleven-year-old son and her former husband, James Kirkwood, Sr., served as welcomers. Kirkwood the elder had been acting in a play in Cleveland, and he spent holidays with his son. Jimmy had not seen his mother for three years at this point. Between her institutionalization, her trips around the world, and her profligate lifestyle, she had ignored the boy since he was eight. Upon sighting her, Jimmy ran across the tarmac to give her an enormous hug. Lila Lee decided, partly at her son's request, to take Jim back to Hollywood with her after his grandfather's funeral.

A new stage began in their relationship during 1935, closer and more egalitarian in nature. Those three past years in Ohio, however, had given Jimmy his most consistent and stable period of development, as he attended the McKinley School and learned the basics, giving him a foundation in his primary school years that would serve him for the rest of his life.

When Kirkwood had lunch in the 1980s with Dickie Moore, a child star of the Thirties, he knew Dickie had worked with Lila Lee during one of the years he wasn't under her care. Lila played Dickie's mother in the film they did, *In Love with Life*. Fifty years had passed since then, and Jimmy and Dickie being the same age, Kirkwood was still intrigued enough to learn how his dysfunctional mother managed to act the role of a caring one with Dickie.

But we're tracking Jim's string of corpses . . . Over intervening years, Jimmy Kirkwood found one of his classmates from Brewster Academy dead. They were staying at a friend's home in New Orleans at the time. The boy, named Ted, was the model for Jordan in the classic prep school novel-to-come *Good Times/Bad Times*. A different friend's mother was another victim of suicide he happened to find in a room. While in San Francisco during his military service years, Jim was trudging along the banks of the bay when the cadaver of a Golden Gate Bridge jumper washed up at his feet.

"For a while I thought it would be my life's calling . . . some people find oil, some divine where water is . . ." but Jim's knack was finding dead bodies. The five to which he often referred varied, making it seem to be more like seven or eight bodies. In some retellings, he switched bodies or the order in which they were located. After a while, he seemed to have trouble recalling whom he found or when.

When not finding dead bodies, Jimmy was learning of acquaintances who'd succumbed to suicide, or at least made serious attempts. In 1939 Ruth Morris overdosed on sleeping pills she secretly stashed at the Alameida Sanitarium in New Mexico, and a few weeks after her death, Lila informed Jim that Guvvie Morris tried to kill himself by driving his car off the highway. As Kirkwood frequently noted, "I was not too fond of the dark after awhile, and I thought a lot more about death than other young people my age."

When Jimmy was seventeen, he'd been replaced in his father's life. The Senior Kirkwood, fifty years old when Jim was born, had acquired a common law wife during the late 1930s. He returned to Hollywood in 1941 with a new infant son, who was never acknowledged by young Jim as a relative. James Kirkwood, Senior, announced he was ready to renew his movie career. James Kirkwood, Junior, dryly remarked about the aging man's dream: "Life has got to be one huge joke. To my knowledge, nobody has ever come up with a logical explanation that fits any other alternative. But as long as we've been placed on the joke-board, there's nothing to do but play along with as much humor as possible." He never put both his parents, even in fictional forms, into the same book. "Too explosive for one book," he laughed, and his epical work on his father, titled *I Teach Flying*, remained an unfinished ream of 490 typed pages.

Jimmy returned to Beverly Hills the next year and started attending yet another in his series of schools. He went to the East Coast for his Christmas and Easter vacations, spending both with his father in New York City. The plethora of schools for his education might have proven a detriment to consistent education, but Jim never thought it did "while I was growing up because of moving around." He considered his childhood messy. "I never stayed in one place long enough to make friends. But I always took it for granted I'd be in show business."

When his mother starred in a Manhattan play, he made his professional theatrical debut at age thirteen. He was given a bit part to play on stage with her, and that subsequent summer he worked with her in summer stock. It was a hoary chestnut of a play, *Mrs. Moonlight*, but the experience solidified his desire to take up the acting profession.

Kirkwood frequently described himself as a combination of standup comic, gossip, storyteller, and dramatic performer. If he wished to startle an audience, he'd be naturally outrageous. He had an inborn need to be the center of attention. "If someone had told me when I was 14 that I would be a writer I would have told them they were crazy. People often ask me how a writer starts to write. In my case it was really a total fluke because, at the age of fourteen, I wanted to act." His upbringing was the essence of soap opera, so enacting fanciful stories on stage came easily to him.

Though he professed to be appreciative and understanding of his parents, he expressed resentments. "At best we were marked as eccentric," as a family. He never lost the sense, amid all the future and past husbands and wives of his parents, that he was on the outside, always looking in. He resented the illegitimate son his father sired late in life. What he claimed to despise was his growing up in California. "I always felt alienated there, even as a kid." In Jim's mind, his frequent stops in Ohio with his mother's sister, Aunt Peggy, were respites from the mad whirl of his movie star parents. "Elyria represents the most normal part of my childhood." Of his parents, the future writer said: "My father was married five times and my mother four times. I don't want to subject myself to that."

They separated before he was six years old, and he liked both of them, wishing he could be with each. His parents were often broke while Jimmy was growing up, and he carried a terrible fear of poverty into his most lucrative adult years. He worried "that I'll end up without money, that the bank will fail, and I'll start sneaking into cafeterias and eating a full meal and giving the cashier a check for a piece of pie and a glass of milk."

In Elyria, Jimmy had several cousins; two were girls who kept him company when he studied at McKinley School and participated in drama and varsity tennis. After high school graduation in 1942, his older cousin, Robert, went with him to Los Angeles. Jimmy had by then been a student in military academies, private prep schools, Catholic parochial schools, and country schools. "Since I graduated from EHS, I really feel like I've lived about seven different lives." He once flattered and teased a reunion crowd at Elyria High School by telling them, "You might say Elyria started me writing . . . I'm still going to write that book about Elyria," but his writing always focused on the dead bodies he found, not the happy times in Ohio.

A child of multiple divorces and constant shuttling between transient dwellings, none ever really his home, he blandly commented of his family: "There was always a new step-parent on the horizon . . . My mother made about 120 silent films and early talkies with leading men from Valentino to Lon Chaney. My father was a matinee idol who was in films with Mary Pickford." His mother's opinion of the actor differed. "Your father went through life with an open fly," Lee told her son. In more contemplative moments, Jim recalled them "as a wild, stormy, colorful team, he a real Barrymore-type, she a vaudevillian who made it all the way up to the bright-bright lights."

Despite Jim's protests about Hollywood in the 1930s, the milieu enchanted him. He devoured juicy gossip and behind-the-scenes activities of movie legends. Admitting to James Leo Herlihy, an old friend, "I love all that shit." He confessed how he avidly read "Jackie Phuquing Cooper's book, *Please Don't Shoot My Doggie*," (sic) though he recognized it for what it was: a revenge book. It seemed many Hollywood brats from that insecure world wrote books to avenge their lost childhood and gain some kind of vindication. He thought it was impossible for children of show business not to be bitter. He certainly was: Jackie Cooper was another contemporary boy who played Lila Lee's son in a movie. Jim watched from the balcony his absent mother, giving love to a substitute boy.

When Jim was eight and nine years old, this was the way he related to his mother; she was the figure on the silver screen. He also watched her perform with another boy around his age, Jackie Cooper, in *Lone Cowboy*. He began to learn the only way to relate to the movie star was to be a charming little boy in her orbit. Lila Lee decided, partly at her son's request, to take Jim with her, back to Hollywood in the weeks after the funeral of her father. After mother and son met again in 1935, it began a new stage of their relationship, closer and more egalitarian in nature.

In Jim's Manhattan apartment, his prized memento of that era and his parents was a blown-up, wall-size photograph of movie stars and movie magnates from the Twenties—his mother, Lila Lee, and one of the Talmadge sisters and Charles Chaplin and Howard Hughes and two dozen other legendary faces of a glorious fantasy world. "They look as though they think it's going to last forever." The perspective it provided was simple and direct: "I saw a lot of the sad side of the business—my parents had such ups and downs—but there was no other business I ever wanted to be in."

At the height of her career, Lila Lee was considered one of the most exotic and beautiful of silent film stars, working with Valentino and Chaplin. Her scandalous personal life, including rumored alcoholism, brought her movie career to the skids after the advent of the "talkies." Her son and only child, Jimmy Kirkwood, was utterly devoted to her.

Budding actors always try to work at certain ordinary jobs where they hope to be seen; if one could stand the constant smell of food, waiters sniffed out tips. Attractive ones earned bigger tips. Kirkwood thought he'd be most visible as a friendly doorman at Grauman's Chinese Theatre. Louella Parsons mentioned his handsome appearance in her column, as a favor to his mother. Almost immediately, a few producers at Paramount signed the eighteen year-old to a movie contract—or at least that was what he told his Aunt Peg.

In Los Angeles, as World War II raged on, he got to play a cadet in a typical propaganda film, *Aerial Gunner*. It was a low budget picture starring Jimmy Lydon and Chester Morris, and notable for containing the first speaking role of Robert Mitchum in a bit part. Jim's acting contribution was so tiny, he was unbilled, merely showing up as a trainee soldier, milling about among two-dozen other baby-faced extras in the background. He had no lines, no close-ups, and the briefest of screen time. This film wouldn't bring him any recognition. The experience on location helped sway his thoughts about a way to serve his country during the war. In late November of 1942, not wishing to enter military service in a low rank, Jimmy asked several of his former school administrators to send letters recommending him for Naval Aviation Cadet. None were written for him.

Before long he was back east, making "the rounds" on Broadway. "I told my mother that I wanted to be an actor. And she said I was crazy—and too young. She had a cocktail party one night, and I met my first Broadway agent. He told me they were having auditions to replace young actors in *Junior Miss*, which was one of the biggest hits in the 40s. I went over there and lined up with about 40 other boys. I was so nervous I dropped the script and practically stuttered. At the end of the auditions, I turned to go and Moss Hart—imagine Moss Hart himself said, 'Young man, you.' Naturally I thought he meant another kid and kept walking. Finally he said, 'No, you, the nervous one. You.' I got the job and worked for four or five months. And nobody knew that both my parents were movie stars."

As with many tales Kirkwood related, the chronology was confusing or inaccurate. He was encouraged at an early age to hide his real birthday, partly in order for his mother to claim to be a few years younger. His work in *Junior Miss* came when he was a few years older than he alleged, but he had to be approaching nineteen at the time. According to a *New York Times* news blurb in January of 1943, "James Kirkwood, Jr., replaced Don Keefer in 'Junior Miss' on Saturday night at the 46th street theatre. Mr. Keefer has taken the role vacated by Kenny Forbes who was drafted. Young Kirkwood, who is making his Broadway debut is the son of the silent screen star actress Lila Lee."

During that year's Thanksgiving season, Lila was then acting in *Blind Alley* at the Windsor Theatre. Mrs. Augusta Appel had come to New York from her home in Elyria, Ohio, to attend the opening performance on Oct. 15 and had been residing with her daughter for her visit. At the conclusion of that Saturday evening's performance, Miss Lee telephoned her mother, as per her nightly habit. When there was no answer, she was unable to contact Jim, either, and asked the super at her apartment house at 148 East 48th Street to investigate. Mrs. Appel, aged 65, was found dead; apparently she'd been listening to a favorite program on the radio.

It was a rare night that the Body Finder himself, though in Manhattan, was off duty. For some reason, Jim chose not to claim this body in most interviews.

The strain of losing Mother Augusta led to Lila Lee having another relapse of "tuberculosis." She next emerged in the summer of 1944, performing in a legitimate stage comedy at Lancaster, Pennsylvania. Media tracked her to

Philadelphia, where the former silent film star and John E. Murphy, 45, New York stockbroker, were wed at the office of Magistrate Benjamin W. Schwartz. The marriage was the third for the actress who gave her age as 39.

In 1944, Jimmy enlisted in the Coast Guard for a four-year hitch. He served on the USS Admiral H.T. Mayo, was listed on the crew manifest for its commissioning on April 24, 1944, and was at Okinawa when the atomic bomb was dropped on Hiroshima. One of his shipmates was actor Victor Mature, who played Samson in *Samson and Delilah* and Doc Holliday in *My Darling Clementine*. They were the only two on the ship having Hollywood connections, yet there's no account of their meeting. Neither ever mentioned it. Kirkwood's fascination with Hollywood, makes it likely that he went out of his way to introduce himself at some point. Mature left the ship and service in 1946. Kirkwood's discharge was a few years after, but he chose not to make much mention of his service, which could undercut attempts to appear a decade younger than he truly was.

According to biographer Sean Egan, Jimmy Kirkwood gave an interview on radio that explained his book, *Some Kind of Hero*, about an incident during his military service: "My best friend had died aboard ship in a fire . . . it was a ridiculous accident. They were laying a new floor in the head in the john, kind of macadam floor and they used some kind of tar and you're not supposed to smoke or light a match and some guy got up in the middle of the night to go to the john and sat down and lit a cigarette and the whole thing blew up, combusted. About thirteen or fourteen men were just fried in their bunks and my best friend was one of them. So that was a very bad kind of send off as far as getting out of the service." Log records for his ship supply no evidence for such an occurrence.

This spectacular description flowered during a publicity tour and is not verifiable. So far as his service on the Mayo was concerned, the major episode was the December 31, 1946, heart attack of its captain, Adolph Schulz. His replacement arrived within a day. The new commander was Captain Rinaldo Ballero of San Francisco, who joined the ship in Seattle. Extensive research has turned up no report of any major fire and consequential crew deaths on Jim's ship. In fact, ship floors are steel and painted, not over-laid with tile.

Jim lied about his age when enlisting or forged dates, though this remains unclear. James Kirkwood's DD214 Form, the official discharge paper of the United States military services, has an erasure and retyping of his birthday. He recorded his birth to be in 1930. His birth date was 1924, and he finished high school in 1942, though he did time at both Elyria High School and Brewster Academy that year. His mother endlessly turning younger than her actual age, it seems inevitable he'd claim to be younger, too. This lie affected his draft status during the War. He was certainly not eighteen at the time he enlisted, but closer to twenty-two. At the tail end of the war, he served in the Coast Guard as a radar operator with the rank of S1c (Seaman First Class). He was discharged in December of 1948, and was a naval reservist until 1952.

While Jim served out his term of service, he also learned that Clyde Plummer, lately the warden of Folsom Prison, had died of a heart attack while on the golf course in 1947. It was a troubling name from the past to be crossed off the list, but Jim could not forget any of the cast of characters.

After the war, he studied with the American Theatre Wing under the GI Bill. There he met another young man with whom he shared a sense of humor and style. He teamed with Lee Goodman, and they put together a comedy cabaret act for supper clubs. The partners were hip, high-class, and trendy, a far cry from the antic-laden style of another team that went on to a big movie career—Martin and Lewis. He also worked as a night clerk at the Waldorf Astoria Hotel in New York. Whatever else he did, it was acting that addicted him and offered him attention and expression. "I had fleeting moments of wanting to get out of it, but I couldn't."

Within two years, Lila Lee was again hospitalized with 'TB', divorced again, and her career was effectively over. Some called it "a swift decline" after illness and bad career moves. Louella Parsons continued to give her star treatment, reporting on her convalescence at Lake Saranac. Dorothy Kilgallen reported Lila was "completely cured" at Saranac in April of 1948. Lila was spotted in 1949 at the Reuban Bleu to see Jim in his comedy debut with Lee Goodman. After divorcing Murphy, she spent much time in New Mexico at the ranch of Gouverneur Morris, maintaining her friendship with him.

Kirkwood and Goodman appeared at sophisticated watering holes like the Crown and Anchor in Provincetown, Mass. Their photograph adorned a wall until a major fire destroyed the club in the 1990s. When apprised that an aging picture somewhere else showed him looking twelve-years-old, Kirkwood quickly added, "And that's exactly how old I was in the picture." On second thought, he asked to have it ripped off the wall and was disappointed to hear the image and its frame were nailed in place.

Like many young men reaching thirty and unmarried in the Fifties, Jim began to look around for a mate to help him come into compliance with the social morays of the era. "When I was doing the role of Toby Smith on *The Aldrich Family* on radio, some of us were invited to a party for one of the cast members of the stage hit. I can't even remember now who the actor was or anything about the occasion. I only remember that there was Muriel at the party, and I must have been feeling particularly pepped up after our show."

Jim should have started to give serious thought to writing memoirs in those days, but he never really allowed himself time to try it. Muriel Bentley, several years Jim's senior, and a dancer with Martha Graham and Jerome Robbins, known for her comedic ballet talents, was in great demand for stage and formal ballet productions. They began to see each other regularly—or as much as doing road tours allowed. In terms of positive publicity, each knew the value of putting their "relationship" into the media spotlight.

To eke out his early career, Kirkwood made guest appearances on New York radio shows. Television fame, the new form of recognition, overwhelmed all else. Before long, television dominated Jim's career. When he did his club act with Goodman at the Bon Soir or Reuban Blue, someone would remark to him, "You know there's a kid on a daytime television drama who looks so much like you it's unbelievable. You should watch him some day."

Otherwise, he was under a constant barrage of compliments from women who considered him attractive, according to Muriel, "and how cute!" His workaholic mode and the continual sleepless routine began to take its toll. He was up till 3:30 am each night he did the club act, and then went to the studio to do his live television gig. Before long, sitting in the set on a comfortable sofa under hot lights, waiting for his cue, he couldn't help nodding off.

The heavy schedule took its toll. He started having spats with his partner, Lee Goodman. Kirkwood became increasingly intolerant of hecklers in the audience, and lost his temper, challenging them to nasty fights; he publicly criticized club owners for not respecting his act. This led to fisticuffs with Goodman. They were fairly much finished as a team by then, but worked together off and on. Others also began to notice that Jim had a strange reaction when anyone referred to his age and his money. He was more than a little touchy. "I admit it. I was getting punchy." Observers accused Kirkwood of having a Jekyll-Hyde personality, one for his television character and one for his comedy routines. The same applied to his performing personality and his writing personality.

Of his hectic, non-stop need to perform, he said: "This makes for a very cranky boy at times, and I don't see how Moo—the name I had begun to call Muriel—put up with me at all. When I had a free evening, and we went out together I could hardly keep my eyes open. This was great companionship for her. A lot of the time I was learning my scripts and she had to sit around and cue me, instead of being out and having fun. My mother often came over and helped things along. She and Moo got along famously." Jim delved deeper into his own psyche to figure out what drove him to such a frenzy of living; he followed another trend of the 1950s, acquiring a therapist to probe his psyche for all his demons. What he learned, he traced back to traumas at Manhattan Beach.

Jim could fool many people. One interviewer blithely wrote her impressions: "Actually there are three Jimmy Kirkwoods—or perhaps more accurately, four! The night club comedian, the host to teenagers and spinner of popular platters on a radio program; the youthful Mickey who is trying to take his dead dad's place in the life of the valiant Emersons on television; and the real Jimmy Kirkwood who is a combination of all the others. The real Jimmy is a rather quiet acting, shy-seeming fellow, a lean six feet in height, with dark brown hair and rather dark blue eyes with the suspicion of a twinkle most of the time. A fellow who is a little star struck himself, in spite of being a star, a little afraid to ask a girl for a date because he thought of her as way up there!"

When Kirkwood wanted something, nothing stood in his way. Despite his schedule, he made time to pursue Muriel Bentley. She herself admitted that Jimmy fell in love with her dog, a miniature black French poodle. Jim called him TM, short for Too Much. The little dog would follow Jim everywhere and cozy up to Kirkwood. Muriel mused, "It was Jimmy's fondness for TM, which drew him back and back again." Interestingly enough, twenty years later Jim would use the nickname TM (Too Much) for one of the lovers in the Vietnamese prisoner of war camp in *Some Kind of Hero*. In mid-January of 1953, Walter Winchell reported how the couple was practically married. Because they found the same things amusing and shared a sense of the ridiculous, Muriel and Jimmy planned to marry, but for reasons related to their careers, they chose to keep this private from the press.

Another example of a series of puzzling actions in Jim's life, as time passed, he dismissed the marriage idea as a prank of sorts. He was as likely to have married as to murder someone. To prove how silly was their decision to marry, the happy couple promptly separated in the blink of an eye, each excising the nuptial from their biographies thereafter. It was simply a mistake, best unspoken. He insisted on referring to this marriage idea as a mere joke.

While performing that summer, he learned from his mother that Guvvie Morris had died of a heart attack, after years of living in quiet obscurity in New Mexico. With the passing of Ruth, Clyde Plummer, and now Guvvie, Jim may have realized each viewpoint and potential insight into the death of Reid was silenced. Many other participants still lived, and telling an unvarnished, non-fiction story about Russell's death was not possible yet.

Focused on his stage career, Kirkwood performed in *Dance Me a Song* on Broadway, and toured in *Call Me Madam*, appearing in locales such as Newport, Rhode Island, and played second fiddle to stars like Martha Raye for months on end. He grew to have great sympathy for the 'gypsies', dancers who trooped along as a chorus in these musicals, who supplied the foundation for his most famous hit, *A Chorus Line*. When he finally stopped performing in troupes, he lamented how, "I miss the camaraderie . . . That's what I miss: the company."

During the 1950s, television provided work for many actors in New York. Jim did television commercials and "even a V.D. film for the Army Signal Corps." He wrote, "I was never what you call a star—but I was regularly and luckily employed in one of several branches of show business." Steady employment and instant recognition came from work on the daily drama shows, also called 'soap operas' because of their reliance on sponsors like Proctor and Gamble.

On October 12, 1953, Jim joined the cast in the premiere of *Valiant Lady*—and he remained on the show for its four-year run. "Son of Valiant Lady sounded like a race horse," he often complained. Several different actors played the key roles over the show's tenure (there were two valiant ladies; he had multiple actresses playing his two sisters, *etc.*). Jimmy was the fixture on the show, from the first day to the last. It always amazed him to learn how many people saw him and knew him from this least challenging of all his acting jobs.

"After a while it got to be like an office job . . . I played a 19 year-old when I was actually in my thirties." The grind taught him discipline and gave him a nest egg that grew quickly, ready to be used as means to underwrite a future career. Of the show, he said: "It was a good experience. We were paid well, and I think I really learned to act. It was like a 9 to 5 job. We'd learn twenty-six pages of dialogue in an afternoon." The shows in those days were usually fifteen minutes, though some were half an hour per day, done live. "I was always known as the Son of Valiant Lady. I felt like Lassie. All I had to do was bark and sit up."

Groups of writers controlled his fate. Every six months or so, new writers replaced the exhausted ones, owing to burn out. One new addition to the writing fraternity didn't like Jim, and the next development in the script was having his character go on a trip into an unknown Amazonian jungle. Mickey Emerson, Jim's character, was the last to understand the dangers of his adventure. With a sense of foreboding, Kirkwood said to a producer, "Hey, doesn't really look like such a good job up there in Brazil, does it?" They told him *Valiant Lady* would be more valiant if she had to suffer the loss of her son. The actress playing his mother in the scripts, the Valiant Lady herself, tried to convince him not to go. What Kirkwood learned was the writer had the power to reduce Mickey's scenes, make his character obnoxious, or invisible as wallpaper when on camera, or remove Mickey from the story altogether. Jim took notice. When a different writer came aboard, Jim's character was given a reprieve—and not cast into the murky waters of the Amazon.

For Jim Kirkwood the lesson was instructive. "I was told the writer himself had been fired and the new writer liked me and had spared my life in the nick of time." Writers, not actors, had the real creative power. He began to think about setting down all his anecdotes and stories about the business and life. Some were funny; some were sad. He saw both the good times and the bad times wherever he went. His recounting of the tragedy gained credence if he were the storyteller.

Two areas Jimmy intuitively understood were show business and adolescence. Combining the both concepts might give him something creative to do. As it was, radio broadcasts, not writing books, first emerged. With Lee Goodman, Kirkwood did most of the writing for their comedy team; skits and jokes were his métier. When the chance came to do a weekly broadcast called *Teenagers Unlimited* on the Mutual Broadcasting network, out of WOR in New York in 1954, Jim and Lee jumped at it. Patching up their team, they stayed together, spasmodically for a few more years. Jim could do the show in the evenings when his work on the soap opera was finished, parlaying this into live television appearances on television shows like *Ed Sullivan* and *Garry Moore*, which specialized in skits and vaudevillian antics.

Another grand opportunity arose after he had done his soap opera for a while. Lee Israel reported an old gossip magazine version of his first encounter with the singular Tallulah Bankhead, when he arrived at her home for an audition for a role in *Welcome, Darlings*. At this point in her life she was bordering on caricature with her revue that toured the country. After waiting for her in the living room, he heard her at the top of the stairs. He rose and she shouted down, "Don't get up. I see you almost every day on *Valiant Lady*. I love the soapies."

Jim had scrupulously prepared to audition for her with much of his comedy material from both radio and the Goodman team. The best-laid plans were tossed away because Tallulah wanted to talk about the soap opera with him. She wanted all the inside dope on the characters, their motivations, and their possible future actions. She was hooked on the afternoon shenanigans. Knowing this was his try-out, he chucked his comedy routine and chatted. He knew how to talk to old movie stars for sure.

For an hour she told him exactly how she conducted her show. It was tantamount to a one-woman performance, all for Jimmy's benefit. He let her orate without any interruptions. He paused now and then to offer small murmurs of amazement or delight. Then she turned to him and announced, "You're hired. You're absolutely perfect. You're charming, attractive. You have the background, class, and talent."

What followed was the mandatory physical audition on her casting couch.

In her play he was a small asteroid next to an enormous star. Jim was appalled at her frailty and anxiety before the show. At the first performance of *Welcome, Darlings*, they stood waiting behind the curtain. He noticed how old and brittle she seemed. The trouper always emerged when the audience saw her; she came alive in front of those fans. Kirkwood began to envision a story about an aging star having a fling with a young actor. The working title in his mind was *The Angels or Whoever*.

After listening to his stories of old Hollywood and theater life, Bankhead told Kirkwood he was a born storyteller. His embroidery of a tale most amused her. Jim often insisted the older actress of his story was Ava Gardner, not Tallulah.

It was Tallulah who befriended Kirkwood in 1955 and indulged him. After they grew to know and trust one another, he told her about his mother and the scandal surrounding Reid Russell. The actress insisted he had to write it as a story. Because nonfiction was not an option, Jim's talent to embroider meant he ought to consider writing a *roman a clef.* The seed was thus planted.

Sorry to hear about Lila's aimlessness, Tallulah wondered if there was anything her press agent could do to help Lila, but Jim had no suggestions on how to snap his mother out of her depression, directionless life, and health problems.

When Jim's thirty-second birthday in August approached, Tallulah asked him what famous person he'd like to meet—as part and parcel of a birthday gift from her. Without hesitation, Kirkwood gave the name of Eleanor Roosevelt. Unfazed by the request, she informed Jim that they would have tea soon. True to her word, she let him know that Mrs. Roosevelt was coming for an afternoon visit. Tallulah's best behavior "enchanted" Kirkwood, and he found the Former First Lady as warm and kind as he had expected.

Tallulah, always notoriously uninhibited, seemed well behaved until she told them: "Wait a minute. I've got to pee." With nary a shudder, Mrs. Roosevelt shrugged at Jim when Bankhead went down the hall, left the toilet door open, and continued to talk and keep company with them. Jimmy nearly spilled his tea, restraining his laughter. It was one of those silly moments he cherished. When he mentioned the incident to the star, she growled mischievously, "Don't be ridiculous, Jimmy. She didn't mind."

If a line was drawn between friendship and the profession, Jimmy found he could easily cross it. But crossing Miss Bankhead was risky business. She blew up once at Cape Cod Playhouse in Provincetown, where her legendary gay following gathered at the local watering holes, beaches, and took in Tallulah at night. They were her most loyal and enthusiastic fans. A veteran of stage performances, quick changes of costume were what Jim Kirkwood had mastered. On one occasion he was careless, partly due to his urge to liven things up and cause a bit of a sensation. He made an entrance on stage with his fly open and shirttail sticking forth from his pants.

Naturally, this miscue broke up the cast and audience, but Tallulah, like Queen Victoria, was not amused. Laughing hysterically, Kirkwood doubled over on the stage floor, and she came up and delivered a series of swift kicks to his ribs, snarling, "You unprofessional! How dare you break up during one of my numbers?" She then stalked to her dressing room and started cutting up her costumes with a knife. For the audience waiting for the next act, it was sheer entertainment.

Tallulah sulked a while, but she remained his adored liege lady.

Lila Lee was a surprise guest on the Ralph Edwards's popular television show of May 8, 1957, *This is Your Life.* Giving her age as fifty-one, she had returned

78

to Hollywood after a prolonged absence. "I haven't seen this place in a long, long time," she had commented while dining at the Brown Derby beforehand. No references were made to the reasons she left Hollywood in 1940 for New York. Her former husband, James Kirkwood, and her son were behind the orchestration. She was genuinely surprised. The television appearance resulted in a few 'comeback' roles on a few series.

One of the pleasant outcomes of the reunion was that the trio acted together on one occasion, for an episode of *Lamp Unto My Feet*, a popular Sunday morning anthology of moral dramas. It was a decidedly unusual bit of casting for the family and may have indicated what a strange trio they were. Lila was to play her son's sister, and James Senior was to play their father. The storyline involved a father who returned to his son and daughter after being absent for many years to ask for their forgiveness. It also marked the first time the parents of James, Jr., acted together in thirty years.

Lila Lee gave several interviews in which she really disdained a return to acting. "I'm not as excited about what is happening to me as everybody else. I know my son is more interested in a career for me than I am for myself. He likes to see me active." Approached by a publisher to do a tell-all book, she rejected it out of hand. "Frankly I never felt I had a great deal to say." A rash of publicity, engineered by Tallulah Bankhead's press agent, burst forth due to Jimmy's requests, and a number of items were planted in nationally syndicated columns. Jim expected his mother to be delighted by them.

The run of *Welcome, Darlings*, was almost at an end for Jim. Tallulah had optioned a new property, written by a young Southern playwright. His name was James Leo Herlihy, and like ships in the night, these two passed each other for a time, destined to grow into close friends. Meeting Jamie Herlihy was to provide Jim a soul mate, someone from whom he realized "writing novels is really the career for me."

Valiant Lady gave and took away at the same time. When the plum role of Patrick Dennis came up in the legendary *Auntie Mame* musical, with Rosalind Russell as the eccentric and beloved figure, Kirkwood joined the cast as her callow adult nephew. Since he was finishing up his tour with Tallulah, he was a week late for the Dennis play's rehearsals. His "miracle of miracles" role suddenly disappeared. Despite permission from the producers for him to miss the rehearsals, Miss Russell did him in when he finally showed up.

Jim said she was a "pussycat" at the outset, but turned into a most unfriendly star. After he rehearsed three lines with her, the grim lady requested a break. The director and producers were told to meet in her dressing room. Someone whispered in Jim's ear that he was too funny, upstaging her. When he came back to the theatre after the break, there were twenty young actors resembling himself waiting in a queue at the stage door to take his place. "My God," he thought, "they all looked like Patricks. They did and they were." The humiliation burned inside him.

On August 16, 1957, Jim made his final appearance on the soap opera. His long running series had finished its course; live television plays and New York theaters were losing audiences as Hollywood movie studios cranked out multitudes of filmed television shows. His financial security went down the drain with *Valiant Lady's* termination, and Jim wasn't about to give up the comfortable existence to which he'd become accustomed. He'd resume his career as the son of movie stars. At long last he knew, "I had gotten into show business for all the wrong reasons—none of them connected with wanting to be a fine actor."

Before the mid-Fifties, New York actors had begun streaming to the West Coast because that was where the best paychecks and work were most available. "I thought I was going to be a movie star." Jim's roles were rare, far and few between. He appeared on popular western TV oaters like *Lawman* in parts that any young actor could play. "I went for six months without work and got spooked. I was getting into my 30s and I wasn't living a life of any dignity."

He suffered a commonly shared disappointment: "One morning when I awakened it occurred to me to ask myself why I was getting out of bed. For what? To wait for the phone to ring, to go surfing at Malibu? Surfing is fun but it should really be a hobby, not a vocation . . . It struck me there was a forlorn lack of dignity in not being allowed to work at my profession. When you have to be given permission to work—say even a three day guest shot on a bad TV series—by the combined approval of an agent, casting consultant, director, writer, producer and sometimes the star, it's rather like winning the Turkey Raffle and about as calming as a brisk game of Russian Roulette."

The actor exodus from New York made Kirkwood's competition for roles fiercer than ever. He faced an endless round of "cattle call" auditions, the one element of the business he most hated. Gone were the days of business suits and ties; the Industry dress code was dirty sneakers and faded jeans. Men whose feet were often propped atop their desks lolled back in creaking office chairs as they tiredly interviewed tense actors. "Everybody was going there . . . I went up for movies and tested. They'd say: Show us your teeth. Turn around. Walk. And I thought, My God, it's like starting all over again. And I didn't work one day in six months, and my agent committed suicide. And I got up at 2 o'clock one morning in a cold sweat and thought: I can't sit around and wait for the phone to ring. I'll write a novel."

Not many friends thought of Jimmy as a writer or novelist. He was the joker who dealt with disasters by laughing them off. He saw a good side to every bleakest moment. As he made the party circuit of Hollywood, currying dozens of invitations, networking the right people, the process of Making It In The

Business reverberated in his head. Oh, he enjoyed the fun and the creativeness; he fit into Hollywood life, didn't he? What was missing?

All he'd written so far were comedy routines, sometimes original and sparkling, but nothing having the length or sustained plot of a novel. His acting career was undergoing a prolonged dry spell. His first novel was intended to be about his senior year in Elyria, but as he developed the storyline based on his own background, it curbed the original idea. None of the drama and compelling moments of his life had happened in Ohio. He was a child of Hollywood and show business. There were his stories.

Jim happened one night to catch Alfred Hitchcock's black comedy, *The Trouble with Harry*, about a young boy who found a dead body in his back yard. Among the revelations, everyone learned someone else had motive to murder the boyfriend of the little boy's mother. Since the body wound up buried and dug up several times, the parallels of Harry to Reid were startling. The film detailed, with nasty humor appealing to Jim, how everyone was suspect in the man's death. He knew immediately where the story had come from—and that he could tell it as it really was, if not better. "I know what happened or would have happened," he once stated.

Jim said he then bought a typewriter.

Once more, variations appeared in his recollections. He also claimed he began his novel the night he drove home from his first writing class at UCLA. "I came close to wrapping myself around a telephone pole speeding home that night in order to slam a piece of paper in the typewriter and spell out: *There Must be a Pony!*" He also stated he wrote the first chapter that night, though sometimes he indicated he made spurts and starts years before. Once that chapter was begun, however, "I stopped caring if the telephone rang and I was called for a series of guest shots on shows like *December Bride.*"

Whenever he mentioned writing about Manhattan Beach, his crowd seemed more interested in old Hollywood juicy gossip. He couldn't forget harsh realities—like finding his mother's fiancé after he committed suicide. Throughout his life he often referred to Reid as engaged to his mother. If so, it was strictly unofficial. Sometimes he called Reid "a friend of my mother" and insinuated his revelation broke up his family. Whenever it suited him, or if he were questioned too closely, he altered details accordingly.

Knowing he was on the right track, Jim wanted to have his own quiet place to work. No sooner had he used his savings to purchase a little house near Sunset Boulevard, he received horrific news. His mother was near death. In August of 1958 she had a terrible accident. While house cleaning, she passed out, falling into a tub of boiling water, splashing it over herself.

Hospitalized, she was in great pain and needing skin grafts. It seemed the floodgates of cruel fate had once again struck Jim and his loved ones. He hurried back to New York to tend to her. While flying cross-country, he realized how very much his mother meant to him. If he were to write about Lila, he wanted to present her and that delicate psychology in the kindest light. What son would do less for a tormented mother? Jimmy remained at her side during her first desperately ill days in the hospital.

After six weeks, she was well enough to travel to Ohio for recuperation and a series of skin transplants. She stayed with her sister, Peggy, who could best look after her. Another month was spent in therapy at the Elyria Memorial Hospital, and Jim was able to return California with a different impression of his mother.

Everything having to do with Lila must have filled his thoughts uncontrollably . . . as if he were doing an autobiography. To protect her image, he chose to write fiction in order to shade the real facts. It wasn't the sole reason. He was aware of the deaths of Gouverneur Morris and Clyde Plummer. The one person who could take issue with any memoir of the Manhattan Beach episode was Mrs. Victoria Russell, still residing in Pico Heights. He couldn't risk rekindling her anger.

The Reid Russell case, though closed for twenty years, could always be re-opened as an unsolved homicide. Because of his mother's fragile health, Jim wanted to avoid upsetting her. His excuse for writing about the incident so often was that "almost every novel I've written has been based on something that's happened in my life" and he had to make sense of his experiences. He insisted he always told the truth in his work, unless it might hurt someone. Jim frequently interpreted that clause broadly.

His mother's accident gave him something substantial to consider. Lila Lee was the "hard-luck girl of the movies," and he was involved with her in one of the most gothic of Hollywood mysteries of the old days, where her fate once again left her bereft. He began to think of revealing what he knew from behind the scenes, and dealing with his own role in a conspiracy of silence. "I am concerned with the hero's handling of his problems—humor is an important element." He gave that spine to all his stories. James Kirkwood always suffered anxiety during his show business career that "I might bore an audience." The story of his mother and her boyfriend's peculiar death would certainly not bore anyone.

As he often explained during his lectures, "I like to write. I've had this fairly bizarre existence, and it helps to exorcize the past. I grew up in Hollywood, California. I began acting when I was 14 and didn't start to write until well into my twenties." He considered acting a virus, and found writing to be the only antidote to the pathology of performing. "Writing is turning life's worst moments into art, sometimes money. Writing is mystical." His path had led him to the fork where writing was a choice. "Given pen and paper—or even a typewriter, a writer can write."

And, when Jim started, words poured out of him.

Kirkwood certainly required the catharsis writing afforded him—as he was couldn't stop mulling over the bizarre incidents in his life. He believed he'd overcome his emotional injuries of childhood. The novel could show audiences that he enjoyed a happy adulthood. He'd parlay the worst moments into the best ones. "If my works have any theme it is that, although I'm not sure why we're here, we must try to get through what life presents to us with as much grace and good spirits as possible."

Back in Los Angeles, not far from where Russell's strange death in 1936 occurred, Jim was depressed over his mother's condition, and feeling a tad sorry for himself. Unable to sleep, he woke before dawn one morning. He was facing endless empty parties, and failing to do something of lasting merit. He felt he should, and he must; the rudiments of *There Must Be a Pony* were coalescing in his mind. He resolved to work on the book steadily for six hours each day, starting at 8am.

Jimmy's friends weren't impressed. After all, he had nothing to show indicating he had writing skills. When he spoke of his intent, "Friends greeted this news with derision. Some doubted I had ever read a novel." He wasn't rattled. Once committed to an idea, he would not be dissuaded.

If he felt truly inspired, he'd work until 6pm, but by then he lost his concentration. It was too taxing and wasn't his best prose. Without pausing to count pages or words, Jim simply wrote the story from start to finish, as best he could recall. His most peculiar habit as a writer was a response to his endless energy and hyperactivity. Because he could not sit still, he chose to type all his manuscripts while standing up. He found a high level table, put his typewriter on it at elbow height, and thus he wrote all his books, stories, and plays to come. Razzing him, some wags referred to him as "Hemingway."

When the book was done, Jim was staggered by the thickness of his manuscript. Pages upon pages piled up on his desk. It was rough and it was raw, the guts of his past spilled darkly across those sheets of paper. Tallulah Bankhead's words reverberated in his head, "Darling, you're a fantastic story-teller," and he contacted the new friend he'd met through Bankhead. James Leo Herlihy was now both writer and director. He was working with Tallulah on a play called *Crazy October*, and they were traveling on an eighteen-week long tour. Herlihy encouraged Jim and suggested that his story might possibly make a play. Herlihy was writing his first big hit, *Blue Denim*, and Kirkwood worked on *Pony*, simultaneously creating two classics of the adolescent angst genre to come out of the 1950s.

Jim also enrolled in a short story/creative writing course at the University of California at Los Angeles, taught by *L. A. Times* critic Robert Kirsch. The college rules on the syllabus stipulated only short fiction would be considered.

The class had an enrollment of dozens of students, and Kirsch was not overly friendly. He laid down how he planned to conduct the class, if he felt like it, and when. Kirkwood was overwhelmed that he was unknown to the man, and Kirsch seemed to have no personal interest in his students. Jim wondered how much over his head he was, and whether the ridicule of his friends was apt. Who was he to think he could be a writer?

In this class Jim tried the short story form and found it untenable. His works were autobiographical, with a narrative voice flaring up in Salinger fashion crossed with Hollywood brat. One tale he wrote was entitled "By the Time You Read This, I Should be Dead." It was of a boy who played sports poorly and once tossed a baseball bat during the game. It hit the catcher, a young girl. She was rendered unconscious, and the child's mother berated him, screaming, "You're a murderer." It would be a hallmark of many Kirkwood tales to have the main character be accused of manslaughter, accidental or otherwise.

One night, Kirsch came to class and announced that every once in a while he read something that made the experience of teaching this dull and plodding class worth it. He had just read such a work. He then asked, "Who in this class is named Kirkwood?" Jimmy gleefully stated years later, "Well, guess who raised his hand?"

After the session, Kirkwood spent some time with the critic/instructor, who blithely told him that his wife also loved Kirkwood's piece about a movie star mother "who hadn't made a movie in about a century." This fifty-page story also featured a large segment, which would be used as a seminal moment in *Good Times/Bad Times.*

In his own inimitable manner of outrage and rebellion, Kirkwood plopped down several heavy pounds of typescript in front of the critic. Within the mass of words was the essence of his first novel. This was the version Jimmy often gave over dinner and on the lecture circuit. Evidence indicates the contrary: he wrote several short stories and submitted them to Kirsch. One of these was a fifty-page effort, *There Must be a Pony.*

"I dragged it back to my professor at UCLA, Robert Kirsch, who did not thrash me for turning in a novel, but instead stunned me by sending it off to his agent, Phyllis Jackson, and his publisher. Within two weeks a telegram arrived." Jim framed it as a mantle piece.

He had to travel to Amado, Arizona, to find a quiet refuge to finish the novel before submitting it to the publisher. The original short story was not much changed for the novel. Mostly, he altered names—and took out chunks that would appear in subsequent novels.

This early short story version was an autobiography rather than work of fiction. Though he kept a few names of the participants, Kirkwood formed the piece as a work of memory. He called his narrator Josh Kirby, a boy living in

Elyria, Ohio, with his aunt. The experiences he revealed were mostly his school recollections in between stays with his problematic mother. He noted that the longest he lived with her during his life was nearly the whole year he was thirteen. Josh Kirby, like Jim Kirkwood, attended St. Mark's in Los Angeles, a Catholic military academy as well as a fancy prep school in New Hampshire, Beardsley, thinly disguised Brewster Academy.

One segment of this short story turned out to be the notorious rub-down scene, reprinted nearly verbatim in *Good Times/Bad Times*, in which Peter (Josh here) is given a rubdown, not by the headmaster of the school, but by the history teacher/football coach, a tweedy pipe-smoking masculine man named Mr. Wright, who showed up drunk late at night in Peter's room. He claims to be following doctor's orders by helping the star tennis player and his bad back. It turns into a highly sexual encounter that Kirkwood changed little in the subsequent novel. Josh also talks of the "Circle Jerk" club at the prep school, which also became part of the second book.

A few other details are slightly altered; Lee Hertzig is renamed Monty Hertzig—but his nasty demeanor at Ocean Park causes Josh to get sick. There he meets Ben, as in the finished novel. There are several other references to their growing friendship, such as horseback riding in Paso Verdes and other activities that didn't make it into the finished novel. Some incidents were too graphic—such as Josh's memory of his friend Boots who makes perverse appearances in *Good Times/Bad Times* and in *Some Kind of Hero*, where a more accurate version of Reid Russell takes Josh and Boots on a camping trip. Though Kirkwood despised being embraced as a "gay" writer, he admitted he enjoyed putting "little signposts into my novels."

Kirsch gave Jim advice on what to alter, what to cut, and how to make the work a cohesive novel. Much of what Jim wrote in excess would become the basis of his second novel. Nothing was wasted. When the first novel was finished, Jim packaged the manuscript for delivery to Little, Brown in Boston. He selected that publisher because they had a reputation for quality and had printed several books that Jim thought were special. Robert Kirsch put Jimmy in contact with his own agent, who had ties to the Boston-based publisher. To his surprise he was contacted quickly by telephone.

The publisher wanted to buy the book, but he needed to come to Boston to do editing. Little, Brown's representative noted that he was over their traditional length by about 500,000 words. Most of their novels were at least 120,000 but seldom passed 200,000 words. He must cut the story down to a reasonable size. More reliable sources said the book came in excess of 110,000 words and was cut down to 90,000.

Though this may have been one of Jim's exaggerations for dramatic effect during interviews and storytelling lectures. He always treated interviews like performances. He saw no difference between the stage and using his stagecraft to conduct a book tour. Jim may have seen all of his stories as one long connected rendition of his life. He had begun *Good Times/Bad Times* under the rubric of Josh's life—and the second novel may have been part of the original story in his mind.

In his usual disdainful mode, Jim went to Boston with the attitude that he really could not cut anything from the work. He met an editor with whom he had great rapport—and the work was limited to about 180,000 words after some hard decisions. It took several weeks of dickering to reach that point. Then, Jim asked if the original 200,000 words could be restored. He confessed to the editor: "The truth is I didn't think I had said enough and while waiting for you to buy it I thought of an extension to the original length. I don't imagine you'd like to see the extension?"

"I don't imagine," said the editor.

On Monday, Sept. 6, 1960, *There Must Be a Pony* was published.

CHAPTER FIVE

PONY UP ON STAGE, 1962

"Writing, for me at least, is retreating into a dark place, where you take off into the corridors of your mind. It's a very private trip with your imagination. A secretive jag, the specific secrets of which no one will share until you've told the entire story. (I could no more discuss a novel or play I was working on than I could deny taking the bound and printed copy of my first book to bed with me the night it arrived.)" The act of writing supplied a release for Jim in ways acting never could.

As his book went on sale, Jim Kirkwood told Louella Parsons he was writing a play version of the novel. He said the plot was about his mother and the old scandal. "You may remember it." Jim said his updated version took place during an unspecified year in the novel, likely 1954, the date he gave to his earliest play version, which contained a reference to the Frank Sinatra song of that year, "Young at Heart." Subsequently, he removed many date references—making the setting a more amorphous and generic Hollywood. A couple of years later, he wanted to update the play to 1956, but decided to keep the plot timeless, and instructed producers to do the same.

In 1960 few critics dared explain the joke of the *Pony* book title, in polite terms. Euphemisms abounded. A few referred to the barnyard reference. Partially a hesitancy for family newspapers and magazines to mention the impolite, it was also simply regarded as tasteless. Scatology as a philosophical concept was hardly in the ken of most readers. It would take another ten years of film and literature, brazenly using expletives openly and with cavalier humor, for the concept of horse manure to become less shocking and a clear message.

During interviews at the time he said his first novel was "very autobiographical, about how I found this body of the man my mother was engaged to," and it cast Jim Kirkwood as a writer in a strait-jacket. Critics planned never to let him out. He was not a member of the literary cognoscenti. Salinger, Updike, Mailer, Capote, even Irwin Shaw and Gore Vidal, all received more respect for their literary output. Kirkwood was more or less dismissed as merely an actor writing about how his mother wound up in the Menninger Clinic, ostensibly for tuberculosis, but likely in combination with acute alcoholism.

British magazines reviewers thought highly of the novel. Some called it an "impressive literary debut," though the *London Times* complained the book quite old-fashioned, and rather "garrulous and meandering." Back in the United States, newspaper reviewers, like one from the *Nashville Tennessean* called the work "a first rate job." Another critic would dismiss it as "artifice rather than art."

With a post-card advertising campaign, Little, Brown sought out a few comments to stress: "probes deeply into realms of fear, horror, shock—" hardly described the coming-of-age tale. Another phrase bandied about said the novel had "wild humor with incredible suspense," which represented more accurately the juxtaposition of emotions in Kirkwood's Hollywood fable. Reviews then, as now, were not deep or truly insightful.

Kirkwood represented a new group of authors—those whose credentials came from the world of show business. Other actors, Errol Flynn and George Sanders in the 1940s, had tried their hands at fiction, though their efforts were considered a joke. Jim's new breed of Hollywood writer seemed able to move naturally into the world of literature from in front of a camera or scripting movies, and meeting as much hostility as a film star actor attempting to be accepted on Broadway. More and more frequently, the literary lights of the American scene, like Gore Vidal, shuttled between movie writing and novel writing.

The first two printings of *Pony* sold between 8,000 and 10,000 copies. Kirkwood resented the publisher for his paltry advertising budget. If more money had been spent on promotion, his book would have been a big seller. He wasn't shy about expressing disappointment with the sales because of the American publisher's weak support, whereas his British version received far more attention—and sold briskly. It also gathered better reviews there.

Kirkwood loved telling his stories, "But it's a lonely profession, which is why lecturing and an occasional acting stint permits me to air the gregarious side of my nature. It gives me a lift and allows me to share some of my life's more fascinating episodes. I do it because I enjoy it and I think my experiences might be of help to others. There is still that entertainer in me that wants to escape now and then and put in an appearance. It's a totaling invigorating high to entertain an audience; I don't ever think I'll lose my taste for it."

After the book's publication, Robert Kirsch, the man most responsible for discovering Kirkwood and shaping his first novel, reviewed *There Must Be a Pony* for the *Los Angeles Times* and his column, "The Book Report". Kirsch stated that the young writer tapped the "rich Salinger vein." Calling the work "the best first novel of the year. This account of the time of decision in the life of an adolescent who manages to survive what is one of the most grinding and corrosive childhoods in the history of fiction is effectively written, filled with compassion, and a depth of feeling, yet never self-pitying or maudlin."

To Kirsch, the story was frightening; he did not allude to its veracity and historical basis. He labeled the world Kirkwood depicted as the "unreal world of Hollywood" where children are reared in a dubious environment. "The youth faces not only the injustice of his own experience but an injustice deepened by the essential persecution of authority." He described Kirkwood's narrative style as colorful, yet maintained the purpose of catharsis as well as entertainment.

The underlying message of Kirkwood's work was predicated on the notion anyone can transcend the degrading or discouraging situations of childhood, that the horrors of adolescence do not need to dampen human spirit or prevent adult successes. Kirkwood, he thought, "refuses to be cowed and defeated by fate. Love is not merely an empty word or a panacea; it is a quality, which pervades and overrides all barriers." A lone critic compared Kirkwood, for the only time in Jim's career, to Kafka and Proust. Despite the eccentric surroundings, Kirkwood managed to show the universality of the experiences Josh had.

Referring to superficial resemblances between Kirkwood and Salinger, particularly in *Catcher in the Rye*, the *Los Angeles Times* reviewer thought *Pony* was a better novel in innumerable ways. "Not only does it give us access to the mind and experience of a young boy facing the battering rites of passage, but it goes deeper into motivation and forces and it illuminates a theme never stated or implied in Salinger's work." His glowing review recommended the book and insisted readers would not be disappointed by Kirkwood's work.

The easiest of all literary comparisons quickly dismissed Kirkwood as an ersatz version of J.D. Salinger, only a pathetic attempt to parallel a genuine writer. In the 1950s everyone was compared to and fell short of J.D. Salinger—and it would take years for that yoke to fall from Kirkwood, if it ever did. Few academic critics took issue with Salinger's use of radio shows, child prodigies, soap operas, and other Hollywood sell-out concepts that were the hallmark of his stories—despite the fact that Salinger had never been part of the entertainment industry. His style may have been an urban Huckleberry Finn, but the Kirkwood voice came right out of the disturbed womb of show business.

Implicit in Salinger was a demeaning of dream factory Hollywood, where in Kirkwood, it was the glamorous ghetto of his livelihood, just another American community, though one of great influence. Kirkwood's narrative was familiar in its evocation of Salinger. Every urban, sophisticated teenager adopted the Holden Caulfield vernacular during those years. It was a voice no one else in literature could be allowed to echo.

Another attack centered on the familiarity of story Kirkwood told. It had some vague sense of being tabloid, something heard about in a conversation, or mentioned in a gossip column. Literature that wasn't condescending towards Hollywood was somehow less important.

"One of the miracles of it all is: you're never quite certain where your thoughts or the characters come from. At the end of a day I look back on the pages I've written in wonderment, often thinking: my God I don't ever remember thinking that thought or imagining that character. I write out of blind faith and the more I do it the more I realize much of it comes from the subconscious. Writing can be joyous, uplifting, painful and torturous, all in one day. And I absolutely love it." Alas, his protests were accepted on face value; instead of realizing that he did give deep thought to the chessboard details of character and plot, readers presumed anything that easy to read could not be dealing with complexity.

This led to oft-heard academic snobbery about Josh's incredibility. Time and again critics seemed bothered by the rendition of Kirkwood's voice. Most critical readers did not trust their own judgment to delve deeper into the problem—why is the voice so disturbing? Might that be the point of the tale? If Josh's witness to the death of his mother's love rings false, it does so because Josh is not forthcoming.

The innocent narrator has to be believed. No critics worked hard enough in their analysis to consider that Josh is using mendacity so freely, his story borders on the ridiculous. It simply could not be possible; Murray Schumach, a Los Angeles critic, thought Kirkwood was "superficially effective." In 1960, he found it hard to believe a sixteen year-old boy is able to manipulate the sensation-seeking media with the alacrity Josh uses.

Critics for the *New York Times*, siding with Schumach, decried the pop psychology of the writing—using the same trite theories of human motivation as a basis to chastise Kirkwood. Those who found the story line unreal may not have read the headlines twenty-years earlier, when mythic beings in a fancied domain dominated the tabloids doing exactly what Kirkwood described in exactly the way he related it. "Thank God I fell into writing. It has saved my somewhat hectic life, given me stability, an outlet for emotions and allowed me to mine the past."

Tallulah sent Jim a charming note to say she bought twenty-five copies of *Pony* to give her friends as gifts for Christmas. And, she confirmed his determination to avoid a movie deal until there was a hit play. That would increase the asking price for the rights to the picture. If anything, Jim was acutely attuned to how much he should be given for his work. If his play fell in disfavor, Jim would not stand a chance in the literary world. He'd write emotionally heightened, crisp scenes with planned exits and entrances, for an absorbing stage world composed of vivid incidents. The concept of a drama queen comes from drama itself. Kirkwood's sympathetic homosexual characters transcended the world of beauty parlors and interior design, where the 1950s society condemned them. It would take another generation before such troubling creatures could openly populate a regulated society.

Jim was utterly convinced his book must become a play before being made a movie. He was "anxious to push this because I need money to help pay Mother's medical expenses." He made the case to Lila about the importance of doing the story on stage. When first he presented her with the idea of the novel, she had been reluctant. He worried that, despite fictional disguise, words about her experiences could be "adding insult to injury have her sit down and read a book based on her." It would be worse for his mother to have the open secrets of her life depicted on stage nightly.

They agreed there was "no dignity in acting," and his story shows that. He admitted, "I was terribly nervous when she first read it because there are many personal things in it." The book—he explained to her—might give them financial freedom. Though she was a former movie star, she was not well off—after a lifetime of irresponsible living and illnesses. Kirkwood promised to take care of her. But for him to assume responsibility for her, he needed the success a novel, play, and then movie about Lila would provide for them both. She nodded; she understood that. To his great relief, "Mother loved the book." When done reading it, Lila Lee "was in tears," asserted Jim. Without much choice, Lila Lee said, "It was a good book." Thus, she gave her full approval to the book and all subsequent projects Jim planned to pursue.

The process of taking the novel and translating it for the stage took Jim another year and a half, though he was never satisfied with the structure of the play. He was to tinker with details and scenes, key moments, for years to come. He added and subtracted characters, making it a permanent work-in-progress, but allowed Alan Pakula to see his typescript.

Having a reputation as a humane and supportive producer and director, Alan Pakula was fully cognizant of the energies and efforts of writers and actors. As a director in the 1970s, he was referred to as an "actor's director." Under his tutelage actors won Oscar nominations and gave the performances of their careers. By the time of his death, he had been celebrated for films like *Klute, Sophie's Choice,* and *All The President's Men.* Those greatly overshadowed his earliest work on stage in the late 1950s and early 1960s. A graduate of Yale, where he majored in drama, he moved to Los Angeles in the 1950s and worked as an assistant producer under Don Hartman at Metro-Goldwyn Mayer. When the opportunity to become one of the earliest of the bicoastal producers, he jumped at the chance.

In 1961, living in East Hampton, Pakula was given a book written by an actor known to him, and whose life was already legendary. The Hollywood community, not yet undressed by the Babylonian revelations through tabloid television and Kenneth Anger, still held deep secrets within the guarded limits of the Industry. Whenever Pakula wanted to know the latest gossip of the movie world, his East Hampton source was neighbor James Kirkwood; their next door tie, like so many in the creative circles of New York and California, took on both social and business aspects. Another element of Pakula's work was his emphasis on different styles—from *Fear Strikes Out*, transcending a baseball story into a psychological profile, thence *To Kill a Mockingbird*, that took a coming-of-age tale about Southern children and made it a coming-to-grips tale about a great nation.

Alan Pakula read Kirkwood's show business novel and was taken with it. He was always interested in weaving a message within entertainment. Any story that dealt with "the frightened child," attracted him. In Jim's book he found both a boy facing death and the disturbed family life of a great actress, unable to mature, and unwilling to identify with the realities of her existence. They were the enticing ingredients of *There Must Be a Pony*.

Upon inquiry, Alan learned that Jim had written a play version of the novel and was twice as intrigued. What clicked for the film and theatrical producer was the chance to combine a stage drama about movies and theater with a major star. Having produced a mild Broadway drama starring Brandon de Wilde, entitled *Comes a Day*, he was ready to put together a major Broadway production. He was thirty-two years old, long out of Yale, but bitten by the bug of theater. Though he'd majored in drama, it was said he fell in love with show business after working at the Leland Hayward Theatrical Agency in the Fifties.

One of the best stage directors and close friend to Leland Hayward was Josh Logan, who brought the world *Mister Roberts* and *South Pacific,* and more recently had guided James Leo Herlihy's *Blue Denim*. Kirkwood's connection to Herlihy also aided Pakula to interest Logan in the play. A number of well-heeled friends and connections convinced the director to make a pitch to Lucille Ball while she was in New York.

Lucy recently finished six months on Broadway in the strenuous musical *Wildcat*. She missed many performances, bedded by exhaustion and flu. Hedda Hopper's column announced that Lucille Ball had regained her health after a terrible series of viruses hit her while in New York City doing a Broadway play. New York's weather didn't help, and she was preoccupied with divorcing her real-life husband, Desi Arnaz, while re-establishing her career in a different way. Contacts at Leland Hayward Productions informed Alan that Miss Ball was looking for a television play vehicle, and he may have thought Pony could be it. Jim was certainly excited by the possibility of having Lucy act in a television version of his play. She chose, instead, to do *The Good Years* with Henry Fonda—a lackluster television special, which aired at the start of the coming year. Pakula was back to square one

A distraction arose for him; his agent brought him another novel rapidly climbing best-seller lists—and without anyone having secured the movie rights—to a lyrical character-study written by a friend of Truman Capote. Harper

Lee's *To Kill A Mockingbird* was intriguing, and Alan promptly took out an option on it. On the verge of diving into a stage play production, he thought nothing of juggling two projects at once. Ties between Pakula and his social friends were the basis for his working relationships in both film and stage. For his major adaptation of Harper Lee's novel to film, he planned to hire Robert Mulligan, the director of Judith Anderson, Larry Hagman, George C. Scott, and Brandon de Wilde, in the stage play, *Comes a Day*.

It was that summer another movie icon surfaced as the prime candidate. Alan and Jim attended a summer theater circuit play in Westport, Connecticut, starring Myrna Loy. She got involved in this theatrical venture at the behest of a close friend, Alice Boatwright, a publicity agent with Universal with whom Myrna shared similar political views. At supper one night, "Boaty" suggested Myrna try new horizons, like the burgeoning dinner theaters or theatrical road companies, to revive her flagging career. Surrounded by friends and supportive production people, the star should flourish in a new medium. Under pressure to regain her former stature, Loy was more than anxious to show her talents had not waned. Never shy of ambition, the suave leading lady was aimed towards a Broadway goal.

Alan no longer felt the sting of Lucy's rejection when he and Jim scouted the film legend in *Marriage Go Round*; she was better suited to the role in *Pony* than Lucy. The two impressed men had permission to call on Miss Loy privately in her dressing room after the show. Pakula had known Miss Boatright during his studio days, when both worked in production departments, and she was glad to arrange the special session and vouch for the trustworthiness of the young, budding producer. When Pakula and Kirkwood raved about Myrna Loy's stage presence, the veteran film star was overwhelmed by their flattery and optimism. They boosted her ego tremendously. After a few minutes with them, she began to believe she could tackle any role in legitimate theater.

As the summer stock season was coming to a close for the year, Pakula discussed Loy's success and charisma in the play with producer Joel Schenker and others before approaching the actress about his new production. Pakula's interest in her was so strong that Robert Mulligan told author Jared Brown that Alan was "very taken with Myrna Loy." Interviewed by Sam Zolotow of the *New York Times*, Pakula said what most impressed him about Miss Loy in the Connecticut production was her star power, filling the house to Standing Room Only.

A true professional, Loy dominated the play. She had that stubborn streak of pride and ambition, which kept her a major film star for a generation, and had come East fully expecting to transfer her motion picture success to theater stages. It was no surprise to her for setting new box-office records at the Westport Country Playhouse. Additional performances had been added because of Miss

Loy's following among women of a certain age, and she was a gracious nonpareil, greeting film fans and audience members alike after the shows, taking time to shake hands and chat. All this convinced Pakula of her commercial appeal and audience draw.

Myrna was leery of spreading her wings over Broadway without first playing many smaller theaters. Combating her indecision, Alan argued she was ready for New York, and swore he had exactly the right property for her. She was given Jim's play to read. She went through it that night. *Pony's* script took her breath away; it was not her usual kind of role, and would certainly make a splash if she were to do it. She was familiar with the plot, having lived in Hollywood during the 1936 scandal. She and Lila Lee had each done co-starring roles with William Powell that year in separate movies.

The part of Rita, a veiled Lila Lee, did have its drawbacks. After having played the mother of a thirty-year old actor, Loy expressed little concern about depicting a mother (and former movie star) of a 16 year-old son. The idea of playing a has-been actress, down on her luck, hit closer to home. It could be a serious career error. When *Screen Stories* asked to do a layout on Myrna Loy, she was thrilled, but refused upon learning that regular magazine feature was "Where are they now?"

Well, where was she? Touring the sticks. By portraying a has-been, Loy could prove she was certainly the opposite—if she had the guts to tackle Broadway. It was too difficult to decide. She didn't know what to say to Pakula when she saw him next.

In order to win Miss Loy's commitment, Pakula had to guarantee the production wouldn't rush to open in New York. That was her main stumbling block; the actress was worried the nit-picking snobbish critics might reject her as a novice. Performing in charming little theaters was easy to face, but to take on a role in one of the venerable temples of Broadway was a formidable prospect. She was reassured by Pakula's promise that the play would remain on the road, touring out-of-state venues, for four or possibly five months of previews before making its debut in Manhattan. The producer pledged he would not open the play there until it was in perfect shape.

Pakula used his influence with Boatwright to get the apprehensive actress to agree to star in the adaptation of a first novel to stage. He toasted Myrna at Goldie's New York for pooling their talents. On October 28, 1961, columnist Dorothy Kilgallen issued a glowing anticipatory tribute to Myrna Loy, who celebrated her signing of a contract with Alan Pakula for the leading role in James Kirkwood's play in a room full of attractive women supporters. Among these fashionable elites, she was the one who gave off the aura of someone special and looked every inch the star.

Despite Pakula's unabashed confidence in Myrna Loy, Jim had reservations. The role of Rita was unlike any she'd "complexity presents a challenge" to a usually staid and dignified comedic actress. Although she'd been cast in less sympathetic roles in the few films she'd been getting of late (including Paul Newman's alcoholic mother), playing on the boards to a live audience created an extra hardship for her. Movies were made in bits and pieces of disconnected scenes over many weeks or months; plays ran straight through a few hours from Act One to final Curtain. Jim told reporters her role was "very strenuous" and "very dramatic" and contained a certain amount of comedy.

Whether James Kirkwood ever felt Myrna Loy was right to play his mother may be moot. Indelibly identified as the socialite sleuth Nora Charles, wife of the Thin Man, Myrna Loy was a star from the Golden Age; her presence in the play generated much public interest. It was blazoned as a rare attempt of a major film star to desert the picture business and begin anew on the stage. Many aging film personalities would follow suit in years to come, but Miss Loy's name was attracting considerable attention, exactly the effect Pakula and his prospective backers appreciated.

Josh Logan having accepted other offers, Alan sought out John Stix for his play's director. One of the most respected and thoughtful men in theater, John carried the wisdom and lore of theater history with him, and believed performers must reveal the truth, whatever the cost, however harsh the reality. Like Pakula, Stix was a Yale Drama School alumnus. An academic with extensive knowledge of the operas of Verdi and how they related to Shakespeare's plays, he was not a traditional theatrical director, but rather a visionary. He saw the uniqueness of Kirkwood's play.

Stix brought legitimacy to off-Broadway productions, causing the *New York Times* to give them recognition and be able to use Actors Equity members for his performers. He worked with Helen Hayes twice, and directed J.M.Barrie's dramas. His credentials were traceable to Joshua Logan and August Strindberg. In years prior to taking *There Must Be a Pony* to stage, he worked as a director on the epitome of high-brow television, *Omnibus,* which bolstered his respectability within all facets of the media. He would have been at home helming a Steve McQueen movie, but chose to spend the final decades of his career as a professor at Julliard College.

In late March of 1962, a twenty-year-old Canadian actor named Peter Helm was seriously considered for the part of Josh. He'd played a small role and understudied Brandon de Wilde in *Comes a Day* a few years earlier, and after acting with Joey Heatherton in *There Was a Little Girl,* he remained in the producer's memory. As a result, Peter was front-runner for the pivotal role of Josh from the outset. Kirkwood approved Pakula's choice because Peter started acting at age twelve, much like himself. The youth had studied acting in Rome under Burgess Meredith, who was there for *Enrico the Fourth,* and Peter played a small role in *Holiday for Lovers*, filmed while he was in Italy. Though the buzz put out by press agents was that the role of Josh was subject to a nationwide search, Peter was already pegged for it. Press agents continued to play the game of keeping the production in the public ear by insisting the plum juvenile role was the season's hottest goal for any newcomer.

Earl Wilson, noted Broadway columnist, suggested a nationwide search was likely and director John Stix and Miss Loy were looking among Hollywood's acting community for the right performer. The desire was to cast a teenager to play a teenager. In early April, through Alan Pakula's West Coast office, Hedda Hopper was tipped about the casting of Rosemary Murphy as the Press Agent in one of *Pony*'s supporting roles. Names for both Pakula's projects were beginning to fill columns. The producer gloried in the abundance of work he was doing, never confusing decisions for film or stage, though both productions were beginning to run neck and neck.

The plot of the play called for a gay pal named Merwin Saltzman to be foil to Myra Loy's character. Pakula chose an Oscar Levant clone G. Wood, a noted pianist, entertainer, and actor. Always using the initial instead of his full name of George, he played in both the movie and television version of *M.A.S.H.* Mary Patton was cast in the thankless role of Mrs. Nichols. Adelaide Klein played the acidic Ardeth, and young Edward Terry, protégé of director John Stix, took the role of Sid Traylor. Terry would play Luther the Geek in a bizarre cult movie nearly thirty years later. Others added to the *Pony* cast included Zero Mostel's niece, Barbara Mostel, and noted character actress Jan Miner appeared as Marguerite's confidant Sally.

The pivotal role of Ben was given to Donald Woods, a character actor with hundreds of film and stage roles to his credit. Woods joined the cast as the romantic interest for Miss Loy. His earnest, B-picture persona was vaguely familiar to the public from a series of forgettable motion pictures dating back to the earliest days of talkies. He could play a trustworthy father figure, right out of television central. Previous to *Pony*, he came off a popular triumph in a low-budget film called *13 Ghosts* for William Castle's gimmick horror picture. After the Kirkwood play he'd simply return to Hollywood and work in the latest Elvis Presley movie. His most famous film was likely *The Bridge of the San Luis Rey*, in 1944, based on Thornton Wilder's novella.

Pakula explained in a press interview: "Because actors, directors, and playwrights have been complaining for years about the lack of adequate rehearsal time, we hope to counteract some of the pressures of the ordinary pre-Broadway tour . . ." These were the words of a man whose reputation as an actor's director would be his legacy, but it displayed his talent for winning the support and trust of his troupe.

About mid-May, Pakula finally announced officially that twenty-year old Peter Helm, with whom he was most familiar as an actor, would be making his third Broadway appearance with the pivotal role of Josh, the sixteen year-old son who found himself suffocating "in the shadow of his movie star mother" in the comedy drama. A few reports incorrectly stated that Helm was sixteen, not merely playing a teenager.

Pakula also revealed the play's world premiere was scheduled for July 16 at a trendy resort town with a large gay tourist population, Ogunquit, Maine. The somewhat rigorous tour of smaller theatres would continue at the Falmouth Playhouse on Cape Cod, then to Mineola and Millburn, New Jersey. Scrubbing a trip to New Hope, Pennsylvania, Pakula now thought the play should stop in Philadelphia, previous to the Broadway debut. John Keating of the *New York Times* cracked that the stars would be "a troupe of heat-resistant thespians who will begin working out the kinks." He wondered if there would be "a breakdown in the home stretch."

Preliminary opinion was not optimistic.

As star of the vehicle, Myrna Loy took on certain responsibilities. She felt ethically that she must assume blame if the play did not work out, and her work ethic from movie days did not allow her to sit around idly—or play the star. She was active in promoting the play, as she had promoted her pictures. Doing interviews with local press, she was eager to present herself as she always did, as an upfront, direct personality, with a good head on her shoulders and filled with the wisdom of common sense.

Undeterred by catty charges that she was not considered major film star material any longer, Loy accepted her maturity with enthusiasm. "I shed no tears for lost youth." Her work was paramount, not any concentration on her private life. She found unemployment boring and recommended that all women find activities to contribute service to humanity and community. She thought to do otherwise was to have an unhealthy preoccupation with self. She herself was highly involved with United Nations charities. "My work with the UN has taken me all over the world, but I live in the present moment, not the past ones."

With the press on her role in Kirkwood's first play, Myrna Loy spoke of rather insubstantial matters in her interviews. "I'll wear divine clothes in it. I know what is right for me. The difference between being well dressed and not is in what you reject. There are so many influences you must resist." She knew instinctively how to look every inch a star, whether in performance or in public. In the play, she'd be damned certain Rita, too, dressed the part.

If Miss Loy fretted about her performance or reception of it, she never expressed it to the press. If there was any issue foremost on her mind, it was the daily grind of the summer tour. Facing small towns and cities, rather than the great metropolitan areas with their fine restaurants and hotels, Loy's concern was again her physical condition. "I find it difficult to eat well when I am traveling.

I enjoy food that is not good for my figure—who doesn't? But when you are planning your meals at home it is much easier. Everyone has to find her own way of controlling weight. I try to balance indulgence with disciple But I never allow myself to go more than five or six pounds over."

There Must Be A Pony opened on schedule in mid-July at Ogunquit. Myrna Loy was delighted. She had a stage success there the previous summer, performing in *Marriage Go Round* with Claude Dauphin, and enjoyed her stay at Dunelawn, a Georgian manor with small guest cottages and sweeping vistas of the Atlantic Ocean.

However beautiful the actress appeared as a middle-aged star playing a middle-aged star, the shocked reaction to her work on stage didn't take long to manifest itself. Those long-time movie fans weren't watching the likeable smart-alecky Nora Charles they had adored seeing trade barbs with the Thin Man on the silver screen. Myrna herself admitted, "There's no question that the role was a departure for me." She had known the real Lila Lee as part of their Hollywood community, and the two had little in common in professional or personal lives. "Lila, as depicted by her son, had a drinking problem, a flamboyant temperament, and a mean streak. The kind of vulnerability that made her palatable was hardly my forte." She may well have added they were oil and water in personalities, but an actress should to be able to don another personality. There was now some question whether her fans might agree to the transformation.

Donald Woods usually did his best work in legitimate theater; in rehearsals and performances, he brought a sober, trusting quality to the role of the bounder, making Ben's hypocritical nature incomprehensible to the audience. They never smelled the rat, as intentionally written in the play-script. Donald was too good at deceiving the audience. In real life, the Manhattan Beach crowd who knew Reid Russell could not comprehend his behavior. The dramatic shock of learning all Ben's secrets hit the audience too abruptly. They could not process the amount of irony so quickly—within a few minutes of the conclusion of Act One. Kirkwood calculated shock, and in this he succeeded wildly.

Much to the surprise of everyone, the Ogunquit critics were hostile to the play and to its star. The first small-town criticism, which Pakula hoped would be positive, put it bluntly, if not unpleasantly. The work "does not display enough quality," chimed one local critic. And, far worse, there seemed to be no future for this effort. Rather than attack a popular icon of Hollywood, of course the barbs were aimed at the hapless playwright, the least known of the lustrous cast and production crew. "Kirkwood has taken what might have been potentially absorbing theatre fare and marred it by inept dramaturgy."

In Jim's version of events in There Must Be a Pony, *Victoria Russell, mother of Reid, became an older wife with a severe drinking problem and an obsession that her son was murdered. Mrs. Russell's lawyers tried to portray her as a victimized mother, sentimentally depicted.*

Desperate to please everyone and make his play a hit, Jim Kirkwood threw himself into fixing it. This was more than a first effort to take a work to Broadway; for Jim this was another effort to justify the behaviors of his mother and himself years ago in Manhattan Beach. As a result, Jim rewrote, and rewrote, replacing scenes wholesale. The time period of the 1962 play and screenplay was that of April to April as one full year.

The true situation had been far more compressed, measured in a few months. The play ran the gamut from three acts to two acts, from one intermission to two intermissions. The complicated scenes in Act One jumped from the present to the past, from one night in Scene Two to the next night in Scene Three to two weeks later in Scene Four. The second act was just as dizzy, going from five weeks forward in Scene Two to ten days after in Scene Three. The dramatic strain of the scenes left audiences somewhat bewildered as to the timing of events.

Jim tweaked scene dates resembling those of his life; and he had a problem deciding Josh's age. In various versions, the boy is supposedly fifteen and other times, that was crossed out and Jim substituted "sixteen" in his large curly scrawl. But Jimmy had been only twelve at the time and. as he often said, big for his age. He had grown almost an astonishing six feet tall by his eleventh birthday. In some ways he looked older, but had a pretty face (something he deplored), which made a puzzling contrast between his size and his real age. This made him a frequent adult sex object in his early adolescence. Snippets from nearly every book, flashbacks and episodes, indicate how he was pursued and wooed by adults. This made an uncomfortable transition to the stage work.

The most startling change from both novel and future play versions was Kirkwood's decision to put the *Pony* anecdote early in the first act. He had Ben relate the tale, rather than have it revealed in the suicide note at the end of the play. This didn't work for Jim, and he replaced the anecdote to the end in all subsequent versions. The 1962 screenplay used the word "horseshit" (not the euphemism of manure), which would never have been allowed.

Jim both used the four-letter word in various productions in 1962, but frequently went with words like "manure" or "crap." He admitted these substitutions worked just as well in his mind. Words like that didn't reach the traditional movie screen until almost 1970. Within Kirkwood's anarchist view to try to break through the censorship, it may seem hypocritical he'd challenge language on scatology, but be reluctant to use the word "homosexual."

Jim also had problems naming the District Attorney. In the novel the D.A. remains unnamed, but he used several in the play and screenplay versions, including Simmons (crossed out and rejected), and Keathley. Since he usually kept names beginning with "K" reserved for his lead characters in nearly every play and novel.

Also transformed in the play, the barbecue pit became a setting rally point in his several play versions, though its ashen hearth was featured more prominently in the case of Reid Russell than in the novel. Most interestingly, and probably for theatrical construction, he moved Ben's suicide indoors to the Game Room for nearly all versions of the play.

In both novel and future screenplays, that action took place outdoors on the swing, more accurately in line with the chronology. In all Kirkwood's screenplays the dead Ben, with his hideous bullet hole to the head, is covered in ants, which writer Mart Crowley simply avoided in the RJ Productions version. And in all versions the body was found within a short period after the suicide, except for the novel, which indicated he was there for at least twelve hours. (Kirkwood sometimes said in his lectures that the body had lain undetected in the backyard for as much as four days. The Police coroner estimated Reid Russell had been on the swing for as much as twenty-four hours.)

For another pivotal action of the narrative, Josh picked up the gun where he found it on the ground next to the body. In several versions, he discovered the body, but did not commit that well-known rule not to touch anything at a "crime scene," especially the weapon. In Kirkwood's first draft play-script, no one witnessed his discovery of the body of Ben. In subsequent rewrites of the 1962 play, not only did Josh hold the weapon, he was holding it as Rita walked into the room.

Jim was to spend many hours on the ending—changing the words, the order of episodes, the final characters on stage, or their speeches. It went to the heart of his difficulty in dealing with the lesson he learned from Reid Russell and the terrible crisis of 1936. He depicted Rita hugging Josh and saying, "He loved us!" and tried having Merwin offer comfort and companionship to the teenage boy.

After two weeks in the summer resort, Pakula took his production to Cape Cod and the Falmouth Playhouse for five days, leaving there on July 28th to return to another favorite spot for Myrna Loy, Westport, where Pakula first fell in love with the star. During that difficult summer Kirkwood considered myriad lines and conditions to end the play, such as Josh stating: "When you learn the truth about something—like knowing how Ben must have felt—you start picking your brain apart—but it's too late." Another concluding line was, "I'll go on looking for the pony . . . it's the only way to go on living—the absolute only way—otherwise, why even get out of bed in the morning?"

It was apparent that Jim was still sorting through his own memories, his own reaction to the death of Reid Russell, while he was presenting his work to the public. He had begun writing a screenplay of his stage version. If he got tangled in the versions, it was understandable. He was writing changes in the theatrical script, and likely substituting them for those in his screenplay—and vice versa. Whenever he chose to alter events in one storyline, he made changes in the plot, which became rough on the actors. He wrote notes to himself, "I'd just like to finish something, just for once . . ."

Such would not be the fate of his *Pony* story. It would never be done to his satisfaction.

Jim created one of the play's worst problems in the 1962 version. He populated the house in Paraiso Beach with some dogs and a few jungle creatures. The latter were a chained ocelot, a caged kinkajou and a talkative parrot. Once the menagerie was noisily brought together on stage, Kirkwood quipped, "This looks like the remake of an old Tarzan movie."

The author had only himself to blame. The animals created all sorts of hazards for the actors and director. The ocelot was temperamental. It not only frightened Miss Loy, but also tended to upstage her. And because the kinkajou was nocturnal, he was particularly useless in matinee performances, tending to sleep.

As if to give notice that he saw where the play was headed, director John Stix regarded the sleeping kinkajou and commented, "We've already put one person to sleep." He may have inadvertently let slip his lost patience with the zoo of misbehaving animals.

New scenes, according to Loy, were not as effective as the originals. The script she read and wanted to perform was changing into something less interesting to her. The altered endings more or less took her out of the main focus and placed it on Josh. Rita was rapidly becoming a second banana to her own son—a dispute which takes place among the characters in the play when Rita refuses to let the boy try out for an acting role. With life imitating art badly behind the scenes, columnists like Dorothy Kilgallen pointed out that Loy was not the one on the receiving end of the accolades. On August 5, 1962, her column cackled: "Young Peter Helm is getting ovations at all his performances during the tryouts . . ."

By August 7, the dogged *Pony* troupe moved on to Mineola, Long Island. At this point Pakula made a strategic change in the production before the final leg of the journey to Broadway. Because he realized he was needed in California for his movie production, he began to separate himself from the company. It may be Alan decided the play was a lost venture, or that his fate was more successfully tied to the potential of Robert Mulligan's film direction of Harper Lee's respected novel. He was hopping off the *Pony* production. It made the novice playwright more edgy and the uneasy star more insecure.

Pakula announced that his co-producers, Joel and Ellie Bissinger, would oversee the work while he was away. As if to show his confidence in the project was undiminished, he moved up the Broadway debut date from October 1st to September 27. It effectively removed another week of work-in-progress performances that he had cited only a month earlier as the difference in this new production.

Before Pakula flew off, Jim asked Alan to give his father a one-day role in the new motion picture. The eighty-seven year old Kirkwood was to perform in its courtroom scene, but after receiving an offer for a larger role in Marlon Brando's *The Ugly American*, he took that instead for his final professional appearance. Rosemary Murphy's work in the play had so impressed Alan, he would bring her to Hollywood with him, where she was given a featured role in Pakula's classic, award-winning movie, *To Kill a Mockingbird*.

Alas, with Pakula gone, Jim frantically tried to revise the work before the stop at the Paper Mill Playhouse in New Jersey on August 28. The final performance for Miss Loy was on September 8, 1962. A two-week stop in Philadelphia and the ultimate destination on Broadway were never reached. In her log of the play's journey Loy simply crossed out the final two venues in red ink. She made no further entry.

Myrna Loy's autobiography, written twenty years later, admitted how "we started with high hopes," and how quickly all optimism was dashed. Myrna explained the play was stolen from her by the changing script emphasis, and the winning performance of the young actor, who kept getting a larger and more sympathetic role as the play tour encountered bumpy reviews. She accused Kirkwood of hasty and frequent alterations in the script. "Jim, intimidated by the critics, started changing his play. He's a perfectionist, as his marvelous book for *A Chorus Line* attests, but I don't think that many of the changes were as effective as his original script. And he's so quick the actors couldn't catch up with him."

After working with Asta, the wire haired terrier in a half-dozen *Thin Man* movies, Miss Loy would seem at home with a scene-stealing animal in the show. She revealed how the first Asta, named Skippy, never really took a shine to her—and a bite sealed a less than idyllic relationship. Now she had to work on stage with a menagerie. Jim faithfully recreated the bunch of animals living at Manhattan Beach. Unlike the fictional creatures in Jim's novel, who behaved exactly as he described, the real ones had minds of their own. They did not honor the script, even with trainers nearby. When on stage, they did whatever they chose.

The first problem was the parrot, called Chauncey in the story. Always a patient and generous actress, listening to her fellow actors and responding to make them look good, Myrna found her key lines upstaged and overwhelmed by unpredictable babble from the parrot. In her film work, she'd be allowed to retake the scene, but on stage before an audience, when her line was lost amid the unexpected titters, it affected more than her performance. The message and momentum of the play was disrupted. If she tried to banter with the bird, she looked more ridiculous. The squawking parrot exasperated the star and damaged the dramatic integrity of the play.

Within a few days of the play's opening, employment ads appeared in the trade papers. There was a call for a parrot that would remain dumb. They needed a bird that could not talk over and louse up Miss Loy's dialogue. Her nightly performance sank into farce, damaged by an uncontrollable bird. That was the least of her dismay. No one could predict what to expect from a mix of animals on stage at any given time.

Kirkwood's play-script called for a Brazilian weeper monkey, assorted dogs, a parrot, and for added color, a kinkajou. The arboreal South American mammal with long prehensile tale ate fruit and looked quite exotic on stage. So-called "tamed" animals, cannot be trusted. The small playful thing soon displayed extremely sharp teeth. The play wasn't helped to have actors dashing off stage to find medical care for a bite. The kinkajou had to go.

At the end of July, as they wound up their Ogunquit tryout of the play, the last member to join the cast was an ocelot. This animal responded very well towards the Myrna. However, Miss Loy found herself too much the object of the animal's possessiveness. As *Pony*'s tour proceeded, Myrna Loy heard the ocelot "kept growling as we toured and became extremely jealous when I addressed anyone else on stage." The creature particularly took umbrage if Miss Loy stood too close to Helm, her son in the story, or spoke to him in tones the feline did not like. She often berated and argued with her son, which set off the animal's most ugly responses.

When the menacing ocelot received his walking papers from management, Peter ended up owning it, naming it Lolita.

Continuing portents must have made performing the play an excruciating experience for cast and crew. There were constant reminders indicating how the interest of their producers was on the wane. Miss Loy was disheartened by their lack of appreciation for her hard work night after night on stage. To make matters worse, backstage gossip had, as expected, finally reached her. "As I recall, another producer got into it and I began hearing rumors that he wanted to replace me with Kim Stanley. Apparently Alan and Jim objected and never did anything about it."

The idea that Kim Stanley might replace Loy may have been a misunderstanding. Miss Stanley was then being considered to be narrator for *To Kill a Mockingbird.* Wires could have crossed in discussions over Pakula's two simultaneous projects. Overheard conversations in part were repeated at the theater, misconstruing the spotty content. After all, it was Rosemary Murphy who Pakula took with him to California to play a supporting role in the movie he was producing.

According to Jared Brown's book on the life of Alan Pakula, it was Jim Kirkwood who had little confidence in Myrna. The producer's biographer presumed that Kirkwood wanted a change in cast. Pakula and his people disagreed and thought the problem was the play itself, and they wanted to bring in a play doctor—to bolster the young playwright. This likely did not sit well with Jim, who had more psychic energy invested in this play, which he called "near and dear to me."

Another writer might have been called in if Pakula had been independent enough, but the idea was rejected because Pakula didn't have access for funds to pay another writer. The thought was a hard slap at Kirkwood and his life's work. Pakula said, "I have told Jim all of the financial facts of my personal life," and hinted that he might not continue with the production after August of 1962. He used his parents as the pressure on him to leave an unprofitable project and find one that would make money. He began meetings with director Robert Mulligan on the West Coast on *Mockingbird* while the Kirkwood play struggled and stumbled on the east coast without his attention.

By the end of August, Pakula disappeared from the production of the play he set in motion. Some who knew him and worked with him thought this was an anomaly in his career—not of those Broadway flops he had behind him, but of his carefully nurtured image as a producer with a heart. If the Hollywood film had not looked so promising, he would not have so quickly chosen to abandon Jim and his *Pony.*

Finally, after seven weeks of production, and more than a few weeks of pessimistic speculation, the producer of the show called for a meeting with the cast and crew. Joel Schrenk alone faced the group, as Pakula was on the west coast again. The situation was dire, and he told them that he and Pakula were bowing out of this production and were selling their investment. They were actively looking to find someone who would continue the show, but for them the end had come.

A nasty blow to morale, the cast had to do a performance after this unpleasant bit of news. It sent Kirkwood into overdrive as he tried now to find backers and, at the same time, do rewrites on the show as it continued its tour. As a result of this news, the play staggered along for a few weeks, but had lost its impetus. This sort of moment in theater life leaves creative people depressed and miserable, but it was also part and parcel of working on stage. It didn't make the summer of 1962 any easier on the hard-working actors who believed in the plot, the characters, and Jim Kirkwood.

Myrna sadly observed, "Things began to deteriorate as we approached New York. Out of town critics attacked me and the play. There was still that hangover from films; they were punishing me for having been a movie star. No matter how much you work—and I worked very hard—the tendency is to make it difficult for you, particularly if you have the temerity to aim for Broadway."

The actress was blunt in her assessments. When she saw trouble, she called it by no other name. In her opinion, "Another problem was that Alan Pakula, our producer, spent much of the time in Hollywood producing his second picture." In Loy's experience, a professional proved his mettle by sticking to his project and giving it a fighting chance. She saw something many others never saw in Alan Pakula—ruthless ambition and a fickle nature. *Pony* failed for having a producer who abandoned it on the doorstep of Broadway.

The Cort Theatre opening in October was out of the question. On September 22, 1962, came the somber and dreaded announcement that Jim Kirkwood's play was not on hiatus, but permanently cancelled, falling a week short from its Broadway goal with no explanation as to its future. Regardless of this sad outcome, the presence of Myrna Loy had given the theater world something special to watch. She did what was expected of her; brought in large audiences and delivered a gracious rendering of her character. She stated, "*There Must Be a Pony* closed on the road after a profitable summer." If the play had been brought to the Cort in October, it might have failed on Broadway because of its difficulties during the summer try-outs, but it was never given a fair chance.

Myrna Loy was not deterred. She continued her search for a Broadway showcase.

She heard about the play again when told Elizabeth Taylor was to do it as a television movie in 1986 . . . she may have felt sorry for the other legendary actress, saying simply of her ordeal in the first stage version, "It wasn't a very pleasant experience for me."

After the debacle of *Pony*, Myrna Loy went on to tremendous success in *Barefoot in the Park*, putting her in great demand in both stage and film. In late

1966, Myrna gave an interview to the *Los Angeles Times* about her growing success on stage. Asked about Pony, she said: "The book was beautiful and the play had tremendous possibilities—but like many things you reach a point where you have to do more work on it, which Kirkwood didn't. We played much the same circuit (as *Marriage Go Round*) with Donald Woods and Peter Helm as my costars."

The actress added an interesting caveat, "Now it has been sold to Columbia as a picture—and I think it could be great." It almost sounded to Kirkwood like she was still willing to do the role—on film. Typical of what Jim always experienced, the good was tempered by the not so good. Miss Loy added, as an aside, she disapproved of modern plays and films because "there's no gallantry anymore."

Resilient Peter Helm had quickly rebounded from the summer fiasco and appeared on a *Naked City* episode, a prototype of *Law and Order*. His career as an actor foundered after the 1960s. Director John Stix continued to garner a high-powered reputation, though he left off his participation in *There Must Be a Pony* from his resumes and biographies for the remainder of his career. The only person who had not given up on the work was its author. James Kirkwood had plenty of motivation and energy to spare. The next twenty-five years were dotted with Jim's greatest successes, but always he returned to ride the *Pony* one more time.

CHAPTER SIX

ON RADIO, IN ONE ACT, BUT NOT ON SCREEN

Whenever Jim found time, he polished the remnants of *Pony* into a new novel called *Good Times/Bad Times*. In it he planned to deal with two deaths—his former friend, Ted, and the Headmaster of Gilford Academy. Jim admitted he did not kill the prep school headmaster in real life, "though I wanted to." On another occasion, he added, "We can't go around killing headmasters. So, I killed him in a book instead."

Also, Jim was working on a screenplay all this time and had interested Columbia Pictures in *Pony*. His earliest scenario was drafted and ready on October 2, 1962, and it was given attribution to Alan Pakula's production company. At this point, with the novel two years behind him, the attempt to go to Broadway in failure, he could not relinquish his fascination, albeit obsession, with the story of his mother and the death of Reid Russell.

If he noted in his letters that he was beating a dead horse, he asked for pardon because the new paperback had come out, and he felt the need to shill the book. He received $15,000 for paperback rights, most of which he gave to his mother for her medical expenses. His excuse rang false. He would never escape his past, nor did he want to surrender the story . . . "Having been actor, the dearest thing in the world is to see it done as a play. I don't want to sell it to movies yet."

Keeping his liaison with Pakula was important to Kirkwood. By 1963, around Oscar time, it was clear the film producer of *To Kill a Mockingbird* was a force to be reckoned with. It may be that Kirkwood wanted his Broadway associate to take up the reins again, and to make *Pony* into a successful picture. For the next year or two, having Pakula's Productions in the screenplay acknowledgements was calculated to impress studio executives that he was tied to the project. He was not. Pakula had shed any association with *Pony* fast as he could.

The erstwhile Broadway producer took another fling at theater with a musical version of *Portrait of Jennie*, a disastrous staging of an ephemeral story about time and fantasy, an artist trying to capture the spirit in an oil portrait of a long-dead girl, who appears to him. Pakula realized where his fortune and art rested: in Hollywood. It was there he'd make his mark, and that didn't include keeping ties to old failures. He built a house in Brentwood, produced a film with Steve McQueen and Natalie Wood, and flirted with writers like Ray Bradbury and John Cheever. He was moving upscale, and Kirkwood's story of a tawdry Hollywood scandal no longer interested him.

Jim was eager to see his work done as a film. In his view everyone in America wanted to be a movie star, and he may have included himself in this list. Though his theatre connections made him more respected, he preferred movies. He honed the film script, using the experience of the play to adjust the storyline. He played of elements of popular appeal, like the weeper monkey, whom he now called Kong. He also added a snide Hollywood columnist to the story, someone who had not appeared in the original novel at all.

Though he referred to one supportive gossip columnist, another was written as a Hedda Hopper type, former actress and bitter rival of Louella Parsons. Friends of either were automatically the other's adversaries. As Parsons had been an adherent of Lila Lee, Hopper never mentioned the notorious woman or her son, Jim, by name in her column if she could avoid it. The few references over twenty years were either curtailed or slightly misinformed, perhaps deliberately. The character Ardeth Long enters the play and screenplay with all the vituperation Jim could muster. As an accurate example of the issues the Reid Russell case raised, Ardeth Long serves her purpose far better than any character in the novel. She tells Rita plainly how "your past has been anything but tidy."

More critical of his mother, the screenwriter brought out incidents such as attending a police questioning nearly drunk, and slapping one of the officers. Josh harshly criticizes Rita, saying how he finds her behavior appalling. Ardeth also raises the seldom-spoken creation of studio morals clauses, so prevalent in the 1930s that film studios sought to protect themselves from irresponsible actors.

The character of Josh takes a more cynical and adult turn in Kirkwood's screenplay. The exposition mentions how he frequently ran away from home to escape his mother's unpleasant, erratic behavior. There was a covert code in the 1950s: Josh's fleeing to the YMCA for overnight stays would raise titters today, but the disquieting significance was familiar only to the enlightened decades ago. The inference being that the boy was either offering himself for sale to men at the facility, or just offering himself as a prize.

Josh is allowed to express darker feelings about love and family. He deplores his affection for Ben, "I'll never get fooled again!" or "If that's love, you can have it." Rita jealously sees how his tie to the dead man transcends her own needs, "Your whole world was Ben. You hung on his every word." It sounds accusatory, as if Ben were Josh's lover, not Rita's.

Another new detail Kirkwood added to illuminate Josh's motives and psychology was to have Josh pasting his own photographs into a scrapbook. He keeps a record of his press clippings and hides them from his mother whenever she enters his room.

The screenplay ends in a festive celebration of the passing of the dark cloud that had been Ben and his scamming lies. Unlike the book, in which Josh is sad and depressed, the guests toast each other with champagne. Josh acts as their waiter, supplying drinks for the remaining cast. One guest finds it morbid when the alleged suicide ruling is confirmed. There is something uneasy about this finale, and though it could be a metaphor for the inner feelings of the script's survivors of the ordeal, the original participants came across nearly as heartless.

Ruth Morris, Jimmy Kirkwood, and Lila Lee, stroll to the courthouse in Manhattan Beach to be interviewed by the police about the mysterious death of Reid Russell. It was a walk on the beach for these three.

A year after the play closed, Kirkwood's hard work paid off by submitting his screenplay with a line on the crimson cover indicating it was part of Pakula Productions, which it wasn't. Kirkwood interested executives in the Columbia Pictures office. By mid-July, the *New York Times* announced the assigning of the picture to the new schedule. Late in the month, a headline boasted a "Director of Video Dramas Signed" for the big screen version of Kirkwood's play.

Columbia Pictures assigned Elliott Silverstein to make his feature film debut, directing a version of the play. The thirty-five year old director had made a name on television by staging highly respected series episodes in *The Naked City* and *The Defenders* while he was in New York, and on *Route 66* and *Dr. Kildare* on the west coast. He was to start work at Columbia in June of 1963. The new *Pony* script had been thoroughly updated to contemporary Hollywood and its focus would be on an aging film star and her son.

Unfortunately, a movie was being shot, based upon the Harold Robbins novel, *Where Love Has Gone*. This soapy film slightly altered brutality of the murder of Lana Turner's gangster boyfriend by her daughter. It was the Kirkwood tale in sexual reverse. Bette Davis, Susan Hayward, and Joey Heatherton, took the main parts. It undercut chances of *Pony* making it to the screen.

Barely a month after the announcement his play would become a movie, Kirkwood received word from the Motion Picture and Television Hospital in Woodland Hills, his father had passed away. Their relationship had been less bumpy than Jim's ties to his mother, but there was a greater gulf between father and son. Though he saw him far more than his mother for periods of his adolescence, it was years before he made his father a focus of one of his books. Jim admitted the chase scene in *Good Times/Bad Times* was based on an incident when his father, at the age of sixty-five, ran after his young son, and caught up to him. He repeated the scene in his final, unpublished and unfinished novel, *I Teach Flying*.

Kirkwood didn't recall letting his father catch him. In the same novel, he described his father as a broken down old actor, but however old the silent director and actor may have been, he started another family at age sixty-three with a common law wife. After the scandals of the Russell Reid case, Jimmy's father made headlines in the renewed investigation into the death of William Desmond Taylor, another scandalous crime of the 1920s in Hollywood. James Senior was involved with Mary Miles Minter, the accused murderess, and was called to give testimony in the reopened case of 1937.

When the book, *Cast of Killers*, came out, it detailed the crime and the elder Kirkwood's involvement. There was talk Jimmy would narrate or write a documentary television special in the mid-1980s. When asked about this element of his father's past, Jim answered, "I wouldn't go near *Cast of Killers*, never fear. My Dad is mentioned in that several times. He did it with Mary Miles Minter and a few others. And so did I."

Thus, both of Jim's parents were involved in Hollywood murder theories of 1936 and 1937. If there was one lasting effect of the death of the eighty-eight year old man, it was that Jim suddenly became James Kirkwood in terms of his professional name. With the elder gone, he was no longer junior, not Jimmy, nor Jim. All future literary and film work would bill him as James.

When production head M.J. Frankovich announced the forthcoming movies for Columbia Pictures at a press conference on May 5, 1964, there were seventy-seven titles. Most would be produced that year or sometime in the near future. Among those listed was a film titled *There Must Be a Pony*. It was one of fifty-four films in pre-production, being readied for the cameras. Of that number, a dozen never were filmed at all. Kirkwood's script ended up among those.

Meanwhile, nationally syndicated columnist Mike Connolly wrote a column in early September of 1964, in which he tried to create a firestorm of interest in the movie version of Kirkwood's story. Connolly stated that Columbia Pictures executives were trying to interest a member of one of the biggest musical groups in history to break away from the Beatles to start his own movie career. According to Connolly, he was not fomenting the breakup of the group, but there were some people over at Columbia who wanted Ringo Starr to play Josh. Not much came of this sensational idea, and it deservedly faded fast.

Not a month had passed when, in mid-October of 1964, reports around the Industry were circulating, again from columnist Mike Connolly, how Rita Hayworth would come out of semi-retirement to play the role of Rita in *Pony*. One presumed she finally rejected the notion of playing the mother of one of the Beatles. Alas, she was in the early stages of Alzheimer's Disease, relatively unknown at the time, and her uncertain behavior removed her name from the project. She was not thought fully capable of following through on the picture. After 1965 her career was spotty, playing only featured roles.

For nearly all of 1964, Jim was out of the country. He had accepted a role with the road company of *Never Too Late*. The pay was consistent—and lucrative—and he wanted to escape the pressures of play or film production, movie gossip, and the death of his father. He still liked to act and took the part of a bland leading man, recreating Orson Bean's character from the original. Roland Winters, the Charlie Chan of movies, starred in the production, while Nancy Coleman who played Jim's mother during the first season of *Valiant Lady*, now took a role as his mother-in-law in the hit comedy.

The play reuniting the soap's Mickey Emerson with his mother, Helen, was given for audiences who had no idea of their original teaming. The road company afforded Jim the chance to spend nearly ten months in South Africa, touring Johannesburg, Capetown, and Durban, in director Elaine Perry's version of the comedy. (It was Elaine's mother, Antoinette, who had the famous New York stage award named for her: the Tony.)

Jim took the occasion to put together a shorter, one-hour version of *There Must be a Pony* for the illustrious Herrick Merrill Radio Productions of Durban. Once again, Jim had an opportunity to revise and hone the story, its characters and motivations. He penned a thirty-one-page script, distilling the action, but now, away from American eyes, adding interesting new details to the death of Ben/Reid. The radio show allowed him to play Josh, though he was now forty, and his *Valiant Lady* mother played Rita. His radio play was performed on air in Durban under his own auspices.

Never Too Late started a spectacular tour, except for the night of the third performance. Rushing about the stage, Jim broke his leg—and not for good luck. "Listen, if you're going to do it up right, why not have an audience?" He literally limped across the tour. By Cape Town he was retyping his *Pony* play, as well as working on *The Angels or Whoever*, which became *Hit Me with a Rainbow*. In between these titles, he once dallied with calling it *One Phuquing Miracle* . . .

The future looked rosy. After political fireworks and hot water in South Africa, where Jim took a stand openly against apartheid, Kirkwood went to Spain and spent a European vacation with one of his closest friends, James Leo Herlihy. They had talked frequently about working together—and threw themselves into an amusing writing project, while involved in an intense affair, which never abated for Kirkwood. Years after, Jim always tweaked at Jamie to rejoin him, write another play together, live with him, or just send him another letter because, as he said, "I am like a diabetic. I need a Herlihy fix."

Jim suggested the twosome should co-author a wild play script about a secret organization named *UTBU,* which was a kind of Murder, Incorporated, for the average person. Someone could supply a name to this group, who investigated to find out if the person was truly unpleasant, deserving to be offed. The acronym stood for *Unhealthy to be Unpleasant.*

A major draft continued into a second version, yet untitled in early 1965. They called it *Time to Kill* at first, but abruptly dropped that. The final choice was the peculiar acronym of the murderous group: *UTBU.* Kirkwood came to find a dozen humorous variations on the title. Among them was *UBTUPSBOO.* When he was in a particularly nasty mood, the title ran for two lines of weird syllables.

James Herlihy said, "Yes, we wrote *UTBU* together in 1964 in Torremolinos where we had taken a little villa together for the winter. Working with Jimmy was enormous fun, but since I dislike working in the theatre, we made a deal that he could have a giant's share of the royalties and all of the credit if I could please excuse myself and go to Mexico City. Thus (sob!) my name did not appear on this particular flop."

Jim used the play as a pointed barb to needle Jamie in years to come, sometimes referring to it as "*UPTUB,* or whatever the name of that thing was." He mailed royalty checks for miniscule amounts to James Leo Herlihy, to "cut out the middleman." These games were often pretexts for Kirkwood to beg Jamie to team up again, or at least send him a long letter. His dear Jamie never agreed, despite Jim's constant declarations of love. "Can we write another play together? Please, Daddy, please!" Jim sent his requests to Herlihy on a regular basis.

Kirkwood tended to make wickedly outrageous promises if his old friend would work with him again, "blow jobs on weekends." Herlihy knew better than to respond, which often made Jimmy become furious. "Write me a letter when you learn to type again, and make it quick and long." He lamented, "I commit crimes against Nature in your name."

Letters often arrived at Herlihy's address with huge crayon comments written on the envelope or letter itself: "This letter could be injurious to your health!" But Kirkwood loved Herlihy ("you great big beautiful bitch") and admired him for not becoming involved with the "commercialism" of the business, and for separating himself from social madness and endless partying that often caught up with Jim. After years of high-speed living, Kirkwood wrote to Jamie and confessed: "I'm feeling my age for the first time in life." And, Kirkwood advised that if his long, super-charged letters bored Herlihy, "Ho-hum it into the waste basket."

Whenever Kirkwood attended parties in the Hamptons, everyone asked about Jamie. They were a well-known couple. Kirkwood used his usual strategy, by letting Herlihy know, "I tell everyone that you're writing a sequel (to *Midnight Cowboy*) about the cowboy and the gimpy one, how the cowboy goes to Hollywood to become a big star. But his relationship to his friend becomes a problem, and the studio has the gimpy one killed to avoid a scandal." When none of this worked on Jamie, Jim resigned himself to the distance Herlihy kept: "I accept the fact I am a fucking leper."

Kirkwood was cynical about *UTBU* as much as any of his creations. "That play, as far as I'm concerned, is the least personal of my works." He sometimes said the same of *A Chorus Line*, of which he also added he was seldom asked about his "Phew-Litter Prize" winning play. As for *UTBU*, his official line was that Jamie and he "were old friends and decided to meet there, both of us having been in other parts of Europe, and try our hands at writing an entertainment." The play was the illegitimate child of their love. As he wrote to Herlihy, baiting him yet again over a refusal for a second collaboration, "I'm glad you have crabs. They make nice pets."

Jim's whimsical humor had led him to name one of the characters in *UTBU* after his beloved Aunt Peggy, calling the woman by Peggy's married name: Tufford. When asked about this habit of assigning names to characters, he confessed: "I suppose, however, you are right about certain names I use in my books. I snatch them out of the air, and sometimes from a character I have played, obviously, like Mickey Emerson. I really don't plan things that way, it's just sort of the way they come out." He then proceeded to call himself "Sly Boots," a reference to a recurring character in his novels.

Kirkwood had many co-authors in the theatre, part of his perception of stage work as a communal project, and one that required more than a single creative force to make it successful. This may have contributed to his icy hostility to the ego, which finally engulfed *A Chorus Line* when Michael Bennett went out of control, hogging credit for the work. That was unlike writing with Herlihy, who wanted no credit, and with whom Jim spent a torrid time. Their mutual affection sparked the sole creative project between them, leaving Jim wanting and wishing for more.

"*UTBU* was the result. I think it's a funny farce comedy and I've seen some productions in little theatres around the country that have been very gratifying. The production was a befucked one on Broadway with a cast of prima donnas, and a very talented lady, Nancy Walker, as the director. It was her maiden effort at directing and she was somewhat stunned by the cast. The production was not nearly as good as it should have been." The play offered Tony Randall, Thelma Ritter, Constance Ford, Margaret Hamilton, and other faces familiar to movie and theater fans. That assembly of talent should have delivered a classic hit play, but didn't. Typical of Jim's luck, the New York opening night took place during a blizzard and transit strike.

The reception of his show inspired Jim to take out a black-bordered ad in *Variety* in memory of a certain critic. "As for Stanley Kauffman—it was the very first play he reviewed for the *New York Times*, and I suppose he was just letting everyone know that the *Times* had this new critic who had a lot of hand grenades to lob at anything that might land on Broadway in front of him. He certainly threw one at me—the prick!" In his indomitable style, Jim added with cavalier shrug, "Isn't it great though that I'm not bitter!"

If there were a candidate for bumping off by a secret organization, the critic certainly put himself at the top of the list. Jim would have paid any bounty, so to speak. "About the only thing I haven't done yet is kill someone. And every now and then I get the feeling."

Not to rest on his royalty checks, and never one to forget his *Pony* story for long periods, Kirkwood started to work again on the subject. This time he intended to write a one-act play, possible for productions with small budgets in regional theatres or high schools. If any individual or group wanted to put on a production, he'd happy to tailor it to budgets and needs. He'd drop everything to work again on Reid Russell and the bizarre circumstances of his childhood obsession.

The smaller production written by Kirkwood offered a few interesting alterations, some determined by the medium. The character of Sally, a hard-as-nails press secretary, was developed strictly as a device of exposition. She held scenes together and brought disparate time frames into some chronology. Together with Merwin, Sally often put forth background information about the plot. And

Jim gave more of the play to the character of Marcy, an ersatz girlfriend of Josh, who—in various versions—typified a slutty teen girlfriend who questioned Josh's masculinity and provided sexual tension in terms of a subplot. She was there primarily for conversation while Josh received odd phone calls from a mysterious woman whom we learned was Ben's wife.

In this speedier shortened play, Ben becomes drunk in short order, and wrecks his car before traipsing over to the beach house to kill himself in the game room. Mrs. Nichols appears in this version, belligerent and drunk herself, confronting Rita. Kirkwood was already jettisoning the more complicated and unworkable flashback system of the old play.

The characters are more open, outrageous, and illuminate the original plot with their behaviors. By Act Two, Josh sees how Marguerite slaps one of the investigators who believes there really is no motive for suicide (off stage). One of the cops is a close friend of Rita—with a hint of past romance and tries his best to cover up the situation to protect Josh's movie star mother. In exposition, rather than drama, Josh delivers monologues indicating his mother's friends in the police department took the body away hastily, and the coroner cleaned it up before letting her see Ben. Nevertheless, she became hysterical upon viewing the body as it was removed from the premises.

In this version Kirkwood took an unusual approach on another point. In nearly every adaptation he did of the story, Marguerite's studio was upset and not inclined to keep her under contract. The exception to the "morals clause" concept was in the 1960s radio play when the studio wanted to cash in on the controversial death by putting Rita into a television series.

With his condensed and revised script, Kirkwood stressed the celebratory feeling of Rita and her friends, Sally and Merwin. She has garnered steady work for the first time in a while, though friend Sally worries that she may have to do her TV series from San Quentin Prison. The fly in the ointment in the short play is Mrs. Nichols, the wife who uses power and influence to act out her vendetta against Ben's lover. Here, too, Lee Hertzig is said to want to dump Rita as a client, or euphemistically "turn Rita over to another lawyer." He's actively pursuing the public relations card, trying to find a Hollywood columnist who'll stress that Ben hurt both Rita and Josh. Rita had alienated public opinion by having the local police and coroner cover up the death with a ruling of suicide. He wants to build sympathy for her by suggesting this is not happening just to a spoiled, self-indulgent movie star with a string of messy affairs, but also to her emotionally vulnerable son.

Additionally in this view of the inside strategies of the household against the police charges are the discussions and opinions of the dead boyfriend. Marguerite, shortened here to Rita, is faced with a character smear of the deceased man to save her own reputation. Both Merwin and Sally, coded versions of Gouverneur and Ruth Morris, decry the fact that Ben has left no suicide note, has no motive for killing himself, and that Mrs. Nichols stresses how her husband, a devout Catholic, was opposed to suicide. The inference is that upon hearing Ben was ending their affair, Rita became incensed and killed him.

Though Rita's uncomfortable with much of the talk in front of her son, Josh protests that he's no child and does not have to "eat Fig Newtons and watch Captain Kangaroo" on the television in his room. He wants and needs to hear what is going on. Remaining present, he hears what Lee Hertzig's private detectives determined about Ben's past. The crimes and sins against Ben far outdistance anything in previous versions.

Ben was guilty of having an illegitimate child, crashing a sports car (perhaps deliberately), playing drunken Russian roulette with others, and running up exorbitant gambling debts. To the indictment of Ben, Rita protests, "He was not a psychopath." His list of misdemeanors causes Merwin to label him a "crazy, mixed-up, middle-aged kid." He certainly doesn't sound like a man in his late forties, as the play description indicates. Rita refuses to paint him as bad as that, "No need to make him into another Jack the Ripper," though during their arguments she begins to see another side of him, informing him: "I suppose you couldn't be Prince Charming always."

The hostility between mother and son grow palpable in this version, especially as Josh realizes his mother still loves the bounder. At this point, the complexity of protection emerges since the audience cannot know or be objective. Josh's anger may be resulting from his jealousy at the loss of Ben, or from his mother's continuing bond with the dead man, despite all Josh felt he gives her in terms of love. Rita is aghast at the interview her son gives one newspaper, telling the press, "I wish she had shot him. He deserved it."

As if to dismiss her son as a juvenile with a lack of understanding of the deeper feelings involved, she comments that Josh could not fully grasp the situation. (If so, and if Jim were present during discussions, he may well have seemed too young, at twelve years.) Josh, however, is nearly sixteen, and he answers bluntly: "I'm not confused. What's there to be confused about?" He rejects being shipped to Ohio, or being dismissed from the strategy sessions his mother holds with her closest advisors.

The anger between mother and son reaches a crescendo in this version wherein Marguerite makes the statement that she wants only the best for her son—whether it is sending him back to Ohio or intervening to shield him from the press in the scandal. The young man strikes back at his mother with the sharp retort that he doubts she ever knew what was best. When Rita accuses Josh of a "hateful attitude," he tells her: "I can't take any more of you either."

In this shorter play more characters witness the crank calls allegedly made by the mysterious older woman with ties to the victim. In several instances, the recipients of phone harassment, Merwin and Josh, try to protect Rita from the abusive calls. It's possible that notorious publicity unleashed abusive callers other than the wife of Ben Nichols. Rita's ultimate problem is that, despite who or what dispatched Ben, she still loves him. "He's gone and I don't understand why," was her pathetic lament. And, she pleads with her son, "I didn't kill Ben. You know it. I know it."

Jim also had his fictional counterpart challenging his mother, as hostility and suspicion between them became more evident. In the novel he made Josh far more supportive of his mother. At a pivotal moment near the climax of the play, Josh complains: "I won't go into mourning for him. You'd think he died in the war—memories of SAINT Ben." Rita does something not done in the novel: the boy's mother slaps him across the face when he points out she's been nothing more than a convenient sex object. Rita lectures him on the meaning of true love. "You want to be loved so badly. You hope, you rationalize, you interpret every little sign, but when you are loved, really loved, you know it."

After finding the notes in the newel post, by accident when he leans on it, Josh is able to provide closure to the incident for his mother and for himself. The greater operatic styles are gone, as are the happy-go-lucky endings when Josh served as a bartender for the rest of the surviving cast, expressing his happiness. Now, Kirkwood had mother and son silently sit side-by-side, comforted with the knowledge that Ben had really loved both of them.

In one of the greater understatements of all his *Pony* plays, Josh says at the conclusion of this one: Ben "was the master of the little white lie." More emphasis is placed on Rita, as she has a mental breakdown as a result of the strain of all the tabloid sensation. Always ahead of the curve, Kirkwood with smug humor has the gay Merwin give Josh his final line as he leaves at the end, saying: "I wish I had a son like you." With the oncoming permissive age of the late 1960s and 1970s, this seemed a brazen message. By the more conservative social era in the post-AIDS world, the motion picture retreated from one.

Merwin reminds Rita early in the play of one of her favorite phrases, the expression: "press on." It's the dictum by which she always faces adversity. Before the denouement, during the reconciliation of mother and son, she says to Josh, "We're going to press on. Have you got that?" As for the author, he certainly took that philosophy to heart from his mother. When he was naming a production company to head his creative projects, he decided upon "Presson Productions." He typed it onto manuscripts that went to the studios.

As often happened to Jim when the floodgates opened, he was struck by news of another figure from the past. After decades of silence, Jim learned Reid's mother, Mrs. Victoria Russell, who tormented him and Lila so long ago, had died on February of 1968 in Pico Heights, CA, where she'd resided for over thirty years. She was the biggest motive over the years for Jim to fictionalize his life story. The woman, who originally cried "Murder!" and held a threat of reopening the case as one of a capital crime, was gone from the scene.

Mrs. Russell's death brought the subject of the unsolved crime back to the forefront of Jim's thoughts. The truth was that this sad lady, so protective of her dead son, had been beaten into quiet submission for decades. Her passing meant little now, as Hollywood and its scandals had long since buried the incident of a young man's suicide under more outrageous scandals and killings in motion picture history.

Over the years Jim's boyhood interest followed infamous murderers and their trials. He described himself: "I've always been a trial freak. I've read all the headline courtroom cases with hunger. Being an actor I realize the essential drama of Candy Mosler and Ma Duncan who had her daughter kidnapped and buried alive out in California, and good old Dr. Sam Shepherd." As an actor, he gleefully appeared on *Divorce Court* and *Day in Court*.

On the horizon for Jim was the court case of the decade, if not the century. The playwright-novelist-actor and "trial buff" had been insisting he was too busy to go anywhere or do anything. Jamie Herlihy decided to test his friend by phoning to invite him to a special dinner in New York City. "I had told him the night before that I wouldn't leave my East Hampton cottage for New York if Marlene Dietrich asked me to an intimate supper for G. Garbo."

What Herlihy had cooked up was even better: he planned dining with a man facing the worst criminal charge in recent American history. He offered Jim a chance to meet Clay Shaw in a social setting. Shaw had recently been indicted in the conspiracy to kill President John F. Kennedy, and was allegedly a friend to Lee Harvey Oswald and part of a bizarre crew of New Orleans underworld life. It was an irresistible offer; "Herlihy knew," said Kirkwood, "what an arch-fiend I am when it comes to trials, and the actors in them."

Meeting Clay Shaw in New York while the man was there on business and hearing of his predicament awakened disturbing memories for Jim. Kirkwood had utter sympathy for anyone facing an intensive police investigation and a monomaniacal District Attorney. Add to this the frenzy of a media blitz, and Jim saw it as what happened to him and his mother in Manhattan Beach in 1936. He could not be objective. "My bag is so full of human frailties, how could I be objective?" His belief that Jim Garrison harassed and hounded Clay Shaw led to his writing the book, *American Grotesque*, one of the most unusual of many studies of the Kennedy Assassination and possible conspiracies.

Whether Shaw was guilty to any degree didn't matter to Jim. He saw a man who couldn't get fair treatment. Kirkwood first wrote an article for *Playboy* and called it "A Farce in Three Acts." He examined the case as if it were a bad play. "And what a cast! Dope addicts, pimps and paranoids. Why, if you put them on stage, no one would ever believe you." Becoming friends with Shaw and his circle, Jim always spoke despairingly about the case and justice in America.

Ancillary to Kirkwood's obsession with trials and murderers, or typical of it, was his insistence that he wanted, albeit needed, to meet Ted Bundy. In the late 1970s when Bundy's antics were followed closely on television, through court trials and escapes, Jim became fascinated. Bundy's list of murdered victims, young women of a certain style and attitude, grew to dozens, with intimations of others to come. Bundy tried to gain reprieves from his death sentence by promising to reveal more victim names and specifics.

Among his letters to Herlihy were requests for him to use influence to arrange an "exclusive interview" with the killer for Jim. Kirkwood wanted to be alone to milk Bundy for the truth. For several years Jim repeated the same petition, recounting to Herlihy the specific details of the cases surrounding Bundy. Jim never received that interview, nor did he write any articles, books, or plays, on this prototype sociopath killer. He believed he could create a special bond with Bundy—achieving an interview of historic proportions.

James Kirkwood raved about the musical, *Sweeney Todd: the Demon Barber of Fleet Street*, which he listed constantly as his all-time favorite, the morbidly amusing musical of a serial killer, a la Jack the Ripper, whose practical wife baked his victims into kidney pie. Certainly he recommended the musical play to everyone, and he'd be greatly disappointed to hear that the ghoulish mix of music and mayhem didn't become the personal favorite of everyone who went at his request. The subject matter, he said, gave him "giggles." When Jim was preparing to do *P.S. Your Cat Is Dead* with Sal Mineo, he told the actor he was the only one in the movie house to laugh out loud when Sal, as Plato, admitted to drowning the puppies in *Rebel Without a Cause*.

Jim could bounce between kinky cult writer for stage, and middle of the road oddball elsewhere. For television he pitched a new series with most of his favorite themes, yet slightly off-kilter. The script of *Harold* was about an unemployed actor and the hectic life with his girlfriend. Harold was, however, not the actor. The gimmick show would be seen through the eyes of his dog, whose name happened to be Harold. This idea was taken from his years with Muriel and her dog, named Too Much. He toyed with giving himself a part in a television series, though it would truly have been too confining for him. He needed variety in his projects and freedom to go in any direction, where his moods took him.

Whatever he complained about was not serious. He seemed to be achieving a modicum of success and acceptance by the world, "Life is hectic, life is sometimes fun. Just got back from sailing around the Virgin Islands with some friends on a thirty-six-footer. We had a terrific time." What he wanted most, even with the frustration of un-produced plays and novels to nowhere, was to be in his home at East Hampton, which always supplied him great pleasure. "This has been the most beautiful fall in East Hampton. Absolutely sensational! Tennis weather right up until the blizzards hit us, I think. I love my house here and wish I didn't have to make so many trips into the city, where it is nigh impossible to write because of all the vibrations and the incredible adrenaline that seeps in under the doorjamb."

He was forever interrupted and threatened to give special instructions to his friends. They were to ring once, hang up, and call back. That way he'd know it was a call he wanted to take. With the growing demands on him socially, he still needed time to write. But he was never beyond his friends. He'd offer phone numbers during his travels where he could be reached at all times "in case you get panicky and afraid of death in the middle of the night or anything like that."

Living in East Hampton with many other literary lights had value to a nonconformist like Kirkwood. When he wrote his novel of *P.S. Your Cat is Dead*, it was done after he had finished the play and waited for a production to form. In the meantime he put the story into a narrative form. Not yet a success or household name, Kirkwood's efforts were largely hit or miss. But the Book Hampton store opened in 1971, and Kirkwood, an avid reader, became a customer.

There he connected with other writers and publishers. As a consequence, browsing in the store he let known his traditionally poor experiences with agents and publishers. The store partners commiserated and connected the author to one of their trusted friends. Almost immediately, Kirkwood made the right moves. Stein and Day bought the *Cat* book; then it was sold to two book clubs and was taken up by a paperback house. The work won him a cult-audience. He explained, "It took so long to get a production that I decided to do it as a novel. It's been a bit ass backward." It seemed to be the way his fans wanted it.

Based upon Jim's lackluster career as an actor and crisis in his love life, the protagonist met a burglar—a cat burglar who changes his life in many ways. The plot featured some fairly kinky dialogue and situations, including a major character tied up naked and a sadomasochistic gang that torments all. Kirkwood acknowledged this story was "a little too kinky-dinky" and that the S&M crowd took his message the wrong way. He quickly eliminated the masters of cruelty characters and tried to recover the humor in repartee of two misfits. Unfortunately, the reputation of the play and novel coincided with the burgeoning gay movement, and Kirkwood's work was forever tied into the politics of the era.

Between the liberation of Studio 54 and the wild life of drugs and sex and the notoriety of Fire Island and "Asparagus Beach" in the Hamptons, Jim's play fit neatly into the newly emerging zone of more openly gay sexual themes in novels and plays. Though he seemed on the cutting edge, he resisted jumping on as poster boy for the movement. He kept his privacy and politics fairly ambiguous.

The sexual message caused Kirkwood to spend time reworking the *Cat* play "and about the fourth I've nursed." He oversaw ten productions and put his time personally into much stage-work. "It's done well around the country and audiences seem to like it. This is about the third rewrite and this time I've done major surgery. I used to get scored for getting into SM and for three extraneous characters. Both worked in the book, but productions all over the country all shared the same trouble spots. It's so good to get them out now, and I could kick myself for not doing it before."

As the *Zeitgeist* of the age, the *Cat* play, like so much in Jim Kirkwood's life, seemed cursed. During its pre-production in Los Angeles, actor Sal Mineo took the role he was born to play, the Bronx hustler Vito. After many years of a disintegrating career, Mineo's expressive lunar eyes brightened over the Kirkwood play. He fully expected to take it to Broadway, and then to direct the movie version. Kirkwood grew increasingly respectful of Sal's abilities, and it appeared the two would have their greatest success together. The play seemed tailor-made for Mineo's personality and talents.

Coming home one night from a rehearsal of *Cat*, gentle little Mineo was stabbed to death in his underground garage. All the momentum of the play was also killed by the incident. Though Tony Musante tried to make the part his own when it came to New York, he was roasted by critics; too old, too hard-edged, lacking Mineo's vulnerability. The play did not do well. Kirkwood said he felt "accursed." But he fought those feelings, "I'll deal with the cards life has dealt without too much bitching."

Kirkwood would do almost anything to help his productions become successful. During one of *P.S. Your Cat is Dead* incarnations, at the Promenade Theatre, a critic called it as contrived as a pretzel. As part of the show, Jim agreed to do seminars after the performances on two nights per week. He enjoyed the banter of questions and answers with his audiences, almost always giving his fans a treat. These were time-consuming and draining when he had so much more to write. He expressed disappointment when one literary advisor was unable to come to New York during its preliminary rehearsals to give advice.

While his career hummed along at low speed, Jim once again had the past thrust upon him. In early April of 1973, he happened upon a Los Angeles news story that rang familiar. One of those names from 1936 flooded him with memories again. According to the California media, on March 29th, seventy-eight year old Buron Fitts committed suicide, sitting in a lawn chair at his home in the open doorway of his garage. He used a .32 caliber pistol to do the job.

If Jim wanted to put *There Must Be a Pony* behind him, it was not possible while key players like Fitts on the scene. With Fitts dead, it opened up the chance to rewrite and revise the plot again. The other problem participant in the tragedy, Mrs. Victoria Russell, was gone too. The final major figure, Attorney C.P. von

Herzen, always under legal confidentiality rules, never addressed the case or Kirkwood's writings, and he died in April of 1975, silent to the end regarding his legal representation ties to Lila Lee during the 1936 mess. The sole person Jim needed and wanted to protect was his mother. Jim never gave much thought to his own reputation or appearance of guilt. If anything, he was ready to put his nose into the middle of any controversy.

In 1953 while starring in Valiant Lady, a television soap opera, Jim Kirkwood first began to formulate a means to tell what really happened at Manhattan Beach in 1936.

Kirkwood kept trying to analyze in every version of *There Must be a Pony*, how he and his mother were drawn into a mutual protection society. Whatever occurred between them and Reid Russell was their secret. Police, friends, and press, were outside and came to their own conclusions.

The constant return to the central incident of his life in literature and on stage proved there was something unresolved in Kirkwood's mind. Whether he was trying to figure it out himself, or whether he was trying to find someone in the public to figure it out, remained unclear. He said, "I really don't lie, not in my writing. Sometimes in real life, but then only to avoid hurting people but not in my writing, believe me."

For the next thirty-six years, mother and son were in constant contact with each other, never allowing the other to be away for long or out of reach. Lila Lee may have been responsible for the early distortions in their ages. Though he was old enough to serve in the military during World War II, Jim's constant moving from one coast to the other, and the altering of dates of his birth may have postponed service. Suddenly he was born in 1930, and his mother seemed to become younger too. How could he be born in 1930 and discharged from the service in 1948, with his military records listing that year as his birthday?

Living in Florida in retirement, she came north to view her son's fiasco play *UTBU* and carefully followed the range of activities around *There Must Be a Pony*. She tried acting in soap operas and made a last comeback in a terrible motion picture called, *Cottonpickin' Chickenpickers* playing a Granny Clampitt type in a low-budget 1967 film. On November 13, 1973, she suffered a stroke in Key West and died, having had smaller strokes for several years. Her sister Peg came to live with her and help during the final few years, and she stayed on when Jim gave her a small house in which to live, and he kept an upstairs apartment for himself.

After several months, Jim began to think of having a memorial service for his mother. Rather than something traditional, he considered making a film tribute. He was inspired by the series of evenings with various movie stars that was in vogue: Bette Davis, Cary Grant, Gregory Peck, and Ginger Rogers had one of their film clips shown and they appeared to answer questions to an audience. Jim decided to try this approach, with a multi-media show of slides and film clips, to which he would talk, tell anecdotes, and answer questions about his mother. He called it "Life with Lila Lee, My Movie Star Mother."

East Hampton, Long Island, ran a relatively new film festival, offered by the Guild Hall in town. It was called Filmmakers of the Hamptons. This, Jim decided, was the venue for his tribute. After all, his mother made the earliest legendary films, and he believed she'd be delighted at such a forum. "I thought that showing some of her films and talking about her life would be the kind of tribute she would have gotten a kick out of it." His work would have its premiere and only showing on August 25, 1974.

To pull this together, he had to locate and catalogue any memorabilia that belonged to his mother and father, who had died ten years earlier. In the 1920s they were the equivalent of Burton and Taylor or Pitt and Jolie. Being somewhat of a pack rat, Kirkwood never tossed anything away, but neither did he organize the material. Since their film careers began around the time of the First World War, peaking in the 1920s; a second batch of material related from stage work and Broadway. Much material was beyond souvenir in quality and bordering on antique.

By conducting his scavenger hunt for items from the past, Jim allowed for the fact that he did little or no research in background detail for his novel/play of *There Must Be a Pony*. For the first time in his life he confronted artifacts of his mother's life. Whatever he found, he based his novel strictly on memory of the affair—a suspect tool—rather than news accounts, letters, or other opinions of what happened at Manhattan Beach. "You know how things accumulate over the years. And a lot of it wasn't even mine."

According to Jim, when he tried to mine his mother's past, "I had things in my studio, stuff in the attic, things squirreled away all over the place." Since his primary home for a decade had been a waterfront cottage in the Hamptons, he stored materials there, where much memorabilia remains. Other material was in Key West, where his mother resided for the last few years of her life, and the rest was in Elyria, Ohio, where his aunt, Peggy Tufford, maintained a residence for decades.

Naturally, the problem of Jim's credibility cropped up again. In death, Lila Lee's fictional age stood the test of time. Jim could not let his mother's real age out for the public consumption. He said in an interview about the forthcoming multi-media show: "My mother died in November at the age of 68." That statement was a blatant lie. She was seventy-three, but the impact on his own age was also at risk. At this point he was fifty, posing at early forties.

Like many celebrities, Jim did not collect a great deal of movie or stage memorabilia for its own sake. Most celebrities will agree, had they known of future value of such materials, they would have saved every prop, script, memo, or poster from their careers. "When you grow up in this business, as I did, you don't become a buff, as others might. I never really collected that much myself. And when I decided to do this program—I really had to scramble for material."

Someone in Kirkwood's life more proud of his accomplishments than anyone else—that was his mother's elder sister. Aunt Peg was always there for Jimmy, like a surrogate mother. He lived with her more than either of his parents, years in fact. She notified local newspapers at all his successes and told them of his progress, as an actor, and as a writer.

Peg Tufford gladly added Jim to her own brood of three children. She had a generous heart and was concerned for Jim. She understood his difficult position with two movie star parents, and she suggested to him once that she'd write her autobiography, entitled *Living in a Star's Shadow*. It tickled Jim. Of the family's role in movies, Aunt Peggy had official control of all scrapbooks, "Luckily, my aunt kept a lot, including my mother's things and she sent me a huge stack."

Ready to face the package of materials from Aunt Peg, Jim said, "One rainy Sunday I spread it all out over the living room floor, the newspaper and magazine clippings, 150 or more publicity stills and candid photos and posters, and started going through the pile." Kirkwood recalled that the sorting of the memorabilia was "a devastating experience. For each picture that resurrected a joyous moment or funny anecdote from life with mother there was also an item that brought back the tragic aspects" of the times he spent with his Lila. He talked "of being raised by the Hard Luck Girl of the Movies," meaning Miss Lee, but she did not really raise him, and their moments together smacked more of bad times than good times.

Lila Lee did not see her son for three years at one stretch, and her illnesses and tabloid headline life showed her to be only an on-again, off-again parent. In Jim's mind, she was a good woman who tried to be a good mother. He needed her to be that.

From all the materials the easiest for Jim to look at and think about were the posed publicity stills. From them he could weave any story he wanted about the past and his mother. He preferred those photos to newspapers or magazine stories; those were what they were, and he did not want to think about what really may have happened at Manhattan Beach. His selective memories were particularly fertile for reminiscences. After all, he wrote fiction. As he said several times to one friend, he only lied to protect people. Jim was able to recall or invent a story with almost every photo, and those anecdotes became his narrative to accompany the slides he showed along with clips of Lila Lee's films.

The best example of how Jim felt about written evidence was his comment about one letter he read. "At first I thought it was one I had written." This was because Jim's handwriting, in its weird curly-cue calligraphy, was exactly like his father's, nearly duplicate. For example, when Kirkwood wrote in long hand the expression "I am" in his notebooks, the words almost appeared to read: "Jim." His mother, like anyone lucky enough to receive one of his antic letters, "saved every single one from me. But then when I opened the envelope stationery from a London hotel and it hadn't yellowed a drop even after 40 years—I realized it was from my father."

The effect of confronting the past devastated Kirkwood, and he admitted to "such a clutch in my stomach." He called the correspondence a love letter, written "around 1930 during one of the separations that finally led to divorce after six years of marriage, and it was a touching love letter, pleading with her not to get too involved with John Farrow, the man she was supposed to be having an affair with. The news had gotten to my father in London, and he was frantic about losing her."

For many years, Jim stated he was born in 1930, but here he was old enough to realize: "My God, it was just at the time I lost my family." Ignoring whether these affairs were painful or not, Jim proceeded. Just as he had with the novel and play of his mother, the tribute would go forward, facts be damned.

Though fame as a writer began to grow, Kirkwood was about to be thrust into the pantheon of stage history with one of the top Broadway plays of all time. It would win him a Pulitzer Prize and a Tony Award. Eight months into creation of this play, the young inexperienced writer, Nicholas Dante, was flailing, drowning in the demands of Bennett. As much as it hurt him, he knew Bennett had no heart about this. In an abrupt phone call, he learned the lion's share of the writing was to be done, approved, and credited to Kirkwood who came in like gangbusters.

Jim asserted Michael Bennett thought about directing *Cat* in 1972, and that was how the two originally met. "I later bumped into him in a theatre and he asked if I'd like to do a musical. He said, 'It's going to be about dancers, maybe about auditions.' Nick (Dante) and I had good times. Michael would get us all together and we never broke up in a bad humor. The good thing was we had three months rehearsals. We knew the cast, and it was no problem in writing for them or assigning them lines. It's the ideal way to do a show." As Jim noted, *Cat* was roasted, but the musical became Kirkwood's annuity for the rest of his life.

Bennett was under the gun from producer backers to finish it up and have it ready in five weeks. He believed only Kirkwood could help him. Accepting the challenge, Jim complied. He knew and said on occasion how he enjoyed the stress, the action and danger of live stage work. "Nothing can happen to you," he commented, "unless you're in the game."

Nick Dante, who was already writing the script, had been primed on how to treat the mercurial Kirkwood. He immediately told Jim *Good Times/Bad Times* was his "all-time favorite book." Jim recalled their introductory meeting; he said: Neither knew anything about the other, had never met before Michael Bennett tossed them together. "I thought, 'Oh, God, we're going to cross swords,' But, it turned out we got along fine. Except for punctuation."

Coming aboard the production, Jim relaxed everyone with his demeanor, and Bennett had a top-notch professional writer to doctor the script. After a while, slogging through bad audio transcripts of dancers that made no sense, Kirkwood took up his favorite pet peeve from being a performer auditions. It's what drove him from the performing end. He ran with it.

The final script was permeated with Kirkwood themes, motifs, and concepts. He dominated the characters and gave them wit, energy, and focus. He constantly countered Bennett's urban legend about the play being based on tape recordings. Kirkwood insisted, "Only about 5 percent of the final show came from the tapes . . . I heard the tapes and I leafed through the transcripts. But we'd only get a line here and a line there. Many of the types were there, of course. The girl who's over the hill, the new one, the veteran who finds there are fewer jobs for her charms . . . a lot of the characters were real. One of the big speeches was Nick's own story. The director was a combination of Michael and Bob Fosse."

Almost instantly, Jim knew this was to be a big hit. Usually careful with his own money, he suddenly wanted to join the backers. Bennett told him it was too late. "The pie was all split up by the time I got there," he complained. "I tried to put my money in the show. That's how much I believed in it."

126

Deep down, Dante resented Kirkwood. For years he flooded the press with compliments and cheery comments about how well they worked together and how much he loved Jim. "A lot of sweat and work went into writing it, but we had a really wonderful time," Dante said repeatedly during interviews. "It was the best time in my life and I know it was the best time in Jimmy's life too."

When the play came near the end of its run, after Jim passed away, Nick Dante's tone and words became vituperative and nasty upon mentioning Kirkwood. He thought Jim unfairly received and accepted credit for work done by himself, the younger unproven writer. Dante's callowness seemed to grow over the decade while the production of *Chorus Line* made them all wealthy beyond belief.

Before Dante died, he complained bitterly about "how I kept myself in his shadow. I felt like the secret writer" of the great musical play. Dante never could sustain another piece of writing and took to touring with the company as an actor in the Puerto Rican drag queen role years later. He wanted the world to believe that he was capable of pulling together the script for the show.

The result of *A Chorus Line* was both good and bad on a personal level for Jim. It brought James Kirkwood fame, untold wealth, opened doors, gave him a new platform for his ideas, and after all that, he learned, not much else had changed. He was left with no support for most of his play ideas and only led on to do more work that went nowhere. The Great Booking Agent in the Sky, as he called him, cancelled gigs too soon and too often.

When producers learned a rip-off version of *A Chorus Line* was being presented in Israel under the title *Stage Bug*, Kirkwood elected to go there on a trip, armed with a videotape of the New York stage performance to show to the Israeli courts. They planned to stop any copycat productions. Kirkwood testified to the motifs and parallels that *Stage Bug* had to the original. Though the effort cost over $45,000 in costs, the production and creative teams knew they had to protect their interests. The lawsuits effectively ended this attempt at plagiarism.

A Chorus Line made its way to a movie version, directed by Richard Attenborough and only vaguely resembling the play with its metaphoric line facing the judgment of God. They had taken a huge sum of money for the rights and divided it among the four principals: Bennett, Kirkwood, Dante, Ed Kleban, and Marvin Hamlisch. Upon seeing the film, the group was despondent at first. But after a few drinks, Kirkwood was cursing the filmmakers as "murderers and baby killers."

It didn't improve his relationship with Bennett at all. Their collision course would culminate within a few years, before the noted producer succumbed to AIDS. Around the same time an editor of a gay magazine started a backlash against Kirkwood by claiming he was "too coy" and, if he didn't want to come out, then gay readers ought to pass him by. In the world of theater and the artistic scene with which he was comfortable, he opened up and thrived in terms of his sexuality.

Drugs and sex took a dreadful toll on the twin communities of Hollywood and the Hamptons. Jim's contemporaries, friends, and co-workers in film and theater were spiraling into oblivion. In his most personal correspondence, Jim refused to use the term AIDS. It was something kept unnamed, unspoken. Jim and Herlihy referred to the disease as "it." In the 1980s, the epidemic tore through the creative world. It came close to home; Kirkwood's houseman died of it. He referred to victims as being "shipped off" after contracting it.

Jim courted Phyllis Diller for a role on stage in *Murder at the Vanities*. Part of selling the play was to have her name attached to it as Winnie Clarkson, the wisecracking performer in the Earl Carroll revue. Though the role itself was small or featured, it was pivotal to the plot. Jim mentioned Diller by name in the script to describe the character and how it was to be played. "I have been working extremely hard on the musical *Murder at the Vanities*. We almost have a rough draft of ACT I. It is hard tough mean work but I am loving it. Wish I had the whole summer off but . . ."

The author described his new musical book, "It's a strange genre, set in the 1930s with a lot of showgirls and a couple of murders. We hope to have a draft by fall and then we'll look for backers for production in about a year. We'll need about $1.5 million. It's ridiculous what it costs to produce a show. There are a lot of shows being turned out. Perhaps people are writing faster because the costs are going up every month."

In the era when musicals escalated in costs and producers began to shy away, Kirkwood had the impetus through his big success to push for what he wanted. "It's one of those things everybody tells you not to do, but your nose tells you to." He wrote the book again, and had difficulty mostly with inserting music and lyrics into his plotting. He never felt comfortable writing musicals. The music was by Don Oliver, the lyrics by David Spencer. They brought the idea to Jim and convinced him to do the collaboration.

Despite the familiar title, he revealed: "*Murder at the Vanities* has nothing to do with the old Earl Carroll musical. The title's now in public domain. It will be a musical about chorus girls, glamour, mayhem and murder. It takes place in the Depression. And it will have all the showbiz pizzazz that surrounded the Follies, the Scandals, the Vanities. We started talking about the plot two months ago, then doing research, seeing old movies, looking up facts, toying with fictions. We plan to begin the hard work this summer."

Jim planned to use the workshop system, as producers used with *A Chorus Line*. "The workshop system is unbeatable. It allows freedom, time, and it allows for perfection. Trouble is, I don't think *Murder at the Vanities* will be suitable for workshop. It's going to be too big, too physically demanding." His script used a revolving stage, like a giant turntable "to handle the simultaneous stuff backstage and onstage. This is to be a play-within-a-musical. Anyway, if we can't workshop it, I'm hoping for a long out-of-town tryout. We should be ready to open on Broadway, if everything goes okay, by next spring."

To Diller herself, he sent one of his typical letters on *A Chorus Line* brown stationery in 1981. "I think of you often as I'm burning the midnight oil as well as my brains trying to write this musical. You are constantly in my mind every time I write a line or a monologue or a sketch in which I hope you will appear. The show is extremely difficult to write book-wise because of the heavy plotting involved—what with red herrings, many suspects, and all the entanglements that go with a musical combined with a murder mystery. So it's going slowly." He admitted to her that he loved her by the "buckets."

As he told Diller, this project was important to him, and he was careful and slower than usual in his writing. He was still not a musical writer, and that more than anything else tended to slow him down. "It is an extremely difficult show to write and right now we're in kind of a messy period with it but I have a lot of faith we'll finish it eventually and it'll be good entertainment. It just takes a lot of time and sweat and a few nervous breakdowns."

This was to be his big follow-up to the prize-winning and long-running musical associated with Michael Bennett. Kirkwood thought the public's perception of their chemistry ought to be considered. He went to Michael Bennett once again to make lightning strike twice. The result was not as he expected. Jim was horrified to find Bennett's ego out of control beyond anything ever before. "I had a hard time dealing with him after *Chorus Line*." Their relationship, according to Kirkwood, "turned into a cesspool."

According to the author, Bennett made "outrageous demands"—like co-author of the script for *Murder at the Vanities*, and huge percentages of the profits. He felt his name superseded all others in the production and would win the attention such an expensive musical required. Kirkwood found it all "very insulting to me," and pulled out Bennett's involvement, despite putting hard work into the script. Jim knew it would likely never be produced, but he had endured far worse in his career.

From here on came a spate of un-produced plays and half-hearted efforts. Equaling the success of *Chorus Line* would be formidable for most, but Kirkwood never gave that a thought. He was his amiable and dynamic self. Kirkwood preferred to work with collaborators most of the time, especially on plays. He co-wrote with Nick Dante on *A Chorus Line*, James Leo Herlihy on *UTBU*, Jim Piazza on the final production of his career, *Stage Stuck*, and Jerry Herman on another effort that remained a musical only on paper, *Murder at the Vanities*. The consistent work he did alone, preferring sole credit for writing, was *There Must*

Be a Pony! And, when others, like Mart Crowley, presented a well-delineated adaptation of *Pony*, Kirkwood remained luke-warm. That was his baby. No one could ever handle it the way he wanted.

Bennett was to turn on Jim personally. After the celebrated producer killed *Murder at the Vanities*, he tried to embarrass Jim at a well-attended party, but the vindictive producer was playing with the wrong cat. By making inferences that he was a good lover and greatly misunderstood, he asked Kirkwood to confirm all this in a crowd in a public setting. Never one to be rattled, this false charge startled Jim. Michael Bennett and James Kirkwood had never slept together, and he was stunned by the suggestion. It would lead to a nastier confrontation between the two.

Kirkwood never shied from a fight and was utterly fearless in any situation. When giving advice to a friend, he once expressed the words any brother might say to a younger sibling. "First thing you do is kick 'em in the nuts. Just kick the bastards in the nuts." When reports of a fight between the key creative souls of *A Chorus Line* hit the news media, Kirkwood snorted during a telephone call, "Oh, you heard about my little boxing match, did you? Yes, I have taken up boxing and am quite pleased with myself!" An indelible image of Michael Bennett, writhing in pain, kicked in the groin, was inescapable.

CHAPTER SEVEN

PONY REDUX, 1979 & 1982

In early 1977 Jim began work on a new play entitled *Club Mardi Gras,* about drag queens in a seedy bar on the verge of bankruptcy in San Francisco. He negotiated with famous female impersonator Charles Pierce to play the lead and interviewed drag queens from Provincetown to Tinsel Town to learn their habits, styles, and attitudes. In this never-produced play, he showed himself being ahead of the curve. Friends like John Paul Hudson and James Leo Herlihy sent him leads and provided names of small-time impersonators he could interview for research. He met with and corresponded with many strata of show business performers.

In the years to follow many films and plays about cross-dressers became staples of theatre, while Jim's groundbreaker never made it to the stage. The tale was filled with the bitchiness and rivalries of the cross-dressers, having them play all the famous women of Hollywood—Bette, Tallulah, Judy, Carol, Ava, Rita, and perform in skits and a revue.

In a notebook filled with one-liners, character set-ups, and jottings that would be the backbone of the play, he toyed with the idea of calling one of the characters by the inverted name of "Russell Reed." Manhattan Beach figure, Reid Russell, remained on his mind. How curious it was that he thought of Reid in conjunction with a storyline that featured prostitutes, hustlers, and drug users. It's the only time he wrote the name of Reid Russell in his notebooks. He had second thoughts. In an early draft he changed the name of the character.

Many feuds among the "ladies" were incorporated into his last major play, *Legends*—about two long-ago film queens. Their banter and feelings for each other were at the root of *Club Mardi Gras.* Listed as having Zev Bufman as his producer, the play was supposed to start on the West Coast in a tour before Broadway in 1978. It never made it off the page and to the stage.

Having Bufman as man behind the scenes gave Kirkwood an inside track with the man's rumored paramour and potential spouse; news reports were filled with stories about a Bufman-Elizabeth Taylor marriage. Because Taylor and

131

Kirkwood shared Zev Bufman as their producer, Kirkwood was able to reach the movie star, now considering stage work, and he suggested that she do *There Must Be a Pony* on film instead. As usual, she asked for a script, and may have read the novel at this time.

Jim said to me, "I saw an item on the news last night about Elizabeth Taylor's opening in *The Little Foxes* in Fort Lauderdale. The newscaster said she got mixed reviews, but I certainly want to see it too. That is going to be one hot ticket to get. Also, I think it's a limited run of about ten weeks or something like that. There will probably be a nasty stampede to the box office and old women and children will be trampled to death. That should be amusing. I'll probably stand across the street and watch." After he saw the play, he went backstage with Bufman and chatted with Elizabeth. She appeared on that year's Christmas card hugging Jim. The card's obligatory annual signature was "The Kirkwoods."

In June of 1979, he wrote to this friend: "I have finished the screenplay for *Pony*, and Columbia seems to be pleased with it. I believe this week they are sending the script to Elizabeth Taylor. You said you hoped I'd push for her, but she might be just a bit ripe. We will see. They're also thinking of Shirley MacLaine and Ellen Burstyn." His own strong, personal choice was MacLaine. It was ironic that the actress who played the mother of the little boy who found the dead body in Hitchcock's *The Trouble with Harry*, was his first and primary choice to reprise the role in the Kirkwood version of love and death on the Swing of Doom.

As Hollywood buzz became louder, it appeared that a decent feature film was about to be produced. He was cautious about the film, fearful of jinxing himself yet again. "Elizabeth Taylor wants to do *Pony*, but is not that hot at the box office now so I don't know if the backing will be forthcoming." Instead he put his focus on another, less personal screenplay: "I've just finished an original screenplay for United Artists called *Witch Story*. And about to take on another project, an original screenplay for United Artists—if they let me co-produce it, I'm tired of not having any creative control, but then who isn't?"

Around this time to Jamie Herlihy he wrote, "I turned in a second draft of *Pony*." He told Herlihy that forces at the studio said, "Brilliant." But he had great consternation. "Why, if it was so good, did they not ever get beyond the discussion stages?" It left him increasingly sour. When it came to additional screenplays, he began to squawk, "I'll fucking do them when I feel like it." That mantra was to become his new motto, he said. Those who knew him realized this was only so much talk; there was no way he could resist writing, and certainly he would continue to write screenplays.

With his mother now beyond hurt, Jim could add things to the story he previously withheld. Ben became more of a dubious character, which Rita and

Josh seemed to overlook. Ben announced to Rita, "I'll be your combination butler-lover."

An emphasis of deep emotional commitment between Josh and Ben grew in proportion to Rita's stronger emotional reactions to Ben, and lessened intensity to Rita. Kirkwood added one scene and then abruptly cut it, in which Josh and Ben showed off for Rita. Josh did a somersault by putting a foot on Ben's grip and performed a gymnastic back flip. Whether it was too risky for actors, or too theatrical for the scene, Jim decided not to include this bit of business. This action appeared in both his screenplay of 1979 and his revised theatrical play of the same year.

Kirkwood also made changes regarding the truth following Reid Russell's death. In the screenplay, what happens is shown, but in the play an anecdotal story is narrated by Josh, who tells how he and Sid Traynor decided to sell tickets to neighborhood kids wanting to see where the man died. They bicker over the price, Josh wanting $1 per customer, and Sid, like Tom Sawyer's brother, favors setting a realistic price setting of a few cents. Josh argues he was about to give them a tour of the estate and act out the death scene.

In addition, Jim also supplied additional details about how the boy re-enacts the way the body looked as it lay on the lawn swing. *Life* magazine photographers snap away as Josh feigns the posture of the dead man. He also poses for press pictures away from the eyes of his mother, while at school.

Then, Josh begins to keep a meticulous scrapbook on all the press coverage. His obsession with the case alters his personality from shy to brazen. He signs his first autograph for one of the girls who works at the local supermarket, and Josh's behavior at school becomes challenging in class discussions about love or political issues.

When Josh gets home from school with a bloodied nose, Rita is alarmed at the personality changes in her son. As a result of her worry, she searches his room and finds the scrapbook about Ben and lurid headlines about herself. She promptly burns these keepsakes. It results in a fierce confrontation between the two in which she slaps her son hard across the face for the first time.

Rita calls his interests "ghoulish." Jim's counterpart defends his scrapbook, furious and indignant at his mother's attitude. He confronts her with the complaint that her so-called boyfriend "could have shot me too." At this point Rita considers shipping her son immediately back to Elyria and into her sister's care to prevent any deeper psychological damage.

The other figure from the original case, now deceased, was Mrs. Victoria Russell, which gave Kirkwood freedom to explore more deeply the personality disorders she suffered. In all versions, Josh always receives strange phone calls, almost a prelude or foreshadow to the more frightful horror of discovering the dead body. These calls are anonymous at first, a woman unidentified, looking for Ben. In the updated versions of the play she makes appearances that are pathetically hinted at in the novel.

Now, Mrs. Nichols verbally abuses Rita, visiting the home and tossing objects at the house. In one comedic scene, she bangs on the doors and windows, "Knock, knock, who's there? His wife!" she shouts in a drunken state, "His wife!!" Josh loses his timidity and recoils at her verbal attacks when she screams, "You've killed my boy. You've killed my baby!"

This seems an odd response from a wife, even if older. And, Kirkwood's scripted response, to, "He was my Baby. He was my Baby," was an unqualified witty comment reverberating a truth from the distant past, "He was a bastard." The line only works better when the victim is a mother's son, not a wife's husband.

Jim talked in late 1979 to director Anthony Stimac, who was in his sixth year of running the John Drew Theatre and known for his innovative approaches to stage work. Kirkwood heard of a new series Stimac was floating: a Dramatic Playwrighting Series. This incorporated, not a formal staging, but the chance for actors to deliver the dialogue to an audience as they would during a rehearsal reading. The technique was used to great effect and popular appeal in Guthrie's *Love Letters*. The concept appealed to Jim, and he proposed making *There Must Be a Pony*, the first of this new series at the John Drew Theatre. The play reading premiered on October 29, 1979.

The cast of readers included Barbara Caruso, fresh from her playing Lady Diana Spencer's Countess aunt in a television docudrama about her royal wedding. She was cast as Rita. Bobby Doran, who was playing the son of the star of a daytime soap opera, as Kirkwood once had in *Valiant Lady*, was guaranteed being cast when Kirkwood learned of him, so the juvenile star of NBC's Proctor and Gamble production of *Another World* read the role of Josh. Finding actors whose careers had parallels to his own appealed to Jim's casting sensibility. Doran also came from a theatrical family.

The dramatic reading's delightful success spurred Stimac and Kirkwood to think about another full-scale production, in prelude to an attempt to try for Broadway again. In Jim's mind, money was a motivation. If a play were a smash, the movie rights would also soar, giving him a profit.

Kirkwood told the press he wanted to rework his latest version for regional theatre, and he was interested in audience reaction to revised dialogue. The night of its premiere, he was available to take questions from the audience after 9pm. Jim was at his best under these circumstances, using all his comic timing and quick repartee to handle the audience. He enjoyed rewriting as a process and found it effective during a revival of *Cat* the previous winter. Reaction turned out to be so positive he began to think, as did Stimac, about staging *Pony* for real within a year or so.

There was much good news in the early 1980s, and it began to look like it would be his decade. When told that, he grew sheepish. "Do you think so? Well, Paramount is making sounds like they're really going to do *Some Kind of Hero*. Arthur Hiller directing, testing actors . . ."

When he finished *Hero*, Jim noted how "everyone said it was a good, solid script. But there was dickering among the producers about how it should be cast. One side wanted an unknown actor, who'd be discovered by the movie. Another wanted a star. Arthur Hiller was all set to direct but, after waiting three months for the casting, he gave up and went off to direct *The Thorn Birds*."

One of the most bankable actors at the time, considered suitable for the role, was Christopher Reeve, then relishing his *Superman* success and thought of highly by studios. Kirkwood disagreed vehemently, "I thought he was all wrong for the part but, anyway, his agent was called." The salary offered to Reeve was $150,000; he rejected the script. Reeve wanted a million dollars for his performance. Kirkwood scoffed, "For what—flying?"

During a phone call one day, Jim off-handedly announced, "Oh, by the way, they're finally going to make *Hero* into a film at Paramount. Production begins the first of April. You don't suppose that's an omen, do you? If I gave you $100 and twenty guesses, and told you the actor that was playing Eddie was in fact a movie star you would still never guess who it was so I'll just tell you—RICHARD PRYOR is playing Eddie. Don't ask why! He'll probably be very good and the picture will probably have very little to do with the novel or screenplay I wrote but he seems to be big box office and that's what it's all about."

After years in the business, Jim had accepted how a writer's work was tugged, pulled, twisted, and rewritten many times. Once they paid him for his contribution, the project was no longer his alone, but a communal creative effort. He was fine with that notion. "I wish them well and I will have a small part in the movie." He would play a friendly bartender. But during the filming, he was "busy" with other projects and unable to appear, and something else told him to keep his distance. The movie they were making did not inspire him with confidence.

Jim expressed a desire to have a year off. "There are so many books I want to read." When a well-meaning friend warned him about working too hard, or accused him of being a workaholic, he laughed it off: "because I've finally gone crazy, but I don't care, so don't you be upset either." He also claimed he had to work because he counted on the residuals of films of his novels. He always claimed these never made much money for him.

Kirkwood had a Calvinist view of work. He was a glutton for labor; writing and creating was something magical and akin to breathing. He expressed himself like a constantly erupting volcano. "If I go a day without working, I'm dissatisfied with myself. I feel I don't deserve my Vodka Gibson before dinner."

He wrote plays that never went on stage or screenplays that never went before the cameras—versions of *To Be or Not To Be*, the Ernst Lubitsch classic film, was called *Poland, My Poland*, and was meant for Mel Brooks Productions. *Witch Story* dealt with an actor in East Hampton who finds a coven that could help his floundering career on television. And those were the finished projects; he had another list of aborted, half-hearted attempts at plays and screenplays.

"If *Hero* makes $100,000,000 I will make some money off it. If it doesn't, I'll go back to hustling—even though I'm getting a little long in the tooth for that. Still, if the lighting is dim and people's eyesight is going, I can still make a couple of bucks on weekends." He also typed on the backside of stationery sometimes or in the margins, refusing to use another piece of paper. With tongue firmly in cheek, he told Jamie Herlihy, "One of the road companies of *A Chorus Line* is closing down, and I need to economize."

Making films of Jim's novels had become an increasingly frustrating possibility for him. He was willing to work harder to accomplish goals, and thought more work would spur movie versions of his stories. Instead, it urged his compulsion to work more. On his birthday in 1968 an announcement was released about *Good Times/Bad Times* being bought by Alan Pakula's old collaborator—Robert Mulligan.

The Oscar winning director of *To Kill a Mockingbird* would tackle the complex and bizarre story of the death of a headmaster at the hands of his student. Warner Brothers-Seven Arts expected Mulligan would also produce it, but the writing of the screenplay would be left to Robert and Jane Howard Carrington. Of course, nothing came of it. Jim grew increasingly skeptical over the years of having others write scripts from his novels. His suspicions centered on the conviction they somehow sabotaged his work.

Ten years later, the book was still not a movie. In 1977 his neighbor in East Hampton, Cliff Robertson, having won an Oscar for *Charly*, wanted to produce and star in *Good Times/Bad Times* as Mr. Hoyt. Kirkwood once again became excited at possible casting: "Dennis Christopher will do Jordan if it is made." The more difficult role of Peter Kilburn was up for grabs. Keith McDermott who'd played the leading role in Broadway's *Equus* was a frontrunner. As Jimmy teasingly told one friend, "If *GT/BT* ever gets going, I will make my best efforts to see that you audition for the part of Mr. Kauffman; however, I think I should let you know that I have my eye on that part, so I wouldn't be buying makeup anytime in the near future."

Kirkwood frequently noted how his opus, *Good Times/Bad Times*, had been adapted for the screen seven times, including his own version and screenplay. He accused Warner Brothers of cowardice because they held an option on the script, but were reluctant to pursue the film when the movie of John Knowles's

A Separate Peace, another novel about prep schools, failed at the box office and won little critical acclaim.

Cliff Robertson drove the final hope for the movie of Jim's prep school story into oblivion with his personal troubles. The star blew the whistle on some Hollywood financial shenanigans and was plunged into enforced semi-retirement for several years. By then Jim was furious with Robertson, who had abandoned playing Mr. Hoyt, thereby sending the movie project into its inevitable limbo, except for talk that went nowhere of a group of producers who wanted to make the prep school murder story into a musical in the tradition of *Sweeney Todd* or *Murder at the Vanities*.

Jim wrote a one-act play and did take a role in *Surprise!* It was a one-act work, part of an East Hampton theatrical pageant that also featured a one-act play by Cliff Robertson. Jim's co-star, Dina Merrill (married to Robertson), deliberately stepped on all his lines and made Kirkwood regret his return to the boards. Jim could only glower at the Oscar-winner from the stage.

In his optimistic attitude, having won most important literary awards of theatre, Jim felt all his work was important enough to be produced and desired. Though some might have accused him of ego-tripping or of hubris, he believed sincerely he had a mandate to be creative. Postponing anything personal in his life, he went on a workaholic "Lost Weekend," writing screenplays by the reams. He labeled this "a compulsive binge." Results of his labors came to nothing. None of his plays or screenplays, such as *Witch Story, Club Mardi Gras, Crooked Tree*, reached any stage of production.

Decades before the 'Independents' took hold in Hollywood, Kirkwood toyed with becoming active in producing and directing small-budget films. After the death of actor Sal Mineo, who was scheduled to direct *P.S. Your Cat is Dead*, Jim seriously considered taking on that chore himself. A few years afterward, he wrote a screenplay entitled *Crooked Tree*, which was a stretch from his usual tales of show business. This plot involved an Indian woman possessed by the spirit of a medicine man. In this condition she could influence bears to attack people.

The picture's executive producer David Gentile expected to start shooting in upper Michigan. If he were to learn the ropes of directing a film, Jim decided this was the project to work on. Kirkwood told a few people how being a director had started to appeal to him. "I never thought I'd want to tell people what to do. And also, there seemed to be a great mystique about directing. Like there was some special thing directors had. Then the more I watched the more I saw there weren't that many who had it. So I figured, what the hell."

Kirkwood seemed to accept any bizarre whim that gave him reign to try creative work in another direction. With *A Chorus Line* approaching milestone after milestone for longevity, he continued to push himself. "I think," he says, "It's because you remember the years when nobody asked you to dance."

As happens in the film industry, many different versions of a screenplay go through a tiresome preliminary process, often rebuilding one script upon another. Writers are left off or added to the list of credits in the finished movie. Such was the case with Kirkwood's *Poland, My Poland,* written for Mel Brooks, with Anne Bancroft as star, one of several projects he wrote for Brooksfilms. A different version of it finally got to screen in 1983, using the same title, *To Be or Not to Be,* of the original, classic Jack Benny /Ernst Lubitsch movie that satirized Hitler. Jim did these projects in hopes of trading off on his work; Bancroft might be a possible actress to take on Rita.

Over the years Kirkwood had a done take-off on the Shakespeare soliloquy in his comedy routine with Lee Goodman. A variation of one of his comedy routines appeared in *Good Times/Bad Times.* Character Peter Kilburn twice does the famous soliloquy, dressed in a black leotard. In one he delivers a furious interpretation that hushes his audience, but for another audience he delivers a comedy takeoff on the original. Much of the same scene appeared in his Hamlet depiction for Mel Brooks.

Jim also agreed to adapt *Mommie Dearest,* the Joan Crawford child abuse story written by her adopted daughter Christine, then quickly withdrew. Something in "the deal didn't set right, and in my heart-of-hearts I was haunted by a host of glamorous ghosts silking along *Sunset Boulevard.*" He confessed to Jamie Herlihy, "I made a commitment to write *Mommie Dearest,* out of the blue." As he said it, he wondered whatever had possessed him to do so. He thought it another example of his growing insanity and lack of control. "I need a nurse," he insisted, really meaning he needed a keeper.

Nonetheless, he agreed to appear in the movie project with Faye Dunaway. Kirkwood played the awards show host who bestowed an honor on Crawford. He also did a bit part in the George Burns hit, *Oh, God II,* playing a psychiatrist, of all things. He also showed up in a horror film, *The Supernaturals,* in which he played a demonic Union captain whose troop returned after a hundred years as evil spirits to kill modern soldiers. The first victim of the unseen ghost captain was an unbilled actor whose green fatigues' nametag read, "Russell." Was it coincidence? or subtle Kirkwood humor?

His reluctance to write more screenplays was endemic to his regard of Hollywood in general. When Natalie Wood expressed her desire to do *Hit Me With a Rainbow* as a feature film, she added the proviso that Jim really ought to do the screenplay. Over lunch with Natalie and R.J. Wagner, he simply refused. He was now too gun-shy about committing energy and vitality to something that might not reach the screen. In private, Jim expressed the hope his novel would be made into a feature film or a two-part teleplay, but with a strength of will that sometimes made him frightening, he declared, "It will be made without my participation."

The decision triggered tirades. "Why don't they put film in the fucking cameras?" He railed again and again, threatening to produce and direct his own works, but these were not serious threats, only typical of Jim's need to let off steam. "In every case, not once, not once, did anyone say the work wasn't any good. I could have accepted that. Instead, all I kept hearing was, 'Great stuff, Jim, great, it's gonna make a helluva picture.' And then nothing would happen."

When friends like Herlihy urged him to continue to hope, and believe that his films would be produced and made well, Jim scoffed at the possibility: "Yeah, like I believe my cock will grow longer if I pray." Frustrated with Hollywood, he offered a series of threats "to fire-bomb the studios." Thus began a series of interviews in which his outright hostility to movie studios was palpable and challenging. He accused studios of treating writers like metaphor of the horse manure of his play and novel; only he didn't use euphemisms or polite terms.

The standard empty promises of film producers made him increasingly ill tempered. "I don't want to write for committee anymore—that's what writing a screenplay for Hollywood is, because a studio committee sits there and picks it apart. They say it's a great screenplay, but they're not putting any film in the can. It's demoralizing and degrading." These reasons caused him to leave acting in the late 1950s for the freedom of writing—and he found the identical attitude applied to his creative works in print. He used one word a half-dozen times in a conversation about the predicament: "Hurtful."

Was it any wonder he turned to live theater again? He knew this was not much better than films. People like Michael Bennett could not be trusted. "It's like Vietnam out there," he was fond of saying, yet where else could he turn. He planned to write more stage drama—or in his usual vein, he would re-write a play. He was wary nonetheless. "A play is a work of art by committee. Everyone had advice. The backer, the theatre owner, the orange drink salesman, but I'll still do it. And when I do I'll have an armed guard and a trained Swedish nurse along. But I'll do it. For the hell of it."

Reworking *Pony*, he gave notice in interviews he planned a highly subversive play, movie, or television show. He wanted to call it *For Inmates Only*. He would write it and act in it. If he wanted to toss firebombs, this was as close as he'd get before his final nonfiction book, *Diary of a Mad Playwright*. This time, he wanted the play to be "about my real life, and I'll use real names and slides and everything. It'll be close to a one-man show. Its premise is if I were to have a nervous breakdown, I'm in a sanitarium, and it's my night to explain why to the rest of the inmates. I'm going to do this one. I've finally decided I'm not going to be a hired gun for others. I have my own ideas, my own heart and my own soul."

Suffering from utter frustration and despair over motion pictures using up his energy and discarding his efforts, he returned to the theater. He also returned to the one plot that rejuvenated him in *There Must be a Pony*. What made the project attractive was the notion of producing the play in East Hampton at the John Drew Theatre. He was home every evening, in his own Long Island sanctuary, and now had the power and reputation he lacked twenty years earlier. He believed he had the influence to present, at long last, the version he always wanted.

Once he knew the East Hampton theatre would put on a revival of *Pony*, he formulated his list of possible players. It was a *Who's Who* of actresses who had passed forty. Almost in confirmation of the old rumor that Jim wanted to replace Myrna Loy with Kim Stanley, his list of actresses for the new play started with Miss Stanley top and foremost. She apparently never gave it serious consideration. But the next two names of his list were featured in early summer publicity. Chita Rivera and Gwen Verdon both seemed poised to tackle the role of Rita.

Something along the way quickly dissuaded either from accepting the part. Jim wrote to a friend, "And I have also done a complete rewrite of *There Must be a Pony*, which Gwen Verdon will probably do for a few weeks this summer." Gwen slipped away to another venture. Not a week passed before a press release revealed in one of the major national newspapers: "Chita Rivera will star in James Kirkwood's new play . . . starting Aug. 11 at the John Drew Theater in East Hampton, Long Island. The play, about a film star and her son, is loosely based on the life of Mr. Kirkwood's mother, the actress Lila Lee."

As Jim assembled the production, Chita Rivera dropped a bombshell. She had a chance to do a movie with Sophia Loren. On June 18, she bailed out of the show, leaving Kirkwood to scramble to find another replacement. He was beginning again to feel the old curse; nothing ever went the way he wanted it.

Almost twenty scripts went out to every name actress who had done a play, or wanted to do a play. With the success of Elizabeth Taylor on stage lately, many other Hollywood figures were giving it various levels of thought. Some candidates were simply fanciful. Lana Turner simply would never want to do it, and stuck to television in her last major roles. She entertained doing *Hit Me With a Rainbow* on film, but was already in failing health by then. She'd be unlikely to play the mother of a teenage who kills her lover, especially in the most tawdry of circumstances. Some actresses like Raquel Welch, Alexis Smith, Shirley Jones, and Carol Burnett were happy to try summer stock or return to earlier successes in acting—live performance.

Barbara Rush, Vera Miles, Evelyn Keyes, Dorothy Malone, Ann-Margaret, and Dyan Canon were nearly exclusive film stars, but again the roles on screen, either big or small screen, simply did not allow them the chance to perform. They were targets of Jim's interest. No matter what film star took the role, he would tailor the role to her needs and abilities. Far down on the list was Mary Tyler Moore, who had great success with *Whose Life Is It Anyway?*

The most interesting addition to Jim's hall of fame was a hand-written entry: in his large, expressive, cursive script was one name, no surname needed: "MYRNA." It was sheer hubris to think she would play the same role twenty years after the initial performance, but Jim thought it worth a shot. He remembered her with fondness, though Myrna Loy's memoir indicates the playwright never followed through with a request, however well-intended, to have the actress reprise her performance.

Nearly at the bottom of the list was the nominee for Best Supporting Actress the previous year for her work in *Only When I Laugh*. She was now nearly fifty, but almost unchanged after two decades of film work. Her quirky character actress demeanor made her an intriguing choice: her name was Joan Hackett. If he wanted her, he certainly had the connections. Robert Mulligan, once set to direct *Good Times/Bad Times* in past years—happened to be Joan Hackett's former brother-in-law. And, she happened to be available. Jim made a few phone calls.

The director for the latest *Pony*, Anthony Stimac, was a fairly bold innovator who had tackled unusual authors and works previously. He'd collaborated with the notorious Clifford Irving on his first stage work, which received critical damnation; Anthony was accused of under-directing and failing to bring enough innovation to his material and actors. This placed Stimac on the same page as Kirkwood when it came to critical notices. They both suffered barbs for their creative work on a regular basis, and it became their bond, dismissing those judges for lack of appreciation of hard work, and failing to recognize what ghastly effort it took to produce a play.

Stimac had started a forum of workshop sessions to nurture creative people. They'd ban the critics they despised from any role in such a therapeutic learning environment. Both recognized the loss of summer stock and similar training grounds as part of the problem. Actors, writers, directors, were thrust into the open range of critics without having any place to grow, to experiment, or make mistakes. As managing director of the John Drew Theater, Anthony Stimac learned his philosophy from the work he did in East Hampton as well as from his off-Broadway experiences.

Off the beaten-track road companies used to work wonders for testing shows with an audience years earlier, and long tryouts for Broadway-bound plays were the norm. But out of town play doctoring was no longer practical and hardly secret; the media made a public execution of each failed change. There could be no trial and error. Plays, especially musicals, as Kirkwood could attest, had to be perfect on their first night. Stimac's remedy for this was his Musical Theater Works, the school and rehearsal workshop to allow young artists to grow. Commercial pressure, according to Kirkwood and Stimac, was the cause of theatre's demise. They wanted to offer a sanctuary and shelter for young creative souls.

"We're really talking about an emergency situation," Kirkwood mourned, when signed on to be a lecturer at Musical Theater Works, after his play had been done that summer of 1982. "When I came up in the business, there was still a lot of summer stock and you could try things out. That doesn't exist now—those theaters are booking Johnny Mathis or Joan Rivers. So where do you go as a lyricist or a composer or a book writer? It seems we're all on our individual icebergs trying to make contact."

Whether Kirkwood had felt his latest revision was ready, or whether it was still a work in progress, he had a director who also believed a play may never be in finished condition. "Our philosophy is that you can't do anything without a place to practice it, so that if you get it wrong the first time you get it right the second." Stimac concluded, "We don't want to sell shows. We want to see how they work."

Stimac possessed the gift of persuasion, as was proven by his ability to encourage students to attend his Musical Theatre Works and convince patrons to donate more than $100,000 to the project. He inspired confidence in actors and writers, as evinced by the numbers of talents wishing to work with him. But he also had a gift of dealing with ordinary people contributing material, props, and accoutrements to his plays. He epitomized the producer—someone who made things happen. No wonder Kirkwood fell under his spell and opinion that all plays needed nurturing.

After casting was complete, Anthony Stimac and Jim Kirkwood set forth a schedule. The first rehearsal began near the end of July. A dress rehearsal was scheduled for August 9th, and the preview the following night. Opening was August 13 and would run for two weeks, enough to garner the attention—and achieve an extended run after August 28th.

One sidelight of redoing *Pony* was that it awoke new interest for a movie. This time, the focus was not on a theatrical release, but on a television motion picture. "I am slaving over a new screenplay of *Pony* for CBS-TV." At the heart of this he wondered if he was being suckered again. In the meantime, a short run in East Hampton would be an audition for taking the play to another level, the ultimate version on screen.

Kirkwood despised critics and hangers-on, and Stimac confirmed his view that critics were to be barely tolerated and certainly not welcome to rehearsals and planning discussions. As a result, in July of 1982, Jim sat at the John Drew Theater, watching a run-through of his brand-new re-write of the play-script of *There Must Be a Pony*. His original excitement over the work was heightened and rekindled. He firmly believed this would be the version of a suicide at Manhattan Beach that best explains what happened and why. He was still consumed by the death of Reid Russell and his participation in his friend's demise.

Now, he was going to relive the messy scandal and restage the inexplicable suicide. He said with a little self-satisfaction, "There were 12 actors and a director and a model of the set, and I was sitting there with the script, and I thought, 'I'm the author of all this.' I still don't believe it."

With Chita gone and Joan Hackett assuming the duties of the leading role, the play had to be pushed back a week or so to allow for the new star's schedule. Kirkwood told friends: "We're reaching for the tranquilizers right now." His revision of the play was a more optimistic picture of survival. He wanted to stress the loving bond between mother and son more than earlier versions.

This production would be almost an hour shorter than the 1962 play with Myrna Loy. Kirkwood wanted to focus on the central drama—and eliminate many subplots and minor characters. He admitted how his previous Broadway-bound effort was the work of a callow playwright, "too long and overwritten."

The contrite playwright assumed all the sins of the Pakula production. "I was younger then and more stubborn than I am now. I guess I needed to get away from it to find perspective. I guess twenty years is enough perspective. It is a leaner piece now, and I've cut out some of the over-melodramatic moments."

One of the most striking casting decisions was the hiring of Dean Devlin to play Josh. Jim recognized and intuited more than a few characteristics of Dean from his resume and from his interview for the role. Josh, of course, was a variation, though not a big difference, of Jim and his own personality. Nearly all the quirks of Josh were those of Jim, with the main exception being the age of the character at the time of the story.

The most obvious sign to Jim that Josh must be played by Dean Devlin was the simple fact that Devlin was the son of show business parents. His father, Don, was an actor and producer (*Witches of Eastwick*), whereas Kirkwood's father was an actor and director (many Mary Pickford films). And each had an exotic, young, and dynamic mother—Lila Lee and Pilar Seurat. It was that background which convinced Jim that Dean Devlin understood the strains Josh faced.

Dean Devlin made his feature debut in 1980 at age fourteen, serving as a production assistant and entering the ranks as a performer, playing "Boy" in *My Bodyguard*, produced by his father Don Devlin, a movie most notable for bringing Matt Dillon to the screen. Kirkwood's first film was *Aerial Gunner* at age eighteen. Josh is offered a budding Hollywood career in the versions of *Pony*, despite his mother's objections.

Josh despises his pretty looks, claiming they cause him nothing but grief, while both Dean and Jimmy shared similar good looks, a kind of dark, exotic sex appeal. Kirkwood had black hair and always maintained a deep rich tan, while Devlin, being half Filipino, had the biracial exotic appearance popular in a Hollywood of other young male performers like Dean Cain, Mario Lopez, and

Keanu Reeves. Appearing to be an adolescent well into his twenties, and playing one until his thirties, Kirkwood exuded youth during his life. In the same vein, Dean knew he was limited by his juvenile appearance, and the competition for boyish roles was limited and fierce.

Kirkwood himself never went to college, despite his spotty education having covered the rounds of eighteen schools, including every conceivable sort of educational institution—private, public, military, prep, parochial, and one-room. His aunt claimed he graduated from Elyria High School and was on the National Honor Society. Dean Devlin may have had a slightly more stable educational experience, but his curricular efforts did not result in good grades. He was turned down on his application for film school, sending him to New York after an acting career instead, which also happened to be Kirkwood's strategy at the same point in life.

Both young men attended schools on each coast of the country, and they shared matriculation at Hollywood High School, decades apart. Kirkwood easily saw the comparison of Devlin to himself and Josh. Each had absorbed every morsel of knowledge, read and improved his personal standing, and each epitomized the concept of the self-educated. Their sharp, incisive minds were always self-evident.

Devlin was able to turn his dynamic personality into an asset networking with others in the business. Like Kirkwood, he had that knack, and it shone through during the *Pony* rehearsals to impress the writer. Just as Kirkwood worked, early in his career as a "caddy" for Tallulah Bankhead, Devlin served as a "chauffeur" for Al Pacino while in New York. Connections like those served best to increase recognition, and both youngsters used every means to ease themselves into the theatrical world.

Devlin appeared in bit parts in films like *Harry and Walter Go to New York* with Diane Keaton when he moved to the East Coast. As a gregarious performer, Dean tried his hand at comedy and teamed up with John Storey for a presentation entitled the "Something Clever Revue." This echoed Kirkwood's comedy gigs with Lee Goodman and likely struck a chord again with the author. Dean also appeared in Los Angeles on stage in a more sophisticated comedy show called Comedies by Shakespeare.

Discussing his first acting role with Devlin in an early major part, Jack Hannibal recalled, "Even back then, Dean Devlin was a hustler. Always talking, always moving. He was a really happy guy. I remember once on break we walked into town for something to eat and the whole way there and back he regaled me with bits from his comedy routine."

At twenty Devlin was showing the bravado he'd need to become one of Hollywood's top producers. Hannibal said, "Dean was curious about everything and I remember marveling at the surety he had about what he was doing. Dean didn't question himself, he just did things." Devlin also shared Kirkwood's workaholic dictum; he produced creatively and lived for the chance.

Nevertheless, after the break of appearing in Kirkwood's play, the young actor discovered the frustration of being typecast. He was cast in a series of roles as a callow youth, much as Kirkwood had some decades earlier. The biggest problem was the limitation those roles put upon Devlin. He took a part in a recurring nighttime soap, *L.A. Law,* and then played a cub reporter in *Hard Copy.* He also played an illiterate orderly in a medical drama called *Island Son.* If Kirkwood thought being *Valiant Lady's* son was limiting, Dean was slightly worse off. He had the onus of dealing with playing Asian roles when that store of actors was already fully stocked.

Each shared a philosophy about entertainment as the bottom line of their work. Though Kirkwood believed he was writing material with merit, he never wanted to lose the appeal of pleasing his audience. Director Mike Nichols was fairly snide in his dismissal of Kirkwood's plays having no message at their core. Similarly, Devlin's writings were audience pleasers, reaching into the archetypal images and echoes of familiar work to put the assembly at ease. Recently Devlin said: "I think that's the best service that we can do. We're often accused of trying to manipulate opinion or that we're trying to elevate society . . . I think that the greatest thing we can do is to give you a vacation."

Each man found his work the object of critical scorn. Unlike Kirkwood, who grew utterly intolerant of critics, Devlin commented, "I'm just used to having my ass kicked by the press, but everybody's been so gentle and nice . . . I keep waiting for the other shoe to drop. I think we have a culture that creates heroes and then needs to knock them down, and then you have to see what the third act brings . . . I just think it's the nature of our society."

Devlin also learned, as Kirkwood had, to deal with others taking his work and changing it. He also saw a parallel to the loss of one of his babies. "If you create something and then someone else does something with it, it's like you give birth to a child and then someone else is doing plastic surgery to your child; maybe it's making your child look better, but it's not your child anymore." Though he never cried, "baby killer," as did Jim, Dean felt a kinship to the creative control issue. "It's always hard to watch something you create be put in somebody else's hands."

As an adult, long after he was done with acting, Kirkwood took on recurring roles that gave the gregarious side of him an outlet. In this way, Dean Devlin also has taken on guest appearances to help his need to perform. Devlin has appeared in *Predators from Beyond Pluto.* Dean, a self-proclaimed Trekker, has said: "I would act in a *Star Trek.* I would come out of retirement and play a Vulcan for them."

Dean met future collaborator Roland Emmerich in 1989, while acting in the director's West German sci-fi feature *Moon 44* with Michael Pare and Malcolm

McDowell. Roland and Dean's interest in science fiction mixed well as the two went on the make *Stargate, Independence Day,* and history. Devlin found the concept of one genre the best to follow, and it gave reign to his knowledge and imagination. By the same token, Kirkwood stayed within his métier—the comedy, however dark and with or without music.

As an actor, Dean Devlin shared similar insights about plot and character that Kirkwood often employed: "I think that first it's about story, because if you don't care about the character and the story ñ no matter what effect you do, it doesn't have any impact. So the story is the first thing that has to happen in the effects shot. Second is what is the most cost effective way to do the shot that gets the most impact at the end of the day. Sometimes, it's still old-fashioned techniques."

Devlin continued to grow in his writing and will improve his scripts as time and practice allow. Among his rules of literary concepts, the character is paramount to any special effect in the storyline. He found that to ignore this dictum is to lose the audience favor. "I've made that mistake, and I've tried not to make that mistake again." If he learned anything from his stage and television acting, it was the importance of "characters that belong" in the plot and bring the storyline forward. "These are the perfect kind of characters."

In many ways, after *Pony,* Devlin went through a crisis like that which plagued Kirkwood so many years before. He did roles offered him and not much of importance or quality. ". . . Right after that I had taken a period where I wasn't acting for while . . . I had gone about six months without any work."

After six months of unemployment, Kirkwood made a geographical change—and so it was for Dean, when he went to Germany and met a director who changed his life. It was there that Dean offered to "improve" stilted dialogue in the script (written by a German whose English was dubious). They hit it off, and Devlin discovered what fun it was to write screenplays. Other actors in the film wanted Dean to improve their dialogue, too, and he realized he was on his way. The work with Roland Emmerich on *Moon 44* was a moment of truth. "Then we started working together behind-the-scenes, and we had a great partnership. We made movies together for the next eleven years."

Dean Devlin developed a remarkable capacity to work hard and often. His screen writing with Emmerich continued. Like Kirkwood's partnership with Herlihy, Devlin and Emmerich worked together, but in a far more successful way. Their projects reaped great profits. In 1994 while promoting *Stargate,* they rented a house in Puerto Vallarta, Mexico; spending three weeks collaborating on the rough script for Independence Day in a parallel to what Herlihy and Kirkwood did to write their collaboration. Devlin continued to work with Emmerich, "We still have two projects together. I consider him one of my best friends in the world."

This Hollywood producer quoted Robert Browning to explain his career and his dramatic shift into production, "Your reach must exceed your grasp; otherwise, what is heaven for?"

Joan Hackett took on the role of Rita or Marguerite, as her friends know her. Hackett was a quirky actress known for her dark looks and non-traditional performances. Like Myrna Loy, she did not obviously mimic or seem like the real Lila Lee; neither woman portrayed the stereotype of how an actress behaved. These two ladies were quiet, professional, and down-to-earth. The consequence was that it gave their characterization of Rita something more difficult to perform.

Playing against type made it appear that the police actions against Rita, by suspecting her of murderer, were all the more bizarre and typical of the unfairness of life. In the real case of Lila Lee, the suspect celebrity deserved the attention. Lee and Rita were glamorous figures, the Hollywood star as egocentric diva. She did not show regret, remorse, or anything other than cavalier indignation over any police investigation. Was it a clever ploy by Kirkwood to win more sympathy for his mother's alter ego? Joan Hackett did not hint at the glamour that Myrna Loy brought to every role she played, though the quirkiness and eccentricity of her acting made her Rita more apt to do something spontaneous, like shoot a boyfriend.

At forty-eight years, Miss Hackett was at the peak of her career; the previous year she won an Oscar nomination as Best Supporting Actress for her work in *Only When I Laugh*. She had moved between leading roles and supporting roles easily for over a decade. Her latest role finally brought her a Golden Globe for Best Supporting Actress.

Years before she made a splash in motion pictures in the Sidney Lumet version of Mary McCarthy's *The Group*, a film introducing a new generation of actresses to the public (Candice Bergen, Shirley Knight, Kathleen Widdoes, among others). She went on to show versatility in comedy, like *Support Your Local Sheriff*, or in mystery, Stephen Sondheim's clever *The Last of Sheila*. She did westerns, performing in *Will Penny* with Charlton Heston. Her versatility was a marvel.

Hackett's career began in the late 1950s in New York. On stage she won accolades, but did daytime drama *Young Doctor Malone* before reaching evening television audiences in a prestige show, *The Defenders*. She also remade Daphne DuMaurier's *Rebecca*, playing the weak and timid second Mrs. DeWinter. She won an Emmy for a performance on the *Ben Casey* series and was on her way, recognized as more than just another starlet or glamorous figure in pictures. If she was involved in a project, it gained depth, resonance, and respectability.

Directors seemed inclined to indulge Miss Hackett. Her winning personality and their need to elicit her best work may have been at the root of the treatment she received. It's doubtful many associated with the play had any idea of how sick she was at this time, suffering from ovarian cancer that would result in her death in little more than a year. At the time, she looked healthy and energetic. If she were distracted by illness or medical reports, it might have affected her performance, but she was always a little offbeat anyway.

Jack Hannibal had only the most shining and wonderful recollections of her. "I was told Ms. Hackett was a famous actress but I didn't know who she was. She too was very kind and incredibly sensitive. She seemed to have no governor on her feelings and no ability to hide what was going on inside her. I think she also may have been very ill. I had enormous sympathy for Joan and wanted her to like me very much. Joan had this tremendous sense of grief about her. It wasn't that she was without joy or never laughed, not at all. She loved to laugh, was funny herself and was a great appreciator of wit in others."

In her final film shoot, earlier that year, she indulged her study of paranormal, using a clairvoyant on location, at production expense, for herself and others on the crew. Her director on that film, Dirk Summers explained: "Joan Hackett is so great to work with and so perfect in her role, that I would have flown in Uri Geller if Joan had wanted him." Her final films tied into her belief in paranormal. Both *Harnessing the Sun* and *The Escape Artist* seemed to transcend the constraints of the temporal world.

An impending ill health could have been chalked off to bad vibrations, or she may have chosen alternative methods to deal with her cancer. Only as her condition worsened, did she check into the hospital—and even then she was not constrained. Despite all, she was more than willing to host a wedding for her celebrity friends at her home. She was not the sort of woman to let personal health problems interfere with the affairs of her world.

For everyone concerned, Joan Hackett's participation in *There Must Be a Pony* was fortunate. How she interpreted the role of Marguerite enhanced the play. To a young actor beginning his career, she was supremely special. As Jack Hannibal said, "Once, walking into rehearsal, I pretended to lose my balance and slip on the stairs. Joan was in front of me and wheeled around to catch my fall. Realizing I was just fooling around, she laughed with delight and told me what a wonderful actor I was. I was in heaven. It sounds cliché to say it but Joan was a woman who knew about life. You knew it just by looking at her. Her eyes were sad and mercurial, forever looking at something too precious and fleeting for the rest of us to see."

She brought unseen dimensions to the story that sparked additional interest in a film version. Alas, no one seemed to understand—except Miss Hackett—that future versions of the play, on film or stage, would be without her. As testimony to her spirit and idiosyncratic portrait of Kirkwood's immortal movie star mother, Joan Hackett had her tombstone at a Hollywood cemetery inscribed with the line: "Go Away; I'm Asleep."

Jim learned two lessons from Joan Hackett for his future. Her extraordinary courage in facing cancer made a vast impression him. Miss Hackett turned the disastrous news into something only she needed to understand. Outwardly, nothing had changed, and she was determined not to let her illness prevent her from working. She fought through whatever pain or discomfort came with the onset of the disease. She would work up to the end of her life . . . when hospitalization forced her to give up the profession.

When Jim faced a similar problem, he had her role model for example. Second, Jim began again to feel there was something distinctly unlucky about himself. Whenever a star or a major player wanted to work with him in one of his stories or screenplays, some horrible fate befell them. He had seen so many falling from the pinnacle: harmless Sal Mineo was murdered while rehearsing *P.S. Your Cat is Dead*; Natalie Wood died before she had a chance to play in *Rainbow*, Charles Pierce fell sick and was unable to do *Club Mardi Gras*, and now Joan Hackett succumbed right after doing a version of *Pony*. When compared to being seen as a good luck piece, Jim responded: "I hope to Christ I am a lucky charm. I kind of doubt it." He suspected he should be avoided because he was cursed.

Tackling another version of *Pony*, Jim considered his literary reputation. Though he seldom spoke of it, his actions indicated how much that meant to him. Scholars and important journals gave little respect to his writing; nor did they show much interest in the extent of his creativity. "I am not considered part of the literary establishment and probably never will be, so I would think it would be most difficult to sell a piece on me. Unless I was presented as a maverick or a cult author or an actor/nightclub comic turned author." He continued to produce an *oeuvre* of wide appeal. "I've been a real maniac about writing for the last couple of years, and I'm not sure why. I just can't seem to stop."

Jim had theories about why he found little support from literary magazines and the scholars who wrote for them. "Some critics accused me of being an anarchist, or claimed I was espousing the individual against the rules of society, that is—Horseshit!" He thought his works generally dealt with people who go through terrible difficulties with their senses of humor intact. In terms of defending the message of his novels and plays, Kirkwood also said: "I am just terrible when I have to talk about my own books. I can tell why I wrote them—because that always comes from life." He dismissed his own analysis with a curt, "Good heavens, I am going on, aren't I?"

Much of the play's advertising first promoted how *Pony* was loosely based on the true story of Jim's mother—and by inference of him. As the summer proceeded and Kirkwood gave press releases, he started to make better use of the word "loosely." He made numerous insinuations that it was closer to the truth than he had previously indicated.

Jimmy felt more open in his telling of the story with his mother gone. This version featured more tension between Rita and son. He notes her ever-buoyant optimism with a sneer, "They could be strapping you into the electric chair—and you'd wave and say: "Don't worry." Josh and Rita clash over Josh's hostility to the dead boyfriend. "If you think this is fun, you should have found him down there. That was a ball." The author played with his ending, this time making the twosome more equal. In this revision, they sit silently side-by-side after the "pony suicide" note is read, and the curtain falls.

Two principal actors in the play came from different sides of the spectrum. Jack Sydow, a veteran of stage and television, came on board as Merwin. Among his credits for acting were Frasier as a recurring character, late in life. He also made a name for himself in the 1960s as a director of stage productions like *The Crucible* in 1964 and *Annie Get Your Gun* in a revival during 1966.

For Jack Hannibal, who played Sid Traynor, this was his first major professional role. He recalled, "In addition to my youth my part was very small and I was only called to rehearsals as needed." Fresh out of East Hampton High School, he was their most promising graduate with his work in *Our Town* in 1981. At age seventeen, he had impressed many top-level people. He made his way to California and appeared in many television shows. He retained an indelible memory of "my experience working with Jimmy Kirkwood back in 1982. It was such a long time ago and I was very young. I honestly don't have any specific memories of interacting with Jimmy. My memories are quite general. Of Jimmy I remember him being witty and kind. At times, he had about him an air of fatigue or world-weariness. At the time, I remember thinking it because there were problems with the play and that he was reluctant or lacked the energy to do the work required to fix them. The thought of it exhausted him."

Because of the passing of his mother, and her reaction to the story, Jim had freedom to concentrate on Josh's feelings in the play; Josh reads the letter from Ben to Rita, who slowly disappears from scene, and Josh goes off with an arm on his shoulder from Merwin. The scene is decidedly less operatic, and its focus has swung to Josh, which is what may have led Joan Hackett to swing more from the heels with her role, dominating scenes whenever she entered.

Dean Devlin's individual style and performance certainly inspired Kirkwood to re-focus the action on Josh. Appearances and interruptions of Ben's wife were cut to a minimum, allowing more stage time for Josh. Young Devlin was Jimmy's spitting image at that age. Quite a few observers were taken with Dean's work in this early important role, one requiring the actor to be the mainstay of the storyline. Descriptions of Devlin ranged from the quality of his nervous energy to the requirements of dominating the stage with his presence. Devlin, it was said, gave an accounting "forcefully, skillfully, constantly."

The reviews of the production were decidedly mixed, or done in that mildly complimentary style of critics who want to seem supportive but use phrases that could be interpreted differently on second reading. One opening night critic claimed the play and performers "stunned the audience." The chemistry between the actors was part of the evening's interest as "sparks do fly" among the cast members.

One of the fairer judges of the show stated the first act remained somewhat scattershot and "needs tightening." Among other flaws were contrived bits of business the actors performed at the behest of the director, such as folding napkins for a party while they held a conversation. This led one critic to cite the "haphazard direction" of Anthony Stimac. The second act caught the audience with its growing tension and suspense, as was "as good as theater gets."

Jim Kirkwood's nemesis, the New York Times, again reared its ugly head. This time it provided a slashing review of the work on Sunday, August 22nd, on Jim's fifty-eighth birthday, something he loathed to acknowledge. The assessment of the play presented unhappy returns.

Jack Hannibal was one of the few singled out for his winning performance. He recalled: "When the New York Times review came out, I'm pretty sure I was one of the only things to receive favorable praise. I was terrified when I came to the theater that night. I thought the others would hate me. Coming in the stage door I walked right into Jimmy and the director, Tony Stimac. Both of them looked at me and smiled. Playing it cool I smiled back, said hello and kept walking. With a twinkle in his eye Jimmy whispered as I passed, 'You little fucker.'"

According to the Times critic, this was not a play—but a screenplay, with all the action needing to be filmed, and the best of that happening off-stage. After watching one of the performances, Alvin Klein ripped into the story as novelistic. He dismissed direct address by Josh of his situation as un-dramatic. Once more, the experimental theatre crowd dismissed and disparaged the well-made play as some kind of anachronism.

Though another critic lambasted the first act as overly melodramatic, if not operatic, the other critic reversed his opinion. In the view of the Times reporter, the second act was the operatic one, and the first act was "mellow." It seemed a no-win situation for Kirkwood. The allusion too was made to the "loosely based" profile of Lila Lee, though the latest version probably was the most accurate picture of the woman and her predicament.

Can we dismiss the idea that Rita is so self-absorbed in her career that she does not notice her son has run off to the YMCA for a night? Is the concept one of bad writing, or does it say the mother is a dubious parent? Are we looking at the truth, or the boy's version of it? The narrative again is wrapped in Josh's coloration of truth. He claims these "facts" to confound police and to commit the perfect crime.

The double joke on the audience remained in effect if no one told the pack of lies questioned them. Kirkwood's bravado caused audiences to nod with Josh in commiseration. As a boy, Jimmy escaped any suspicions with the press and police when it applied to Reid Russell, and night after night, in novel and play, James Kirkwood threw the same scenario into the faces of the audiences, and walked away with a pardon in his pocket.

The nature of a snake-oil salesman, whether somewhat akin to a rainmaker, is his ability to fool people. Whether or not one presumes oneself gullible, the issue may be how many others are likely to succumb to the oily charms. Though shallow Ben is thought to be the disappointing liar in the tale, the audience may be purchasing the real fake elixir, sold by the boy who seems distraught and innocent. For the narrative by a less than credible teenager, the question ought to be why anyone has accepted his version of the death of Ben Nichols.

The critic did, though there was enough in the clues to make the story seem a concoction of alibis and rationalizations. The point of the story always ties into the stretch Josh puts on the truth. To find the story incredible may be the author's intention. Woe to the critic or viewer who heard the plot and dismissed it as an issue of dramaturgy. Kirkwood needed not to tip his hand to the audience. Those with ears to hear will hear.

The critic dismissed "a small sample of Mr. Kirkwood's overwriting" without pausing to consider the hyperbole that an adolescent may use in his vernacular, and worse still if he is a pathological liar. Yes, indeed, Ben is "too terrific to be true, this Ben, and he, Rita and Josh make an idyllic threesome." And, the thoughtful viewer might well ask how this love affair added up to a threesome. If it was a love affair, where did Josh fit into the love? What motive lurked in the boy's affection and alienation of affection? In many ways, the story seemed a love story between Ben and Josh more than Rita and Ben. The viewer's responsibility must be more than passive. Josh has reason to distort his intense emotional ties to Ben and to cover up his ultimate reactions.

Also lambasted as a hoary, old tale was the climactic pony anecdote. Though shocking in the 1950s when language was tamer on stage and film, the point of the note left for Josh was now trite, according to the reviewer. The joke was stale, he contended, though when first spoken as a punch line by Kirkwood, this was hardly the case. Rather, the *Times* assessment was that the years of social development had rendered the ultimate comment in a "suicide note" to be irrelevant. It seemed a snide dismissal of human communication, which often is tawdry or inept. For the critic the tagline was the most unneeded part of the play.

In his own way, the critic may be on to the truth, but was so inept in his logic that he missed most of it. Kirkwood's tone "is self-consciously clever and ceaselessly sentimental." An examination of the scandal and death is "half-hearted" for a good reason. It may encumber mixed feelings, and the familiarity of the case was the point. Ripped from the headlines of an actual case, there remained an aroma of a long dead mouse in a trap. He dismissed the characters as types, not people, though the plot and dialogue were actions and voices of the people whom Jim knew and loved.

For an actress, whether it was Joan Hackett or Myrna Loy, she had to rely on her innate interpretation of the character she portrayed. The critic in East Hampton noted Joan Hackett was "quite wonderful at reaching out and holding on and giving herself to a feeling, and she can do a comic take to the quick. It is a performance in spurts, however. The actress and the role haven't made a complete connection."

Many playgoers saw Rita as a deranged Auntie Mame, lively and irresponsible, unconnected and disconnected to real feelings, "madly irreverent and irresistible." The role's demands related to the straitjacket that Josh, not Jim, put on her words and behavior. He made the character suit his own alibi in regard to Ben. When the character appears uncertain, it is a clue to the boy's tentative ploy to dance around the death of Ben. This unreliable narration made it nearly impossible for the actress to give a consistent performance; some may understand intuitively what happened in the telling, but most aimed at reality, rather than comprehend the playwright's tricky game of chess with the audience.

As for Josh, victim of his mother's midlife crisis and his own insecurities sexually, Dean Devlin gave a performance that suggested "chronic discomfort." One cannot imagine Jim giving advice any more cogent than that to the young man who played him. Merwin and Sally, Rita's friends, are never more than comic relief, in a way that Charlie Ruggles or Eve Arden provided in their roles. These two weren't meant as genuine or important characters. It is their lack of dimension, which makes them able to deliver plot exposition amusingly.

Jack Sydow and Barbara Bolton, like others who gave character to those two roles, were lambasted for the limitations. And how unfair to pick on the actor playing Ben, in this case—Edward Power—a daytime drama star and familiar face of calm authority on television.

Of all the cast, Jack Hannibal thought most fondly of his time spent with Ed Power. "The person I remember most fondly would be my dressing room mate, Ed Power. Ed played Joan's love interest in the play. A big macho guy, Ed was full of himself in a very charming way. He told one hilarious story about himself after another. He thought I was terrific. Each day we came to work he would ask me about my girlfriend and how we were getting on. I was very much in love at the time and Ed's sincere interest meant the world to me. Each night just when places were called Ed would ask me to do the honors of spraying his bald spot with this black aerosol stuff. I always found this very touching. It was like the king of the lions coming to me to pull the thorn from his paw."

Ben's fall from grace may be unbelievable for good reason: Josh filtered him for the audience, because Jimmy could never present an accurate portrait of Reid. A remnant hatred for Russell lingered within Jim's heart for the rest of his life.

After discussions with the author/playwright over several years, and twice staging the play, Anthony Stimac as director must be cleared of the charge of overindulging or under-directing his actors. Whatever advice Jim Kirkwood provided, it was the acceptance and trust of Kirkwood's vision and explanation for which Stimac was most guilty. The conception required a director to allow actors to teeter on the plot, confusing and contrasting their feelings. It was the purest way to show that the truth of what happened at Paraiso Beach was a mystery no police could solve, no district attorney could indict, and no critic could see.

If Jimmy's endless retelling of his play suffers any chronic problem, it is the blindness of the spectators—especially those whose insights are to be most trusted. To dismiss the deposition of Josh as misshapen and misplaced at Paraiso Beach is nearly worse than police rejecting Jim for deeper questioning at Manhattan Beach.

Mulligan's close friend, Alan Pakula, was directing the future award-winning film version of William Styron's *Sophie's Choice* in the Bronx that summer and was never home in East Hampton to view the play. Having left for location scenes in Yugoslavia, he missed seeing Joan Hackett in the revival of *There Must Be a Pony*. But among the opening night audience were Pat Kennedy Lawford and Ruth Carter Stapleton, Presidents John Kennedy and Jimmy Carter's sisters who came back stage to meet the cast and author. They joined a larger group for a party, typical of the Hamptons in the summer.

The play closed on Dean Devlin's twentieth birthday. He never again was asked, as an actor, to carry a production. Beginning to shift his show business career away from stage and acting, he proved he could do it, but next time he was a central focus, it would be behind the scenes when he turned to film, producing the biggest hit movies of the 1990s.

Though an inveterate letter writer, always demanding to receive them, on occasion, Kirkwood became overwhelmed with his various projects and dropped a quick note to insist that he was alive and well, but needed the drug of another missive. He loved letters, and took time from whatever project he worked on to write long and energetic letters. When he received a long letter with wit and humor, he was sent into an ecstasy, which allowed him to dive again into his own creative projects.

Jim became more and more subject to distractions. He was furious with agents who were unavailable. He was always reachable, and as a consequence, producers, booking agents, and financial people, were constantly interrupting his work. He wrote angry notes to his agent about questions on foreign rights to plays, royalty questions, scheduling issues, all of which were supposed to be handled by the agent, but ended up on his lap.

Kirkwood didn't mind chatting with friends or writing long letters of a personal nature. What he did object to was the prattling of business requirements that intruded on his creative time. He complained to his agent: "Why is it that everyone seems to be able to get me, but not you?" He confessed to friends he was "positively sickened by the state of affairs." He felt abused and disrespected when he was a young and upcoming actor, but believed he was entitled to better treatment now. Heaven help anyone who didn't show him that respect.

He did go silent occasionally when the heat of creation flowed like a magma that reached the boiling point. "My silence means that I have still been active—in fact, up to my neck in all sorts of projects. I've finally finished the first draft of this fucking musical, *Murder at the Vanities*. Now I am starting on a new play, creeping into another novel, and trying to get as much ass as possible."

The new novel he started at this point was to be his major epic, a second novel on his parents, and an equal-time novel version of his father's life. He had picked a title: *I Teach Flying*. When he reflected on 1982, ever the optimist, Kirkwood called the chaotic months "hectic. And they were fun in a madcap sort of way." He thrived on being busy.

In March of 1983 Jim managed to convince some backers to put $200,000 into mounting a Chicago version of *Pony*, but it never eventuated. His hope to present Broadway with a polished version, thereby increasing the value of screen rights to the play, fell through. The latest direction, one producing movies on a small-scale, but impressively, was of feature films for television. Once thought of as a stepchild of Hollywood, the TV movie gained respectability in the 1980s as the place where worthy projects found artistic realization—and an audience. Jim turned to Columbia Television Pictures. The last frontier left for *There Must Be a Pony* would have to be the small screen.

Chapter Eight

SMALL SCREEN PONY, 1986

Though Jim cared greatly for his aunt, he was not beyond using her for making lecture points, or in interviews. He called her "a great old gal," and noted that she had a writing bug, "She grew up a shade outside the circumference of Lila Lee's bright light. Just recently Aunt Peg told me she was thinking about writing about Lila Lee. She had the title all picked out, *In the Shadow of a Star.* Isn't that great! I love the old dame a lot."

His Aunt Peg was over eighty-years-old and living in his home in Key West. He had renovated his home, giving himself an apartment there for visits. She was always on his mind and greatly concerned about her. After one hurricane in the Keys, he wrote: "I have been having construction done on my house in Key West and it has been a disaster because I've not been there—builders defecting, flying up the Keys with my money, putting on the wrong decking, leaving roofs open with my seventy-nine year old aunt living underneath the stars, etc. etc. so I'm taking that time to go down there and try to straighten the whole mess up and out and over." What emerged was taking her into the scheme of the false age. She was Lila Lee's older sister, and certainly older than the age he gave for her.

Around Christmas of 1985 Jim went to Los Angeles for the start of the notorious *Legends* tour with Mary Martin and Carol Channing. The exercise left him debilitated and exhausted in ways that he had never before faced. As if in premonition of the horrors of the play to come, on December 10, while visiting Jamie Herlihy, he checked his messages at the Oakwood Apartments where he was lodged. The ominous news gave him bad news. His cousin, Robert Tufford, who long ago came to California with him, informed him that his Aunt Peggy had passed away in Key West. Jim was devastated.

This woman had truly raised him and shown him care and affection as no one else ever did. In the last years of Lila Lee's life, when she was ill from a string of strokes, Peggy had moved to Florida to tend her younger sister. There she stayed after 1974 in a house Jim bought for her. He was unable to return east for services—and thought everyone around him was being kind by not mentioning it until the hard-hearted director made an offhand comment that it never occurred to him to tell them about the death of an aunt.

Jim was fortunate to be with Herlihy, whom he loved in a special way, different from all others in his life. He remained with his play, as there was not much else to do. He said in his *Diary of a Mad Playwright,* "I turn sadness to anger. I am angry when death takes away someone I love. I am angry with whoever runs the whole works and whoever thought up death. What a miserable concept to dangle in front of us all our lives until we finally meet it head on." On December 22nd, he addressed and sent out his annual Christmas card. From the Kirkwoods, it featured a photo of him and his embattled stars, all hugging and smiling, the ultimate in Christmas cheer and folly of the season.

Jim was preoccupied, if not consumed, by his major involvement in the biggest play of his career. Unlike *A Chorus Line,* this one was not a committee of creators. It was primarily his brainchild, and he was deeply involved in casting, with director, and with the stars. He spent New Year's Eve with Jamie and friends, though he went off to be alone at the stroke of midnight.

While Elizabeth Taylor and Robert Wagner made the film version of Pony, Jim Kirkwood was preoccupied with his play, Legends, starring Carol Channing and Mary Martin. His annual Christmas card displayed his early optimism, though it was short-lived. From author's collection.

When the chance to produce Kirkwood's *Hit Me with a Rainbow* fell through after the death of Natalie Wood, Robert Wagner's production team may have been distraught. Howard Jeffrey, who had worked with Wood on *West Side Story* among other projects, as her personal choreographer, was looking forward to producing this big screen film with his old friend.

Kirkwood had written to all his friends about having met Wood and her husband Wagner. "Natalie Wood has bought *Hit Me* and I had lunch with her and RJ a couple of weeks ago. She really seems all het up about doing it. So keep your nuts crossed." Refusing outright to write the screenplay, he took a chance at disappointing Wood who wanted Jim to do it. She usually received her way, and this would be a real comeback role for her. He told Herlihy how excited he was by meeting them. He was as much a star groupie as any fan.

Wagner himself knew that he had to go on, and he did have a strong regard for Jim Kirkwood. They had hit it off, and the star utterly enjoyed Kirkwood's humor and élan, and his zest for living. Though the major film was no longer possible, Wagner was always on the lookout for other projects. With his own interest in old Hollywood lore and gossip, as well as its history, the *Pony* story was made to order. In the depressing years following his beloved wife's death, Robert Wagner needed something to buoy his spirits. The discovery of the *Pony* story struck a nerve for him. He loved the book's optimism, message, and historical roman a clef. It was something he could produce and perform, though the second issue was not paramount for him. As he read the book and an old script by Jim, he thought: "That's the story. It means to look for the good things in life. Look on the positive side." He did that naturally, and other factors also began to make this a viable chance to work on something significant for him.

Asked for a new treatment of *Pony*, Jim Kirkwood had likely felt what was wanted by the new production company could be found among the several screenplays he'd done of it in past years; he was not inclined to write another for them. Though shorter than a full-blown script, the work would take valuable time while Kirkwood had his hands full of *Legends*. Even a very limited treatment was out of the question. "It usually runs about 12 to 15 pages and it tells the story as briefly as possible but still tries to convey the aura and atmosphere of the characters and locale. I never write them because I don't like the form but it can really become almost any form that is comfortable to you as long as it is not too windy or highfalutin. They seem to like them simple." All the writing of the teleplay would be assigned to Mart Crowley.

Wagner's team of friends, like Mart, who had done so much with him on television series, also supported the idea. To an extent this was Natalie Wood's team, but they shared their loyalty with Robert Wagner too. Crowley and Wagner were aficionados of old Hollywood. Mart Crowley would revamp the screenplay to suit the star and producer. More important, if Wagner could entice Elizabeth Taylor to do the film, the script needed to reflect her own interests and focus.

Wagner had the added impetus. The two stars of the 1950s whose lives were socially intertwined had never worked together. "We had always wanted to do a film together and I asked her if I could get this property, would she do it with me. She knew the book." RJ Wagner may have been a little surprised that Taylor had been considering one Kirkwood screenplay. He had re-written the earlier Columbia Pictures treatment again in 1978, playing off that for the public reading in the Hamptons the next year.

Taylor always was fussy about her leading men. She never shied away from autobiographical material, and often played it to the hilt on screen. If she were to be depicted as a movie star on the downslide with a penchant for picking the wrong man, she was as game as any actress to exploit herself. She adored Wagner and respected him. One of their great disappointments was not to have worked together, and such chances might be lessened in the years to come. When he called her about the part, he said: "We've been friends, you know, for years. I can't think of a leading man who wouldn't want to work with Elizabeth Taylor. You have to stand in line for that." He did not have to stand in line. She readily agreed, knowing the storyline and trusting the lead actor who'd also protect her in the production as he took the position as Executive Producer.

Like two veteran actors who have spent their lives surrounded by voyeurs, watchers, onlookers, and crowds, they had learned how to focus on the moment and ignore all the rest. It probably came from acting out intimate scenes in front of stage crews. Wagner and Taylor honed their ability to be oblivious to their surroundings. They had known each other nearly forty years when the *Pony* project came up for them. There was something in their demeanors that made the Kirkwood story real and tangible. They too knew the power of press and the tabloid gossip. If they wanted to make a statement about the world of fame, which had engulfed them since adolescence, the story of Lila Lee and her doomed boyfriend seemed tailor-made.

Wagner first met Taylor in Roddy McDowall's backyard at a party. They had an instant rapport, this generation of young stars and stars-to-be in the last gasp of the studio system. "Elizabeth befriended me. The lady is not only courageous, generous and talented, but she's been a good friend in every way." Many years before Kirkwood bought his little home in East Hampton, Taylor and her husband, Eddie Fisher, vacationed with another superstar couple of the era, Wagner and Natalie Wood. Taylor revealed, "Nat and I were great friends . . . the four of us would spend weekends together. It was RJ and Natalie and the gentleman I was married to at the time. When we were together we avoided cameras. When you are on vacation, you don't like the look of a camera. The train ride east was so luxurious, a great way to get away from things . . ."

Once, the debonair star refused to do an Elvis movie in the early 1960s, after his divorce from Natalie Wood. "Fox hit me with the classic line: 'You'll never work again'." Wagner recalled that low point in his career wryly. When he moved to London and Rome for a few years (1961 and 1962), though his life went "into a tailspin," he could count on friends like Elizabeth Taylor. In those days with Richard Burton, "She would walk into some damned club in Rome and people would go crazy."

As for playing in a tale of Hollywood scandal and tragedy, both Wagner and Taylor experienced public crises throughout their careers. Their most intimate moments had been exposed and headlined, and that may have made this project extremely important to do. The actor and producer said, ""I have been with Elizabeth through the high points and the low points, and she has been with me." Wagner loved the idea of stretching his acting ability. All too often he played the suave, sophisticated, and confident leading man. His looks typecast him, but he knew of suffering. The role of Ben whetted his interest. He saw the chance to act as Ben as "a very big departure." On the surface, all the usual stylish features of a typical Robert Wagner role jumped out, but as the film script progressed a darker side emerged, something hidden and requiring a concentration that his television roles seldom demanded. Though he played another suave sophisticated businessman, the actor/producer was fascinated that the character was "unable to commit to anything. There's a kind of deep sadness in his life. He was an interesting character to play because a lot of it was very, very interior."

Twenty years after he produced *There Must Be a Pony*, Robert Wagner remained a busy man. He traveled alone, without an entourage, to drum up support for projects. Though he often was required to act or to perform in any project, he was eager to express his creative spirit. He lost a key role in John Huston's *Red Badge of Courage* to Audie Murphy, but there would seldom be a case when his style and handsome looks would be denied again. He was on a spiritual journey himself, transformed from young hot prospect in *From the Halls of Montezuma* and the bow of Barbara Stanwyk's version of *Titanic*.

The power of an impresario, or mogul, did not impress him. He loved film and its history. He loved the business he was in, and the appeal extended to the gossip of old scandal. If anyone was aware deeply of his legacy within the Hollywood community, and his role as a bridge between the old and new film industry, Wagner played the role better than anyone else. "I don't want to be a mogul," said RJ. "That's not the idea at all."

Robert Wagner understood the foundations of how the business worked. Like many stars, he made up for his lack of formal college training with an acute mind. He knew he needed Taylor to guarantee the money backing for the TV movie; she still commanded press coverage and financial people still remembered the girl from *National Velvet*. Though the budget for such a television movie in 1986 was small in comparison to major films and what stars commanded, the production for *Pony* was set at $3.2 million, which in her heyday was what Taylor commanded as her total salary.

With Wagner at the helm, all Elizabeth's hesitation of recent years and frequent balks at performing in television movies like the *Pony* film disappeared. With him she knew her image would be protected and the story would not be watered down. If nothing else, Taylor was always courageous about her film projects and wanted them done right.

In the 1970s it seemed that Taylor and Wood were playing roles the other disdained, but the parts were growing fewer and the challenges and quality dropping off badly. Elizabeth accepted *The Mirror Crack'd after* Wood turned it down. Each was crawling into television movies in the last years of the 1970s. Natalie did *Cat on a Hot Tin Roof*, with Wagner, a remake of Taylor's 1958 film. They were resorting to small budget and small screen. Taylor claimed, "I must say with all candor that I am not made for television. It's hard. I don't know how people who do these series keep up. I really don't."

If *Pony* were done on the big screen, it could be truly freewheeling and open about some of its message. Television, especially network shows, meant dilution of the words and scenes. Taylor definitely was against that. Wagner assured her Crowley would make use of every nuance from the novel, no matter how unsuitable for television. To her credit Taylor who trained like an athlete for the film did not mind playing a mentally broken film star, destroyed by her own career in Hollywood. She informed one interviewer, "All of us actresses are a little crazy."

As always, Taylor was subject not so much to reviews as to public ridicule. One of the issues of modern celebrity was the denigration of creative achievements or work, all overshadowed by the complications of life and biographical detail. In Taylor's case, her desire to use her own life as fodder for her film projects drew more reviewers to seize on the parallels for the grist of jokes. One inaccurate critic said, the film "hints of *roman a clef* and heaping spoonfuls of plot complications spice up this Elizabeth Taylor vehicle in which she plays a child star turned movie star turned mental patient turned unstable has been looking for a comeback."

During the first week of January in 1986, syndicated columnist Liz Smith pronounced, likely with a tip from her friend Jim Kirkwood, that Elizabeth Taylor had been cast in the new television movie version of *There Must be a Pony*. The contract and agreement, meeting all her stipulations, was not signed until late May of that year. Taylor demanded and received top billing and a share in the profits of the picture, which was scheduled for European release as a feature. Soon thereafter, with her friend Robert Wagner in charge of production and costarring with her, Miss Taylor felt comfortable enough to jump into this version. She was a new sleek and thin self, looking better than she had in twenty years. On May 28th she began rehearsals for the filming.

Following on the heels of *Who's Afraid of Virginia Woolf*, Edward Albee's scathing depiction of a self-delusional and self-destructive marriage, Mart Crowley fashioned in 1968 an equal time version in the gay milieu. His biting wit with all its movie references and dastardly wicked characters won him accolades and fame from every quarter. He became another Southern playwright in the mode of Tennessee Williams, but with a outlandish and outed personal style. Though more than a decade younger than Kirkwood, Mart and Jim shared a birthday date, August 21ˢᵗ for Crowley, and August 22ⁿᵈ for Kirkwood, which gave them another example of their compatible styles.

In 1980 each chose to do cameos in major motion pictures, Crowley in *Nijinsky*, a sensational depiction of the great dancer's sexuality, and Kirkwood in *Oh, God, II*, a light-hearted satire of the Cosmic Joker. There was no better writer for Kirkwood's message, outside James Leo Herlihy who appeared in Arthur Penn's film *Four Friends* that year, causing Kirkwood in competition to jump into *Mommie Dearest*. Where they differed was in the openness of their sexuality

With Kirkwood deeply occupied and distracted by *Legends*, Crowley was able to make the adjustments necessary to meet the acting styles of the principal stars. Crowley left the New York theatre scene and moved to the West Coast to concentrate on film and screen projects. With his longstanding relationship to Robert Wagner, there was probably no writer that the producer better trusted. After years of working with Miss Wood, Mart Crowley had done yeoman service on the *Hart to Hart* series with Wagner and Stephanie Powers, first as the executive script editor and as one of its producers. It proved the most beloved of all Wagner's television work by himself and his audience.

Like Kirkwood, Crowley also never made a secret of his autobiographical elements in his plays. He said in his introduction to the printed play, *Boys in the Band*, "There was never a real birthday party attended by nine actual men . . . However, just before I began to write the play, I had . . . attended a party for a friend's birthday and it gave me the idea of how to frame what had already been on my mind . . . All of the characters are based on people I either knew well or are amalgams of several I'd known to varying degrees, plus a large order of myself thrown into the mix." The friend whose party it inspired Mart now served as producer on the *Pony* picture—Howard Jeffrey. Crowley had met Jeffrey through Natalie Wood, where Crowley worked as her personal assistant during the mid-1960s, overlapping the period Howard also advised Miss Wood on her roles, helped her with her choreography and performances.

In early 1986 Jim read Mart Crowley's *Pony* script, mostly while he was engaged in the chaotic production of *Legends*. His only comment about it was "I have read the script, and to say it doesn't follow the book is a gross understatement." The reaction of the author to Mart Crowley's brilliant teleplay was curious indeed. Though Kirkwood heard before the film aired on ABC how preliminary buzz noted Taylor was going to be fabulous, he intended to tune in and watch it himself; he had not seen a preview of the movie. He reported to others how "less than thrilled" with the finished product.

Executive Producer Robert Wagner took odds with his producer, Howard Jeffrey, an openly gay man, and his writer, Mart Crowley, over the casting and attitude toward Merwin. James Coco was the actor being set for that role. Thinking to have it played against type, Wagner considered having the effeminate Merwin turned into "the Marlboro Man. We never had, at that point, a truly masculine man playing an open gay." This interesting idea also dealt with one of the consistent complaints about the play—the stereotypic "sweetie" dialogue of Rita's close friend. To the credit of all involved, they did give Merwin a closing moment with Josh, showing he wished he could take the boy in as a guardian, but it was impossible.

Wagner himself had played a gay character, Brick, in the remake television film of *Cat on a Hot Tin Roof* in 1976 with his wife, Natalie. He learned an important lesson about how to "act" a gay part when he consulted Tennessee Williams who told the star not to act gay or try to. Williams advised Wagner to be natural in his depiction. It stuck in the star's head when he came to produce *Pony*. He wanted to stay true to that advice. In addition, he wanted to cast a perfect actor for the pivotal role of Josh, knowing that this would be Kirkwood's main concern.

For the job of director, Joe Sargent was chosen. His steady production of films for television rendered him a master of standard storytelling. He went right for the money shot, and only added stylish features if absolutely required. Though he worked primarily as an actor during the 1950s in every popular television show, he began directing episodes of *Lassie* in 1954.

By the late 1960s he had moved behind the camera, directing such well-received and stylish films as *The Forbin Project, MacArthur, etc.*, on television he directed James Cagney in *Terrible Joe Moran* in 1984, the great star's final picture. Sargent could give a solid accounting for *Pony*. He was also familiar with the roster of upcoming young actors in the television medium.

Among a number of candidates, Chad Lowe's name was submitted.

Chad Lowe, born in 1968, had an auspicious start in 1984. His television debut was a pivotal role in *Flight 90: Disaster on the Potomac*, an NBC docudrama TV-movie. With the growth of cable, small screen motion pictures were now diverse, interesting, and offered genuine performing opportunities, often rivaling the big screen or Broadway. He also did an uncredited part in his brother's film, *Oxford Blues*, playing a computer hacker. He also learned quickly the miasma of working in a television series. He quit almost immediately, allegedly due to a salary dispute, but the creative differences he had were over the direction he wanted to proceed in.

In May of 1985 Chad Lowe took on the leading role in the stage revival of *Blue Denim* by Herlihy and William Noble. Though the play itself had grown creaky in recent years, no longer as relevant about teenagers, the subject that Herlihy tackled in his novel and play about the unspoken concept of abortion, is more important to people and a hotter political issue. It was another superior choice for work by an upcoming young actor. Not only were his film roles carefully selected, he raised the bar among his generation of actors by going to stage and not being a film and television actor exclusively. It seemed, at first, that Chad Lowe was serious about his work. This was also proven by his desire to move to New York City and study acting, doing off-Broadway. He also went to Williamstown, where the summer festival held prestige among actors. Here he did a play version of *Huckleberry Finn*, tackling the lead.

Such roles during his full adult career had merit and importance, certainly displaying integrity in his work ethic. He made a striking guest appearance on *Law & Order: Special Victims Unit*, playing a grown man involved in an incestuous relationship with his mother. He went back to his roots, the television movie for a chance to play the tragic singer John Denver in the docudrama, *Take Me Home: The John Denver Story* in 2000.

Right from the earliest days of his acting, Chad wanted to do parts like the Josh role. "I believe that the story is the most important element of any medium whether it's theater, film, TV. So ultimately I am looking for a story that has some value and is important and is entertaining."

He knew too that the writer and the writing was the foundation of all creative work. In scripts his innate sense was to seek something "that has a perspective and that comes through in the writing. You can tell the agenda of the writer whether they are doing it just to exploit something and to something made or whether they really have something to say about the subject matter." The history behind *Pony* was told to him, and surely its insider look at Hollywood life appealed to him. "In some ways, I think it's the actor's way of changing the world—"

If he did not see the duplicity in Josh's character, the potential that he was as guilty as innocent, Chad knew something about playing characters with depth. He said, "it was important I thought, and a good challenge to anchor it in reality and try and get inside the mind of the guy who behaved like he did."

Chad Lowe's career has taken a few amazing turns over the years. Not the least was his marriage to Hilary Swank, a two-time Oscar winning actress. Out of this Norman Maine/*A Star is Born* situation, came Chad's ignominy, left off a long list of thanks from his own wife during her second Academy Award acceptance speech on national television and then divorced by her for his drug addiction. The young man cast to play Jim as a teenager in the RJ Productions version of *There Must be a Pony* was fated to parallel, less successfully than Dean Devlin, and more openly than Peter Helm, his ties to a Kirkwood curse on the character of Josh.

Like Josh, Chad had no college education and went directly to show business from and due to family connections. He tried stage work and did early efforts with a more famous member of the family. He went to high school on the west coast, not far from Kirkwood's alma mater. Unlike Kirkwood he'd win some accolades for his acting, an Emmy as a Best Supporting Actor in 1992, and he turned to directing.

Winning good reviews was not enough. He appeared in small budget films with cult-like followings, but the creative success he enjoyed may not have been enough to keep him from the self-destruction of the modern show business world. The temptations of escape through other means, like drugs, put him inevitably on the track to rehab, the concept not available to Kirkwood as a boy. He used old-fashioned psychoanalysis for most of his adult life, and Lowe likely would go the same route.

As a basis for his acting career, the young man from Ohio took the cue from his older brother, Rob Lowe, in whose publicized shadow he always lived. Chad was somewhat like Jim's Aunt Peg, in that he was constantly reminded of his family roots, and that his career was owed to the pioneering success of his brother. It made him resentful, feeling inadequate and overwhelmed. Martin Sheen, father of yet another show business brood, observed Chad's resentments and situational problems. Martin's recommendation to Chad was to try attacking his acting career in a different way from brother Rob.

Connection to such insiders within the business opens doors that others can never come near. Within a few days of making a decision to enter and to study acting, Chad had an agent and job offers. He was not yet sixteen then. They were the kind of details that Kirkwood would certainly recognize and remember from his own life. Had he been involved with filling the role of Josh, the casting of Chad Lowe would have rung all the right bells.

Unlike big productions taking months to complete, or the studio products of the Golden Age, television presentations must come in fast and ready. There is little room for temperament or reconsideration. Fortunately, veterans like Taylor are one-take masters, who learn their dialogue and know what is expected. Her training stemmed from the old MGM contract player school. At her *Pony* press conferences Taylor insisted that television work was too hard, too demanding for her, but this was false modesty. Wagner did not have to exaggerate: "And she was great. Totally professional, always on time." He added, "She made me crazy on the set. She never forgets a line. There I am stumbling, trying to keep up."

"Oh, sure," responded Taylor in an interview. Her dismissal was not of her own ability, but Wagner faking his own inability.

The producer may have misstated when he said, "Elizabeth was the one person I always wanted to play the role," said Wagner. He would have done the film with his late wife. She was certainly the first choice of Kirkwood. Wagner was correct when he added this was Elizabeth's "juiciest role in years . . ."

Though Taylor's career was in the downslide toward retirement at this point, she still commanded respect and attention. Not truly box-office, she had a popularity quotient that made her highly attractive on television. After her public bout in the Betty Ford Clinic to rehabilitate her drinking and eating habits, and after controlling her weight, she looked ten years younger, causing Wagner to effuse: "There isn't a leading man in the world who wouldn't want to work with her. I'm very glad I had the chance."

Whether they had the chemistry to make the filmed version of Pony work or not, they knew from their tabloid days as icons of gossip and love matches that the public would accept or forgive anything in their film union if there was some spark between them. For Taylor their love scenes were pivotal. Taylor recognized, "It happens between the eyes, like an umbilical cord. I was receiving so much from him. I hope they caught it on camera." For Wagner, whose acting had usually been limited to playing one-dimensional characters, he still possessed the power of communicating what was needed through merely a kiss or a glance, both to other actors and to the general viewer. "Hell, when you look in her eyes, if you can't get it, they might as well carry you out." Wagner added. "It was definitely worth the wait."

Part of what made Wagner such a perfect producer and expert actor was his natural sense of support and kindness. As a rock of strength, he reassured everyone. His best talent was to make everyone feel comfortable when stress loads increased. For edgy actresses, or people in work crisis, he exuded that strength and generosity more than any other. He played the hero so often because he was heroic in demeanor. Taylor confirmed, "He's such a gentleman, so considerate." It made his dual role as Ben more complex and difficult. He was playing against type and against his own character.

For example, as part of his duties as executive producer, he escorted Miss Taylor to publicity and press briefings, personally serving as her driver. He had the style to pull the project together. Taylor teased him about this quality of loyalty and strength and how long lasting it might be "unless the film is bad and he never talks to me again."

After the filming ended in May, Wagner was convinced he had done justice to the book and gave, generous as always, credit to Miss Taylor. After spending time giving his personal supervision "in the editing room for three days watching her performance. I think this is her best part since *Who's Afraid of Virginia Woolf.* It really is her picture."

Mart Crowley cleverly included moments that revealed his suspicions about either Rita, or more possibly Josh as a suspect in Ben's death. His script contained several illuminating scenes that transcended the various plays and brought to the surface some truly interesting insights into the characters and situation. Whatever else Crowley thought about Ben's suicide, he added perceptively throughout the film. Many takes never made it out of the editing room. The necessities of time allotted for each section of television movies meant key scenes suffered butchering which wound up on the cutting room floor. What Wagner had to cut from the preliminary reels may have changed the viewers' understanding of possible crime.

Nearly all the excised scenes related to the scenes with Lee Hertzig, played by William Windom, distinguished and powerful actor whose trustworthiness made him an important character. Because those moments were altered or cut entirely, Windom's role in the picture became matter-of-fact and nothing more than a cameo. It also eviscerated the subtle plot machinations that Crowley put in place. On a humorous level, having placed any number of references to Taylor into the script, melding the character and actress, Mart Crowley offered the same treatment to Wagner in an insider joke scene, also cut. In this odd moment, Ben pretended to have a heart attack to win some sympathy from Rita. She found his acting unbelievable and, in fact, called Wagner's performance that of a "bad actor."

One legal decision that Lee made for his clients was removed from the picture in the editing process. He advised them in a scene during the aftermath of the police investigation and the arrival of Mrs. Nichols. Lee banned both Rita and Josh from attending Ben's funeral, telling them he feared their reactions, the press reactions, and the likely attitude of the dead man's wife. The only bit left in place was a fleeting moment in which Marguerite insisted she wanted to express her condolences to the wife when they crossed paths at the police station.

A second scene with Lee revealed his attitude toward the affair between Ben and Rita. He immediately had detectives do an investigation into the deceased man and found his background fraught with dubious falsehoods. The opinion of Merwin and Lee was that Ben must have been "off his rocker" to spread such lies everywhere he went. Hertzig was concerned with making Rita and Josh appear to be victims of a con man. The idea appalled them, as they still wanted to believe in the man who befriended them. The scene was dropped.

Another omitted pivotal scene was one in which Windom and Chad Lowe had an opportunity to convey the subtle message about the "whodunit" nature of the plot. In this confrontation between the attorney and the boy, Lee had to give Josh instructions on how to answer police questions, as if to indicate his worry at what the son might say about his mother. Josh indicated he knew how to protect his mother and would not fail. The scene also implied that the lawyer was concerned about the relative innocence of Josh himself at this point. Dialogue conveyed a more mysterious sense that Ben's suicide was a dubious act, not intentional, possibly involuntary. Whatever the inferences of the Crowley script, they did not sit well with the novelist whose boyhood was devastated by an unexpected death.

Most striking detail of all cut from the motion picture was the brevity of the discovery of Ben's body. Crowley avoided the horror of watching ants crawl over the body, but the most devastating change was the edit that cut the moment Josh picked up the "suicide" weapon.

An exchange with Jim Kirkwood during the production of the film disclosed his growing loss of optimism. The stress of *Legends* seemed to undercut his usual buoyancy; he expressed being jaded about his own work, and felt under-appreciated for his accomplishments. It was part of a long history of disappointment in his creative life. He wrote to me, "*There Must be a Pony* starring Elizabeth Trailer and JR Wagon airs Sunday, Oct. 5 at 9pm on ABC. I haven't seen it but I've read the script and to say that it doesn't follow the book literally is a gross understatement. However, I hear she turns in a bravura performance so by all means turn your set on."

Alas, for Jim and his autobiographical story, fewer tuned in than might be considered successful, but more people watched the story than had seen all the play performances or read copies of the book over the previous twenty-six years. The show aired on Sunday night, but ran opposite the *Dynasty* star, Linda Evans, in a telepicture called *The Last Frontier*. She whipped up thirty-six percent of the audience, as opposed to Kirkwood's *Pony*, which garnered nineteen percent. Considered small by television standards, it introduced Jim Kirkwood to his widest audience ever.

Those tuning in to see Taylor and Wagner may have been surprised at what emerged, expecting to see soap opera gloss. But the show was not about an affair of a fading couple of stars of a generation earlier. James Coco, in a highly toned down Merwin role, played off Taylor as a life-long friend. It was Chad Lowe, who mastered the night with his ability, not only holding his own against tremendous veteran actors, while making his version of Josh merge with Taylor's Marguerite. Their repartee smacked of mother-son ties almost unconscious in style, but is the work of performers who could bring scripted lives believably onto the screen.

Lacking genuine criticism in newspapers, the comments about the film were predictable. Many simply took on the easy target of making Elizabeth Taylor jokes, rather than note her performance or the story itself. The title and anecdote about finding the pony in the pile of manure also sparked a steady stream of witticisms, in lieu of serious assessment (*e.g.*, "Pony Can't Get Out of Starting Gate"). Others jumped on various acerbic lines in the screenplay and threw them back on the actors. Taylor delivered one of Mart Crowley's comments, "Television gives new meaning to the term 'chopped liver'." It became a memorable moment in the morning-after columns.

One of the most intolerant and nasty reviews called the work "a maudlin, pointless drama," and that was the best that could be said. The prejudice and insensitivity of the writer, for he was no critic, featured lines about the film was a "Laughably bad tv movie about a sunset boulevard style actress trying to make a comeback after a spell in the looney-bin, makes chopped liver look mighty fine indeed." Not only were Taylor and Wagner skewered for looking good, but acting bad, also attacked was young Chad Lowe, the one "who plays Taylor's son looks like a sniveling arrogant youth and acts like a sniveling arrogant youth."

Unfortunately for viewers and thoughtful people, this sort of drivel passed for serious criticism in many media outlets that bothered to review the picture.

An industry journal, *Weekly Variety*, gave a more measured and incisive look at the film. Calling the original novel "flawed," without explanation, the reviewer did acknowledge that the 1962 play made "little splash," but failed to note subsequent variations on stage. The opinion of the trade journal was that the Crowley version of the story should make James Kirkwood "proud of the teleplay."

In the opinion of this viewer, Crowley removed Kirkwood's excesses.

Whether the story was really Taylor's or not, she took over the production by sheer dominance of her personality and personal history. That, too, was the result of Crowley's homage to the great film star. The character of Rita in *Pony* had been renamed Marguerite in homage to the usage of Taylor's own first name. In the television play Elizabeth declared in diva style: "There's only one Ava, one Marlene and one Marguerite. Now, then, and forever." She added disdainfully that those who think they know her, call her Rita. It mirrored Taylor's feeling about the shorter name "Liz," which she despised for its use by people claiming to know her well.

Whatever the profligate lifestyle of Marguerite, the play's protagonist had not fared as well as Taylor, who certainly never cut corners in her own luxury. Rita, however, must live in a borrowed house and take whatever television roles come down the pike. She and her son were, as in all versions, unknowingly waiting for the right con artist to fleece them. The line about the name suited both the script's character and the actress playing her.

The real Rita was a smoker, but Taylor refused to use cigarettes on screen, though she smoked in her own life. As a role model, the actress believed she had some responsibility to behave in public. The intricate intertwining of actress and role was part of her creativity. Wagner noted the usual "bits of business" she added to the part, like having Marguerite check her makeup in the shiny image on a dinner knife at a restaurant.

According to the astute *Variety* critic, "The initial problem of explaining the suicide, as it did in both the book and the play, remains. The change of character by the suicide victim is too abrupt, too vague, and too senseless." That was the same feeling the police had about the situation. In another version, critical judgment was on the mark, but unable to understand what really underscored the tale. This victim was murdered. Could there be any more doubt? Just as sharp as Crowley himself, the critic observed, "considering the difficulties the book offers. Kirkwood's intent, or what seems to have been his intent, has been nurtured and developed."

Another critic, like many careful viewers or readers, was left with an uneasy hunch that something had been left out, or that we were missing key information.

The disquieting feeling was genuine and dismissed too easily by many intelligent viewers. After watching the mounting clues, John O'Connor of the Times had to admit: "and there are many more to come in this strange little movie." Alas, he was unable to put the final steps to the crime and solve it, but this was the undoing of police, reporters, and readers, for years.

The script by Crowley generally received probably more praise than any other aspect of the film. The *New York Times* reviewer recognized correcting "each time the movie seems about to settle down to perhaps an illuminating analysis of Josh, the story and cameras shift to Marguerite and, with a svelte Miss Taylor done up in Nolan Miller costumes, nobody else stands a chance."

Josh's psychological state, overshadowed by the spectacular immaturity of his mother, became more deeply obscured to any and all observers around him. Overwhelmed by Taylor's appearance and demeanor, the audience became distracted too. She was a time-tested scene-stealer. Merwin warned her that she missed the picture on her son when they discussed whether he might be "gay" (now updated to the current slang), rather than a "sissy" or "not a regular boy," as he'd been described over the previous versions. Marguerite, to her credit, did recognize something scary in her son, "You're like a little old man."

When a handsome businessman, a New Yorker "in real estate," offers to give Marguerite some money in front of her son, she replies with some dignity, "Even though I'm grown up, I still don't take candy from strangers." These tidbits were the crackling, insightful dialogue provided by Crowley. Both Rita and Josh were ripe for the plucking by any opportunist, whether he sold religion, vitamins, or sex. Ben Nichols was that force, and he deteriorates a bit more in each progressive scene, ending up finally in a drunken stupor, ready to argue with Marguerite, and to leave her.

According to the Crowley script, Josh heard some shouting, awakening him from sleep. Though he fell back into bed for a while, when he awoke, it was literally in a fog with dogs barking in the dark. His stumbling walk to the swing where he found Ben dead was cut sharply. No sooner than he lamented the loss, he was talking to police who carted away the body.

"And then disaster strikes. The problem is it's so unexpected that the effect is merely baffling." This was the original complaint of all the play versions, that the sudden change in Ben seems without foreshadow, confounding audiences. There is enough of Josh's character to indicate that the eavesdropping and secretive boy was not to be trusted. Most viewers felt bushwhacked by the plot development, and their lack of consideration of Josh's odd character once again failed to make a dent in audience's comprehension.

Instead of recognizing Kirkwood's peculiar narrator as a potential problem, the story seemed to tell about suffering among Hollywood's rich and famous: not a sympathetic subject. Marguerite denigrated the movie industry at every step, but won't hear a word against it from her own son. The loopiness of her character became a yardstick of measurement for the tale. The coming-of-age story of Josh fell between the cracks of madness in the star's character, overwhelming the possibility that she has wrought an unstable boy who might turn on anyone who leaves him. Instead of seeing this, the critic found only "a stale essay on Hollywood emptiness."

At least one critic gave it thumbs up: "ABC's *There Must Be a Pony* was a really lovely and poignant TV movie that sure hit home. Elizabeth Taylor and Robert Wagner were brilliant, and Chad Lowe was excellent."

Alas, those accolades were rare.

When I protested to Jim that I stood apart from the detractors of the movie, that I for one, loved the movie, he responded to me with: "I, for one, was not at all delighted with the tv version of *Pony*. I didn't think it came anywhere near capturing the essence of the novel. I thought Chad Lowe was very good as Josh, but that it was really the Elizabeth Taylor show. I didn't really believe a strong love affair existed between her and R.J. and I thought he was fairly lackluster as Ben—so there!"

Whatever did he presume was the "essence of the novel"? It seemed the Mart Crowley screenplay followed extremely closely the novel, to the point where it adopted the name of Sinisonia, the Native American servant. She was a minor character in the novel and worked at the ranch where Rita and Josh moved after leaving Paraiso Beach. This was an example of the specificity Crowley adopted into his screenplay, telescoping key moments in off-hand comments. Did Jim mean the film did not focus on Josh enough? It was there—from his discovery of his mother in breakdown phase, to the hurried uncovering of the suicide notes.

What was omitted was Josh's haphazard and half-hearted affair with a local girl, but that was not a great part of the novel, mostly included in all the play versions in greater form. The closeness of mother and son was clear and well acted with small gestures and eye contacts between Taylor and Lowe to indicate a long-term tie to each other. What Jim may have objected to, in his complaint of the essence, was the issue of making Elizabeth Taylor's personal idiosyncrasies part of Marguerite's.

One of the major problems Jim had in version after version was his vacillation between making the story more that of Josh, or more that of Rita. His inability to resolve this issue made for the swings of focus in play after play. The scene in which Josh found the body was also curtailed; though it was filmed, the final edit removed the moment that Josh picked up the gun, though it was referred to in the subsequent police interrogation.

Kirkwood's negative reaction to the show utterly confused anyone familiar with the novel. The movie resembled his novel far more than Jim's stage versions. It was not his screenplay—which may have featured Josh making a scrapbook of the press coverage and having a closer relationship to Sid Traynor. These were minor infractions.

We began some heated discussions, both in phone calls and correspondence over the Manhattan Beach issues. The movie version precipitated some hard questions. If I was feeling a little threatened, it was not from Jim's lack of trying to intimidate me. I gave him, at long last, a serious problem about the veracity, if not guilt, of Josh.

For Jim, Josh was "quickly dismissed as a suspect in Ben's death." This is an astounding statement, even if misconstrued by him in our conversation. In no official police report released to the press was Josh ever named a potential suspect or even a "person of interest." In the real case, secretly, there may well have been some consideration of this possibility.

In Jim's view, "I think it was obvious to everyone around at that time, even the police, that the boy was absolutely destroyed by the tragedy of finding him." Josh may have been upset, or angered by the death of Ben, but he was never destroyed by it—not in a single version of the story. So far as Jim and Reid were concerned, Kirkwood seemed unfazed by the death—when his smiling face illuminated newspapers across America as he gazed upon the "Swing of Doom." In Jim's story, the boy returned to school and functioned, albeit angrily, with deliberate confidence. This change in personality puzzled everyone.

Jimmy Kirkwood, standing over his friend Howard Jones (Syd Traynor in the story) watched in glee as Tony Mumolo, the estate gardener, rakes the crime scene, all posing for a Wire Service news photo.

Jim also waxed eloquent about how grateful to Ben the boy was. He cited this as absolute reason for the boy's devotion, love, and emotional upheaval. According to Jim, "After all, Ben had helped pull Rita and her career together, had helped

Josh crawl out of his shell, *etc., etc.* "While this was all true, Jim conveniently forgot about Josh's peculiar possessiveness, his strong sense of anger—especially at those who might desert him. He did not want to face the issue of Josh's emotions were he to learn Ben was driving off into the sunset. The boy might become irrational, if not violent. This was a lifelong characteristic of Jimmy Kirkwood, too.

When Kirkwood insisted to me, "also there wouldn't be any possible motive Josh would have for killing Ben," I had to express my astonishment. Josh, in my estimation, had as much reason to kill Ben as Rita. Throughout the story as Kirkwood constructed it, the love affair seemed between the boy and the man. Their many secrets, their emotional bond brought the true happiness to the story. If Josh learned that his hero had feet of clay, the response might be too terrible to contemplate. If Josh had confronted Ben and asked him not to leave, what might have occurred when the boy learned Ben was done with Rita and could no longer see him?

The big issue Jim had to explain in all versions was the reason his fingerprints were on the death weapon. He avoided explaining why the weapon was in Reid Russell's hand when police found him. His arms had been folded across his chest and the gun was in his hand, a highly unlikely posture, determined the police. They speculated the pistol was placed there. Someone thought it would prove suicide. It tended to indicate the opposite. Josh's bizarre answers led the police to inquire, "You been in a situation like this before?"

When they asked why he picked up the gun, Josh gave the cryptic comment: "I don't know. Instinct, I guess."

"What do you mean?"

Nervous and tentative, Josh answered, "You know how . . . you know if you drop something, you pick it up. You don't think about it. You just do it."

"But you didn't drop it," the cop led him on.

In a tiny voice, Josh replied, "Well, no."

Josh then offered information about his mother that did not put her into a good light with the investigating authorities. If Josh wanted to punish his mother—and Ben—he did a bang up job. Was this what bothered Kirkwood? Did Crowley's screenplay hint something more unspoken about the story?

Earlier in the night, Josh was shown tossing and turning in bed with his restless pets. The dogs were whimpering and barking, animal noises enough to wake anyone, but the undertone was an argument. Though it might have been a television in a distant room, the sounds were a man and a woman having a heated discussion. It upset the animals. When I pressed Jim on the failing relationship between Rita and Ben, he grew careful.

"Was that in relation to their argument?"

Once again he seemed to realize my questions were leading him into dangerous territory. Their argument, confirmed in the screenplay, caused Rita to flee the house, led both mother and son to suspect the other to have pulled the trigger on Ben. Kirkwood responded to me about Josh's anger about Ben splitting up with his mother. "Actually, he'd be disappointed and saddened in general because they were disagreeing about something."

When I tried to pin Jim down on the boy's attitude toward Ben, if he thought Ben was hurting Rita, Kirkwood again dashed into his coy attitude: "You mean if Josh would be more disappointed with Ben or with Rita?" The point was a set-up for Jim because no matter how mad the boy would become with his mother, his passion was tied to Ben—or was that Reid? If Ben—or Reid—were planning to abandon Josh/Jim, the boy likely would lose his hair-trigger temper. If his mother were hurt in the process, that would not ameliorate the boy's fury. More than fifty years after the death of Reid Russell, Jimmy was still in a state of blind rage over the man who left them high and dry. Pushing that particular button was not necessarily a safe tactic.

Jim continued to insist that the notes he found proved that Ben was a suicide. In reality, the official note was found by Ruth Morris, allegedly in her jewelry case and burned it. Were there additional notes? Jim said, yes, he found them. "As to the suicide notes, they were handwritten and in my imagination, they would not have been dated. I don't think anyone who writes a suicide note would particularly care about the formality of dating it."

Subsequent to his written responses, Kirkwood and I engaged in more frank debate by telephone over these issues. He repeated one of his favorite refrains, with his usual lilting dismissal. "I am right and you are wrong." Whenever he did not like the tide turning on him, he resorted to the notion that, as author, he could make the final declaration—even if he re-wrote the story in doing so.

"We know what Rita and Ben argued about. They argued about Ben's refusal to go to a party where he would be seen with Rita. And, later, they argued because Rita saw Ben drunk and tried to get him to stay down in Manhattan Beach and go with her to meet the producer of the series. He could not do that because—unbeknownst to Rita of course—his wife had come to Los Angeles and he had to get back to her."

Oh, did we know that?

The simple fact was Ben declined to stay or to accompany Rita. This likely meant he was leaving her. She was frantically trying to find him in the days before his death, as he had disappeared. She was making constant telephone calls and not coming home in her obsessive quest to stop him from his desertion.

With the tough questions came some rocky times. He became furious with me after one phone call. I wished there was a bunker in which I could hide—all I could do was wait and hope he'd cool down a few weeks later. He blew up at one point and demanded: "Stop needling me about this." When finally I wrote to him with an act of contrition, he responded quickly: "Well, Billy boy, I'm glad you finally got the nerve to write me. Bygones is bygones. You are back on the A-list."

When debate points seemed to zero in on the facts, Jim became more and more evasive. Finally, he would stop the conversation. He needed a time-out to re-gather himself. The stakes of the game grew too large and he had to balance too many inconsistencies, some of which he could not always recall. "I cannot discuss the suicide letters with you at this particular time." Sometimes he'd use his humor and quick wit to disarm and dismiss the conversation. "I will explain this to you in detail as soon as I come across some more free-long distance telephone numbers."

Jim could resort to threat, again couched in a darkly funny manner: "I can't discuss this any more in a letter, goddam it, but the next time I get my hands around your throat I will make it all extremely clear to you." When all else failed, he'd resort to an appeal for sympathy. "I must get on to new work and I know you don't want me to hang back up by my ankles in old business."

This response was fairly amusing, considering that Jim had spent the better part of fifty years, his writing career, in the "old business" of sorting out the terrible days of that September in 1936. Whatever was unresolved in his mind and heart, he never seemed to feel inner peace on this pivotal incident.

As the teleplay reached the screen during the first week of October in 1986, Jim wrote to me, "I can't wait to get away from this little baby (referring to the Mary Martin-Carol Channing debacle) for a while. It's almost like you're stuck with a child that simply won't grow up. At least I'm getting a juicy book out of the whole thing. Next week I go to Cleveland, then to California for a few days to read ladies for replacements for the maid, then back to Chicago for the opening there, and then down to Key West."

Anyone who knew him could tell something was wrong. He was not himself. Claiming to some to feel his age (not generally revealed), there was also something deeper and more insidious at work. He dropped his clues carefully and without any overt emotion. "You were right about reading between the lines of my last letter."

Jim may have lost all perspective on the film version of his novel, the one he so wanted and tried so hard to create for decades. He managed to find time to see it among the turmoil and chaos of the *Legends* tour. If anything, he was growing exasperated by the drain on his life and energy. He wanted to do well in all his projects, and worked hard to reach that goal. "*Legends* has exhausted me and I am slowly but surely trying to effect, if not a divorce, certainly a separation from it—and them—for a while. I'm thinking seriously of getting away and starting on the journal about the making of *Legends* (or the unmaking of it), because I have a lot of very strong feelings to get rid of and I am going to get rid of them in a book."

After the many years as the dynamo, Jimmy Kirkwood was wearing down, like a top whose spin begun to weave unsteadily. Never before did he make comments like, ". . . if I am feeling up to it." Something was going awry, and he grumbled about some finality in his mind. He wrote to me, "At any rate, life goes on, and it will be good to have the play behind me and to dive into the book. Your crazy writer friend . . ."

Jim's hope sprung eternal, no matter how many leaks he had to plug. "This won't be a long letter because I'm up to my kishkas making phone calls and writing letters and investigating other actresses. Keep your fingers crossed for us." Matters grew worse, and he began to feel unwell. "Besides all of the headaches with the play, my houseman in East Hampton came down with ARC (AIDS Related Complex) and also one of the producers—the only one with real taste—came down with AIDS and had to be shipped off to California. So all in all it was a disastrous time." Since he loathed mentioning AIDS, this was a shocking admission.

"I will be going down to Key West beginning Nov. 23," and in a note to me he gave me a not so subtle hint: "Here's my address there for receiving Christmas presents . . ." He always hated the holidays. Though his famous Christmas cards were so loved, he himself did not love the occasion. "I hope you've had a bunch of good holidays. I just neglected them down here and kept on working. A little swim in the afternoon, a little tennis, a drink with the evening news, a little reading, and beddy bye."

As a consequence of his joke, and because I really felt he needed to be cheered up, I went looking for the right present to give him. There was no one else I knew who had such a terrible time this year—all the worse for how much optimism he began with. He told me, "Have a whole mess of happy holidays. I think there will be a Christmas card this year. I have to go now—time to shoot up."

I sent him the best gift I could find—and I was so pleased that it brought him a little pleasure. As a child, he had wandered among the lemon and orange groves of Manhattan Beach, and I found something that could remind him of the happiest of his days there. "The Christmas chocolates were terrific, just great, they were mostly eaten late at night, during pee calls in the wee hours of the morning. I loved them. I love chocolate covered orange and lemon peels." If it helped him through writing his revenge book, I was glad. It was the least his trusty spy and helper could provide.

The book he needed to write was *Diary of a Mad Playwright*.

During this year he seemed to hate the holidays more than usual. He was never truly in the spirit of Christmas or New Year. They left him more depressed than anything else, including bad reviews. He told me he wanted so badly to escape to Key West where cold winter holidays could be removed from the mind, a kind of hypnosis of the warm weather. "I'm going to stay there until about Jan. 5th and just work and work and work and gets lots done over this shitty holiday period which I absolutely loathe, hate, and can't abide. So the best thing for me to do is WORK. And play a little tennis and maybe horse around a little, donchaknow. So that's the scoop on lil me."

Jim was not well during the summer of 1988. The real problems emerged, but he would not acknowledge them. He still planned to direct his new play *Stage-Stuck*, though it kept him from writing his novel. He told a friend, "I had a prostate infection, which sent me to the hospital for two weeks and kept me knocked out for over a month. Now I'm okay but it cut the heart out of the summer." It was worse than a prostate infection, and it cut more deeply.

Though he mustered some enthusiasm for the new play, there was a strange governor on his usual excitement: "Our play *Stage-Stuck* is still under option and we're still waiting for the producer to raise all the money—good luck and God Bless us all Tiny Tim." Jim called his final effort a "farce-comedy," but the real tragedy was he distracted himself from his final major novel, *I Teach Flying*. He knew perhaps at the end that he made a bad decision on this. "Incidentally, I am very close to finishing my Daddy book. I would have it finished in a month if it weren't for this play, but there always seem to be some sort of interruption." He told a friend about his new play, calling it "a perverse Valentine to the theater."

Stage-Stuck was so inbred that its appeal could only be to diehard show business insiders, not to the audience and not to the general public. As Jim began to fail in health, his judgment about his work reached a nadir of piquant bad humor. At long last it seemed the power of his optimism was starting to falter. It could only be attributed to the decline in his condition.

Jim's buoyant optimism extended through the summer schedule. Not only did he expect to do a book tour for the expose on *Legends*, he wanted to shape the new play while it was in Boston. "The backing for my new play *Stage-Stuck* is coming from Boston people and that means I will probably be making a couple of trips up there this spring and in the summer . . ." We discussed having a couple of evenings together and eating a Chinese dinner, one of his favorites. He was so up, I wanted to encourage him to drop everything and finish his book, but I mistrusted his mood and went along with the plans for seeing him again.

Kirkwood probably recognized what he was doing, though it did not dissuade him from the folly. He told an interviewer he hoped it wasn't a terrible omen that while writing the play, he and his coauthor "laughed so much, it was embarrassing." The play's intent was dark, laughter at the expense of offending groups, people, actors, producers, and playgoers.

Despite his failing health, Jim thought about expanding his role in the new play *Stage-Stuck*, which he wrote with Jim Piazza. He expected the production would begin in January of 1989 and continue through March. After that, he hoped for a tour of New England in the summer, previous to a Broadway try. "But I also might direct *Stage-stuck*." They had secured the Tennessee Williams Fine Arts Center in Key West for the first performances. "The play—with a cast including Eileen Brennan, Rip Taylor, and Bibi Osterwald—goes into rehearsal at the end of this month, so I will have to be back down in Florida for that period." Because of Jim's collapse, Charles Nelson Reilly was put into emergency director's service.

The play opened a month before Jim died. He stayed and tried to oversee the production as much as possible, but he had to return to New York for medical treatment, and was hospitalized. The play garnered the worst reviews Jim had ever received. At the end he returned home for his last days. In his final interview, he protested about his stories, "People won't believe it, every word is true."

CHAPTER NINE

BETTING ON PONY

I considered myself James Kirkwood's Boswell, but was I merely another fruit fly buzzing around the Top Banana? People sometimes ask me why Jimmy Kirkwood told me so much. The question usually exasperates me.

Why? Because I had his number and he knew it; he joked with me all the time about the insights he gave me, "If you are a good boy, you will be privy to the inside story. And if you are not a good boy . . ." He left my fate to the imagination. He loved the idea that someone was onto him. "You know more about my writing than I do, you devil, you!"

If anyone really needed me to characterize our relationship, Jim Kirkwood and I had an intellectual love affair. It was strictly a textual relationship: intense, fascinating, obsessive, and passionate. I wallowed in his texts, his ideas, and his motifs. He regularly taunted me with comments like, "You're as mad as a March hare." This appealed to his perversity. We were intimate in the ways of literature. I read between the lines with him as with someone else he might lie to between the sheets. He had access to all the luminaries and beauties of show business, movies and theater. But when it came to literature, I blew away the competition for his attention—or at least that's what he led me to believe.

Did he lie with me too? Oh, page after page of letters between us are filled with our mental trysts. I felt such a kinship to him, and I think he did with me. He wanted us to have a literary affair. He tossed metaphors at me like a lover tosses bonbons at his paramour. He surprised me again and again with his insights and his baiting. We met deep in the dark woods of literature and he'd beat me to grandma's house every time. Oh, Jim, what great big teeth you had.

One of the concepts that made him irritable was the issue of gayness. He was, according to gay activist editors of the 1970s, too coy to suit them. Jim wanted his audience of readers to be expanded, not limited, and certainly not limited by sexuality. He was bothered if articles or pieces did more than hint at such matters. The subtle message was there, but—as he revealed—it was its softness and suggestion he felt were important.

When *P.S. Your Cat is Dead* became a counter culture hit, with its appeal to those with a fetish for S&M, he cut scenes out of subsequent versions. When I told him that the most common question I was asked about him regarded his sexuality, he had a pat answer. I assured him I would tell people it was not something I asked him, and he replied, "No, no. If any other students ask you if I am gay or even bisexual, tell 'em to stop by my apartment and find out for themselves." In his East Hampton community, he was far more open about such matters, leaving little doubt. For a man with a confessional approach to literature, he kept those parts of his life private.

Our references with each other to gay life were couched in mockery. "I sent off a couple of photographs a few days ago, which I hope you've received by now. Also I am enclosing a clipping that a friend of mine in Chicago sent me from some sort of deviate newspaper." Of course, he perused all the gay magazines and newspapers, even if he did not want to be in them, or exposed by them.

The interruptions became greater and greater. At long last he changed his phone number in New York in order to be able to continue his tremendous productivity. When I asked him, he said, "I was getting entirely too many sex calls and this was taking me away from my work, and as you know, my work is my life." He offered to give me his new phone number only if I made a promise, "Please do not write it on rest room walls."

The recurring character of Boots in his books became a signpost and a joke between us. When once I had sent him a satiric multiple choice test to fill out on his own books, he answered every question incorrectly. One of the questions had been to translate the name Boots into Latin. As a former altar boy and Roman Catholic, he certainly knew the Latin tongue. He chose "Calvino" when the correct response should have been "Caligula." Though a fallen Catholic, he knew enough Latin to be in on the joke. Oh, Jim, you devil, you. There was no better playmate. He took to signing his letters, "Sly Boots."

He was always interested in how my students reacted to his stories. One semester a student told me he had been assigned the same room Kirkwood used at Brewster. He wrote an essay on it, which amused him, and so I sent it to Jim. "The student whose paper you sent me is 100% right about Brewster Academy. Please tell him he gets an A for research. The only thing that surprised me was that apparently the school is much the same as when I went to it. One always imagines everything is changed completely from those dark days before the Revolution. Christ, if my sisters and I could only make it to Moscow . . ."

Though he told me he was adamant against a biography, I thought he might try his own hand at an autobiography, a better way to control the facts. His own novels were all stories about his life, though he was given free reign to alter the details. In his true stories, like *Diary of a Mad Playwright,* I knew he had a pathological aversion to telling it all. There were passages in that nonfiction that I knew were dubious and mendacious. He professed to me, "You were right about sniffing out the fact that a certain novelist has a lot of juicy memoirs up his sleeve. But I'm not ready to spill the truth or ring the gong right now. I will do that at some future date, however. You may be assured of that."

He requested me to dissect his work and send him the autopsy. He loved my probing and thrived on jousting over the details. He respected my opinion enough to ask me to come to play rehearsals and give my opinion, "Perhaps you could help me solve whatever problems we run into. And if you're not going to do that, at least you could send whatever friends you have in New York City to see the god-damned play."

I am not so sure he ever used the results of our discussions in any way, but it likely served as a stimulus for additional writing. "I can't wait until you start disemboweling *Some Kind of Hero.*" Because insanity was one of the yardsticks he used to judge how much he liked something, he used the metaphor frequently. "If I did as much work writing a book as you do on dissecting it—I'd undoubtedly be enclosed in a strait-jacket at this very moment."

He loved the fact that I read, not what he said, but what he did not say. How often he said to me that I picked up the hidden message and knew what he really was saying. "You're not getting any saner." He begged me to disembowel his books again and again, each one. He anticipated my scalpels digging into the words on every page. "Keep your scalpels sharp please." He became wide-eyed with amazement when I mentioned the specific page number where I caught Josh or Peter in a lie. He loved a good joust. "I get such a kick out of your dissection of my work that I cannot tell you in a letter because it would be too complicated, and I'm off to Pittsburg tomorrow. But I will tell you in person when next we meet."

I attempted to nail him down by conversing by telephone: "You brought to my attention certain themes that reappear that I was truly not aware of." My pressures simply made him promise to be cagier in future stories. No theory and no catastrophe prevented him from writing. "I had a very bad accident—smashed my right hand, rushed the shit out of my fingers, very painful—couldn't write, sleep, shave, fuck, anything. Today is the first day I am off the painkiller and am typing this with my left hand. Not bad—eh? Am working very hard on my next book—supposed to turn it in by Labor Day but no will do. By October probably."

Little really depressed him, though he often made noises about it: "I am in a deep depression today because *Sunday in the Park with Garbage* won the Phew-Litter Prize. Christ, what a yawn. That and the fact that Archbishop O'Connor has been turned into a cardinal by the pope's magic wand really make this a banner day. If everything comes in threes, I can't wait to see what's going to happen tonight."

Psychologists over the decades since Jim Kirkwood wrote his most famous books about dead bodies have come to conclude how memory of a traumatic event may be "unreliable to some degree, whether by failing to remember at all or by remembering incorrectly."

Jim Kirkwood's fictional recall of the discovery of Ben (Reid), and Jordan, a boy named Ted, important people in his life, must be re-read in terms of the possibility his narrators gave clues that the recounted memories, the narration itself, was fraught with distorted facts, a scenario the character—or Jim—recreated to help him deal with the situation he manipulated, far beyond what he encountered.

In the decades before World War II, loss of memory was mostly a theory tied to war experiences, such as shell shock. Not until the Vietnam War did a post-traumatic stress disorder become a recognized condition. The devastating effect of living through incidents or conditions unacceptable to one's mental health might result in the recreation of more tolerable experiences—thus the concept of the "false memory." Lila Lee had, at the time, tried to shield her son, and finally became alarmed at some deeper horror that compelled her to send him away from the scene.

Whatever complications the process of memory create, the situation is complicated by the guise of fictive memory. To use the format of fiction, however autobiographical, always gave Jim the out to avoid telling the truth "under oath." If and when his story became inconsistent or he found himself too closely questioned, he could always bail out of the truth or change the story in any way he wanted. Often under questioning, he altered the printed version to sidestep any uncomfortable issues.

The accuracy of his tale, though written in fictive format, still changed in his verbal retelling, as he allowed in his six play versions, all slightly different from each other and from the novel. In this way his memory was obviously reconstructed and strongly influenced by probing questions. He had a desired outcome to be liked and to be believed. On the other hand, he respected those who could find the loopholes and signposts. It was a dangerous game for a self-proclaimed "danger nut."

In the two central deaths in Jim Kirkwood's novels, the true story is ostensibly described, as he repeatedly insisted to friends. Both true incidents had no witnesses. Jim discovered the bodies alone, and he then provided his own variation on collaborative physical evidence of what happened. The details surrounding these discoveries are not validated, as Jim's physical evidence is questioned or confounded the police, as in the case of Reid Russell.

Though difficult to disprove his contentions, the issue then became his veracity or truthfulness. Alas, in many instances and examples, the characters of Josh and Peter tell fabrications, lies of omission, and white lies. Their credibility, as a witness to a crisis, is compromised, admittedly, by their tendency to distort, to lie, in almost pathological fashion.

Hypnosis can be used to form false memories because this technique can lead to fantasizing and can increase the subjective certainty of fantasy. Jim Kirkwood was certainly under therapy for many years, and he was a sworn advocate of the use of hypnosis to help adjust to unpleasant habits or mental conditions. For an actor, the use of hypnosis can be considered a form of rehearsal, to make an alleged experience (and recounting of the memory) more credible. To relive a trauma, however false, several times makes the brain trick itself into thinking that the rehearsed experience is the actual experience. Thus, future recounting of the event takes upon it an utterly convincing confessional tone.

Jim's constant revision and reliving of the death of Reid Russell, especially by actors and performers, convinced himself of his own version as the years passed. Not only had he the constant rewriting in private of the death of Russell, he had the reliance on the memory of reenactments. From the days after finding the body in 1936, Jim's first performances were re-enactments of the death and posture of Reid's body on the swing. He performed this for press and fellow children of the neighborhood.

Kirkwood performed it in public readings, and in endless play performances that he witnessed and supervised. Each rehearsal with professional actors made his version more acceptable to himself. He could not finally recall anything of the reality of his experience. False memories, according to cognitive psychologists resulted from rehearsal, repetition, and repeated thinking—called visualization—of the false occurrence until it became so ingrained into the brain that it transformed into something comprehensible to the mind of the adolescent.

This moved the bizarre death of Reid into a long-term, highly believable, and convincing memory. By implanting his story about the death of Reid Russell into his own mind by means of staged plays, Jim had experienced the trauma repeatedly. He learned to accept his version as the truth. The incorrectness no longer had any false ring to it for the individual, making him able to function, guilt-free, as it were. One former boyfriend accused him of murdering Reid after experiencing Jim's notorious temper, according to biographer Sean Egan. This rolled off Jim's back as easily as anything else. He was the master of evasion and hypnotized himself to believe whatever the script said.

The two primary cases of finding dead bodies were the hallmark of his first two novels. Not by accident, Jim's original concept for the novels was one super-novel about the Body Finder, himself. Despite the change of names, the anecdotes related in *There Must be a Pony* represented his own false memory that shaped his character.

The first published recollection ("Yes, that's what really happened," he repeatedly told me) was the discovery of Reid Russell, now called Ben, in a novel that he had boiling up in his mind for twenty years. Only in the late 1950s did he have the discipline to tackle the subject. A closer look at the body's discovery by the ostensible fifteen year old (really twelve) may tell more than Jim thought, or exactly what Jim wanted us to think.

Deep emotion content undercoated the new, or false memory. For the most part, the narrator dealt with a horrific moment of great emotional upheaval or turmoil, fear or shock, and so the reaction must fit the situation. Josh noted how, "I can't forget the sensation right then, I had the most terrific impulse to turn around and run back . . . I couldn't even see to where the trees ended because of the fog."

Emotions overwhelmed him, as one might expect. "I didn't know, of course, but I had this unmistakable feeling—that there was something down there." Though a child might be terrified at the prospect of the unknown ahead of him, Josh was unfazed and drawn to the unpleasant scene. What did he remember or what must he explain? Did the boy find himself standing over a dead body and was unable to recall he had shot the man? ". . . the change in the light made me squint and look upwards. The fog wasn't quite as thick as it had been in the grove. It was more dusky-like."

Feelings of psychosis may be also a device spoken by someone with false memory, as it created a situation in which the unbelievable became a keynote. The recounting of the incident cannot be a lie, as it was too incredible. To ask others, "can this really be happening?" played on the falsity, by making the recipients of the lie agree to it in tacit fashion. "I kept watching his face. Although I knew there wouldn't be any reaction, nevertheless, I kept waiting for one. After a while it struck me that the look in Ben's eyes was the same as he'd get when he'd go off into one of those quiet spells of his. When I looked at his eyes I could have sworn he was thinking of something. But when I looked at his mouth, it was too set, the lips too thin and cold and expressionless."

Shock caused a sense of unreality, or heightened reality, and Josh experienced both. "My senses seemed to be more alert than ever before. It was quiet; it was so quiet that the stillness had a sound and I could hear the fog moving slowly . . . everything stood out in sharp, clear focus to my eyes." His fear was palpable, and to deal with the situation of his anxiety, he noted how he must make a "conscious effort" to walk. "I did see an arm hanging down from the end nearest me and the toes of a pair of black shoes pointing out from the far end toward where the dog sat . . . I could feel my stomach constrict; in fact, everything inside me tightened."

The use of vivid examples enhanced his recreated scene in this series of false memories. The exaggeration effect made the experience seem more real to both the teller and the listener. "His face was straight up, and there was a gaping crimson hole to the right side of his forehead, about at the hairline. A coagulated line of blood stretched from there across his cheek to his mouth and on down to his chin, ending up in a cluster in the crook of his neck." The state of disarray bothered him, but "God, even like he was he was still one of the most handsome men you'd ever see. To me he looked like Caesar must have looked after he'd been assassinated." Josh was not frightened. "The whole thing would just about *kill* you, but Ben himself, lying there, wouldn't *frighten* you."

He forced external evidence to fit the situation, imagined or pretended. The artifacts of the death and/or killing were dealt with, however roughly, to explain the new story. "I was perhaps five yards from the hammock." To explain the horror of what had happened, the easiest defense was a note of disbelief experienced by the participant.

A sad plea made the witness sympathetic to his audience. "His eyes were open, staring straight up toward the top of the hammock. He was badly in need of a shave; his chin and the sides of his face were covered with blue stubble. And then I saw the ants. Lots of tiny little ants were crawling around the hole in his temple and around his nose and mouth."

Josh cannot tell whether what he sees is real or imagined. If one experienced such troubling feelings, this dissocializing condition meant lost time must be filled with theories in which the suffering person may understand his situation. It may also indicate a psychosis, an idea at which Jim bristled totally. "I knelt quickly by Ben's shoulder, took the handkerchief from his breast pocket, and brushed the ants away. Instead of getting up, I found myself kneeling there. I was so close to him. I felt the warmth of my breath as it left my mouth. I also sensed that mine was the only warmth; I was getting none back from Ben."

Had Josh kissed Ben? *(Had Jim kissed Reid?)*

"I just knelt there and stared at him, taking it all in. I think I knew to take a good look, as if I were photographing it exactly as it was for all time so that my memory in days and weeks and months to come wouldn't distort the way it *actually* was. If I try to recall my emotions or sensations looking back to that exact moment, it's mainly a feeling of having been hypnotized."

Often in murderous psychotic blackouts an element of "lost time" needs to be accounted for. The memory blackout required the individual, deliberately or unconsciously, fill with the innocent memories and pedestrian story with what he now imagined. Josh complained about his mixed feelings about being drawn to the death scene, "I don't know how long I stood there . . . I felt I was being pulled toward it by some force—almost magnetized. Yet I tried to resist it. Standing there, everything around me seemed to shimmer. And inside my head there was a quivering sensation. Like the chills when you've got a fever. Except they weren't really physical; they were more back behind my nose and eyes and up in my forehead. I don't think I was actually shaking." He cannot leave the scene, and like many people in a state of shock, he seemed unable to determine just how long he lingered at the scene. "I don't know how long I'd been kneeling there when I heard myself saying, 'Oh, Ben, Oh, Jesus, Ben!' over and over, softly, like I was almost bawling him out for being dead."

However long the boy was at the swing, it must have been an exceedingly long time. "I finally stood up, but only because my knees were aching and I was feeling cold and shaky. I kept on looking at Ben because I wanted him to blink his eyes and look over at me and tell me it was a joke. I remember thinking then that I'd have to notify someone . . ." He stayed long enough for the ants to return to the body and climb back up to Ben's face. Only then did he leave. "I must have been down there twenty minutes by that time. I reached over and touched Ben's shoulder with my hand. "So long, Ben" I said. I felt that I'd had my own private farewell with him, I guess."

Certainly in the case of Reid Russell one factor that utterly confused the police was the rearranging of the victim's body. It was unnatural and did not fit the posture and end result of a suicide. Neither did the location of the weapon meet the logistics of a self-inflicted gunshot to the head. When we examine Josh's explanation at finding Ben, we have a better grasp of why the body seemed so out of place. Josh related in his version, "His right arm hung down from the hammock; the fingers of his right hand rested, palm up, on the grass. I took hold of his right arm in order to bring it up and place his right hand on his chest, too, but his arm was stiff. The minute I felt it I let go."

Josh also noted the problem of why the weapon was not where it should have fallen after a self-inflicted bullet wound. "Standing there, I saw the gun for the first time; it was on the grass a little under the hammock, right near where Ben right hand had been touching the ground. It looked familiar . . . I bent over and did a dumb thing—I picked it up. . . . I held it a while; then I put it down on the swing next to Ben's leg."

These feelings found their way into his future story and plot of *A Chorus Line.* "There's an awful lot of my feelings about the business—why you're in it and why you stay in it—in that show." He put his favorite themes into the characters. The success of Pulitzer Prize play finally gave him the freedom and creative control over his own career, but that would not be for many years to come.

In addition to financial security, *A Chorus Line* provided "opportunities I never had before. I'm being asked to write screenplays and scripts. And the funny thing is I really don't know how to write a musical." Years of lack of recognition, cruel treatments, and emptiness made him rail against "mean, vicious critics who use their own wit to attack." He realized too that "I can't go into a tailspin about critics," but his innate sense of justice and his furious temper always snapped. He couldn't keep it in check.

Though some have claimed that professionals as therapists and psychiatrists accidentally implant false memories, the worst-case scenario is the criminal who implants positive memories to cover up his own ill-done deeds. If Jim knew anything about bad memories, he certainly indicated that people with strange and dangerous pasts intrigued him. After a visit to one of the European versions of *A Chorus Line* in late 1987, he wrote: "Just got back from a free trip to Austria, where I was invited to be at the opening of the Viennese company of *ACLine*, which is done in GERMAN and which was very exciting. I spent ten minutes at the opening night party talking to Kurt Waldheim. Very interesting, charming man on the outside. I did not query him about any other questions. Went to Budapest—fascinating to visit but I wouldn't wanna live there, oh, no, it's like 1938 still. Also visited Salzburg, the most beautiful city in the world."

Did Jim Kirkwood have self-interest in creating a false memory by which he chose to live his life? Those who advocate that truth must be uncovered, whatever the cost, may ignore the devastation such genuine recollections may cause. In police cases and court prosecutions, the quest to punish crime-doers is ever vigilant. The pressure to create such a memory that did not happen, or may be misinterpreted, is always a danger to those who want to protect others. How much worse it is for a cold-case crime and criminals who perpetrated their deeds decades ago.

The issue of Jim Kirkwood's fictional accounts of his body discoveries may be partly necessary to keep incriminating information from the readers that could place Josh or Peter's memories in doubt. Jim also raised in each sequence enough self-doubt about the reality of the experience to give him a cloak of secrecy by assuming through trauma that false or repressed memories existed or contributed to any errors in his eyewitness testimony about the bodies of Jordan and Ben.

Jim often hinted at the condition of shock in his narrators as a basis of explaining any inconsistencies that might arise in examination of the details. In both cases, Josh and Peter had lost their primary support base that rendered them isolated. It smacked of the murderer who killed his parents and then pleaded that he is a beleaguered orphan. Jim also liked to turn the tables on anyone who questioned his story by asking whether the "psychosis" could not belong to Peter or Josh, but to the person who doubted them.

One of Jim's consistent falsehoods may have been a jumbled memory. "I don't think I would ever have started to write if I hadn't happened to find five dead bodies at different times between the time I was 14 and 17. The first body I found was a man who was engaged to my mother. I found him in our back yard with a bullet in his head."

Reid was the second body Jim found, according to objective sources. Had he then merely confused the timing? What would cause him to state falsely the order in which he found the bodies? There is always the possibility that he had a hard time keeping track of all the different bodies he came across. It is also clear that he found bodies from age eleven to his early twenties. After that time, he no longer reported on the corpses he uncovered, if any.

Within Jim's letters, I always found an instant familiarity in them for me. Much was coded between us and much was understood. We had a *simpatico* feeling. He certainly said more than once, "Write me a long letter, or I'll kill you." I also sensed and recognized, almost in puzzlement, how much his early stories resembled some of my own writing. Did we share something in syntax and sentence tone? Years later I'd learn how some of my phrases were recycled into his own letters, off to other correspondents, like Herlihy. Was it that feeling in our writings that attracted him? Those recognitions made me feel a kinship to him, a spiritual bond, even if it seemed romanticized, if not downright hokey.

What most amazed me was his time for me. He was constantly busy, constantly writing, or meeting with producers. He'd send me his latest publicity information about how projects were proceeding. "I'm a very busy boy right at the moment as you can tell from the two enclosures."

He wanted and needed reinforcement or approval, which I offered repeatedly. I came to understand that receiving a letter was a tonic for him; by some strange dint of power, a missive sent him into a creative frenzy. He fed off mail, answered with long explanations, and then found himself spinning like a top on his next writing project. I enjoyed seeing his approach from behind the scenes, and he kept me informed of every step. "Enclosed you will find 8 lecture brochures. I know that you will, in turn, do everything within your power to enable me to earn a decent living by aiding and abetting me in setting up a few lectures."

We certainly shared a belief in his Paint Box theory, and I saw it at work in his life. According to Jim, we were all born to paint such pretty pictures and given a little paint box—but in this box, sometimes the brush was missing, the colors were screwed up, and some could not even open the phuquing paintbox. It was this problem that prevented people from achieving their full potential. But he had a big canvas and he was given extra colors, a dozen brushes, and he had the strokes to do a mural of life.

I was his Bagboy in the Supermarket of Literature—and I never put the heavy stuff on top. I always packed his paint cans and his brushes neatly. He did not want a biography, yet he was intensely interested in everything written or said about him. "Lotsa my friends think your article was/is the best ever written about me and I gotta whole scrapbook full of things."

I once told him I was going to write about the cruel joke played by God on famous people by having a curse put on them. The more famous and creative they were, the likelier they'd be visited by a horrid mythological person who'd condemn them to a cruel fate. I mentioned the Wandering Jew—a legend about a man who slapped Jesus and told him to hurry to his death. For that he was condemned to wander the earth forever. Since Jim had met everyone I ever mentioned in late twentieth century film and stage, I threw in the Wandering Jew. "Oh, I met him too." Anyone who met the Wanderer ended up being cursed too. Jim thought he had met him somewhere along the way and left it for me to figure out how and where. "Curses Schmurses," he scoffed.

I saw the Big Joker's cruelty: Jim had been struck down at his chance for a great creative period. His fate left me angry for the longest time . . . that this man nearly at a time of his long-deserved success should be so badly treated by life and the rats in life—that his efforts were so delineated in his narrative about the final play tour. "At any rate, I finally finished *Diary of a Mad Playwright*, which is the book on Mary and Carol and *Legends*. It turned out to be 643 pages and I had to cut out about 200 pages, which I have just now done."

Something had snapped inside him. He was now reckless in a way that made me suspicious about his health. "I think you'll find *Diary of a Mad Playwright* quite amusing. I hope I don't get my ass sued off. But then any publicity is good, I suppose."

Now he began in earnest, under the gun of failing health, to finish his last important book. He told me several times of its importance and its high quality. After numerous delays he forged ahead "on that little baby and loving working on it. I know you will like it." With excerpts from the original *Pony* story, Jim now planned to turn it into a third novel out of the edited materials from the first two autobiographical books.

Though it might seem he had started the work years earlier, the vision to write about his father belonged to his earliest plans. He only carried it out years too late. He told me how he was "working on *I Teach Flying*. Came down here with 140 pages and I'm leaving for NYC next Wednesday with 452 pages. I have about another 200 to go. I'm loving writing it. It's so good to be back in the world of the novel where one has total control, instead of the theatre where it tends to be like Vietnam." The detour of the *Legends* play and the subsequent book kept him from finishing his final great novel. In his last report to me, he said: "I am also way into *I Teach Flying* about 492 pages." In essence he stopped with about two-thirds done. It was not to be published.

When the floodgates opened, the crap came down upon him. He seemed to know instinctively that it would . . . the peak of his success literally killed him, whether it was a bad book tour or a bad play tour. He fought it endlessly with optimism and good humor. He forgave me for doubting him, and he encouraged me to dig deeper into his text. We had text between us at every chance. Unprotected text. Kinky-dinky text. I gave him textual evidence, and he ate it up. After all, he was a Danger Nut.

Unlike the mythic little boy who met the tiger, I had the tiger by the tail and I did not dare let go lest he turn around and gobble me up. He scared the bejesus out of me more often than not. We jousted endlessly about his unreliable narrators, those voices couldn't tell whether they dreamed they murdered someone, or had done it. After all passing years, I suspected Jim could not determine what was real about the case.

So often I declined his invitations to visit—and perhaps he suspected that I had developed a growing fear of his temper and his potential danger. It probably hurt him more than not: "When you come to town, kindly let me know beforehand so I could take you for a drink or a dinner or a drink afterwards. I don't know where I'm going to be in May, but I should be in town about half the time." He invited me to plays, to dinner, to visit East Hampton, Manhattan, Key West, and I always came up with an excuse. He wanted my support—and I failed him.

Jim would tell me he'd "be down in Palm Beach during that run so if you get down there, call up the theatre and ask if I'm around. They will know." I most regret that I did not take him up on his offer to go on a book tour. He said he hated going alone, and there was no one to go with him. How I kick myself today for not taking him up. Yet, as years passed, I became more and more concerned about our Cat and Mouse games. At first, I was challenging a celebrity author, but I began to suspect that I was playing games with a potential serial killer. He frightened me—and I began to see myself as the overmatched mouse.

He was hurt and puzzled by the fact that I thought Josh and Peter not only were capable of murder—but might have genuinely killed people. When I tried to pin him down on the nuances of the crimes, he'd scurry away, rewriting his books and changing the characters' dialogue before my eyes. It was like Jack the Ripper flashing his knives at me and hurrying off to keep an appointment with that old hooker at the local street-corner. "Even the police could see that Josh was absolutely devastated by the death of Ben." He insisted, however different the novel or play was from his memory of it. He used Manhattan Beach and Paraiso Beach interchangeably in our conversations; one was the real place where Reid met his end, and the other was the location where Ben Nichols died. He talked about Ben at Manhattan Beach frequently.

What chance had I of solving anything? I had no *habeas corpus*. I didn't have a warrant. I tried to indict all those dangerous narrators with their own text. "You confuse me when you say you don't believe Josh or Peter." His charming characters inspired faith and trust in readers—except the mad hares like me. He warned me repeatedly that I was misjudging the innocent, "Try to keep your hands off the Easter Bunny, Billy-boy,"

Did Josh shoot Ben? Did Jimmy shoot Reid Russell, or did his mother, Lila Lee, kill the young companion? Jim Kirkwood never did give me a direct answer to the question because I never had the courage to ask him directly if he shot Reid. He said, "Everyone could see the boy (Josh) was upset by the death . . ." or he'd beg off. "I can't talk about that now. Suffice it to say I am right and you are wrong." The comment avoided the question, almost as much as I avoided asking. He was not sympathetic to Reid. "If you're going to kill yourself, you should go off somewhere by yourself, instead of doing it that close to people you supposedly love."

Did Peter go bonkers and kill Jordan when he found out about the book Jordan was writing on him? "Jordan wasn't writing a book on Peter." But I pointed out that the scraps of paper showed that to be the case. "No, Jordan wasn't capable of writing a book," or so he responded. "Peter is telling the truth. He killed Mr. Hoyt but he was forced into it because of Hoyt's more-or-less temporary insanity and his relentless pursuit of Peter. If you think Peter committed the perfect crime under the guise of this—then you are psychotic. I am Peter (or was) and I know what happened or would have happened."

Friends accused me of disloyalty—and worse—when I raised the theory Jim may have done Reid in during one of those childhood lapses. Reid Russell was such a puzzle, yet the ties between the boy and his mother's lover seemed fragile, potentially more explosive than would normally be expected. It made me wonder if Reid Russell were an archetypal pedophile, stalking the hero in every Kirkwood novel as a minor anecdotal figure, usually in the shadows of flashback cameo, a throwaway encounter.

Would the son be more inclined to protect his mother in a crime of passion—or would the mother be more inclined to protect her son? Others claimed Jim saw me as a literary critic and played me to the hilt. He made me a device or alibi, whatever seemed more appropriate. I knew that could not be true from what he had said and how he treated me. No, in our hearts, both his and mine, he knew I would write that book on him in due time—and he wanted me to do it, expected me to pull out the scalpels, and let it rip. "You know what you need to keep doing."

Heaven help me if I were planning to write a book about him . . . at least he made noises that way in the beginning. When Dotson Rader, a friend of Tennessee Williams and Jim from Key West, wrote a kiss-and-tell expose about the great playwright, Jim was incensed. I feared for Dotson Rader's safety when Kirkwood became so wound up. "Friends don't do that," he warned me. If I knew too much, I knew Too Much. He filled me with clues and he expected me to draw a conclusion and share it only with him. I was his personal detective, and he was my "personal crazy author friend."

"Oh, there are little signposts in my books for those who can see them," he giggled at me, as he said he wished he could have met serial killer Ted Bundy.

If I were to accuse him of murder, that charge was the aphrodisiac binding us together. Was I the only one who thought he might kill someone? Was I the only one who dared to suggest it to him? We were like two characters in the play *Rope*—laughing and enjoying the moment of murder, until the body went limp. Every conversation with him was a tonic, bubbly champagne that always left with a little hangover. We were having a clandestine affair of *belles-lettres*.

He called me the District Attorney more than once, and it was funny in one way. He was the star witness on the stand—and I was like Ham Burger, Perry Mason's nemesis, always on the verge of solving the case—but confounded by the lying witness. And, how Jimmy Kirkwood loved murder cases and trials. The highpoint of his acting career must have been the time he appeared on the *Alfred Hitchcock Presents* television show. And how he loved to tweak the truth.

Who was that little old lady he met at a party who said the age of the perfect murder was over? Had she really killed all her husbands? Did he take that as a challenge to prove the perfect murder was alive and well? At least in his books he did . . .

He let me know that no one knew more about his writing than I did, "When you get that phuquing doctorate, does that mean you can perform a free lobotomy on me? But I am so proud of you." He made me regret more and more as the years passed that I did not take him up on his offer to come down to New York and help him solve whatever problems might come up with the plays . . . but deep down I worried about him. *He* worried me.

In fact, he terrified me frequently because sometimes I could see those dark clouds in his demeanor forming before my eyes. He was not a person with whom to trifle. If you were on his A-list, the world was your oyster. If he relegated you to the other list, look out. He once said, after he tangled with people, they never again called him "Jimmy. It was always Jim," thereafter. Sometimes I called him "Jimbo," and he seemed to like that. He could charm the birds out of the trees, and he could practice taxidermy on them too.

He said he'd murder me dozens of times and in dozens of ways, and it almost became like saying, "I love you," but instead he said, "I'll kill you." It was funny and nasty at the same time. I think he did love me in a manner, and it surprised me always. I was in awe of his audacity. What a strange relationship we had. He always had time for me, "I hope you know how to stuff a turkey and stuff it well. And as you stuff it—do think of me." He flattered me with attention, and he gave me more than I deserved or asked for. He said with that leer often, "You little devil."

I didn't mean to hurt his feelings when I grew suspicious, but do friends let friends get away with murder, in a manner of speaking? I suppose they do, or they would not be worthy accessories to the latest serial fad. He told me it was the duty of friends to tell the actor or the writer the dirty little news of critics. So, I'd read him movie and theater reviews on the phone, or I'd send him "CIA packets" when he gave me little assignments to research. "How much does it cost to have a Boston mobster bump off someone?" or, "Find out the name and address of this high school teacher who was fired for assigning his students *P.S. Your Cat is Dead.*"

In suburban Boston a junior high school teacher was in all kinds of hot water for teaching the most kinky cult novel Jim wrote. Jim and I talked about it on the phone while the story blasted over local news and made it into the national gay newspapers. We agreed the story was simply inappropriate for twelve year olds. I did my research job and sent him all the key information he required. He told me, "I've just written to the teacher you put me on to, as it were, by letter, this very day. I am looking forward to hearing from him in the event my letter hasn't thrown him into a total dilemma. He might feel he would be burned as a witch if word got out that he'd been contaminated by anything with my personal signature on it."

When I finished my duty and submitted all he needed in the way of information, I heard, "Thank you so much for the CIA packet. I'm going to be writing that fortunate or unfortunate teacher today. It will be interesting to see what he has to say about the entire matter. Well, we'll just have to wait and see."

Kirkwood could suck the air out of a room. He was an actor and knew all the tricks of staging and performing. "You're also right about Jimmy Zoole's credits. A lot of them are mine, especially the tackier ones." He enjoyed talking about his work, and rationalizing some of his stranger details, "I'll tell you how and I did certain things over a scotch or a vodka whatever."

I think I understood why James Leo Herlihy wouldn't do another play with him. I knew and instinctively felt why Herlihy needed to be away from Jimmy more often than not. Jimmy Kirkwood was overwhelming once he started in. He was unrelenting and powerful, a true creative force of the universe. "I'm sorry about my English and this messy letter but you gotta understand a sick person is writing it. God, I hate to be incapacitated. Hate it." He was only happy when he could write, create, and recreate.

Few seemed to understand that he was as heady as that darling of intellectual critics who wrote *Lolita* and other witty novels, Vladimir Nabokov, playing chess with reader and audience. There were three levels of pawns and knights on his board. Look out for the black queen. He played a mean game. In his weird penmanship, he'd scrawl on the bottoms of letters, or on the margins, or on the envelope, "P.S. I can't imagine what textual evidence you have found for your theory." But I gave him the game he wanted: "Checkmate, Billy-boy . . . and you know what to keep teaching."

Once during a debate on *Good Times/Bad Times*, so complicated with the author of the text, I forgot simply the name of the advisor to the Glee Club. That filled him with such glee that it was a point he wouldn't let me forget again: "It was Mr. Kauffman, Mr. Kauffman, Mr. Kauffman," and he stuck out his tongue at me.

Herlihy said to me after Jim's peaceful death, "So. We should all be so lucky?" When I think how hard it has been and what void there is since his passing, his words echo again and again in my mind. I hear him saying, "The only possible way to get through a day is to face life with optimism—no matter the obstacles. If there is one thing you should cultivate, it's a sense of humor. If you don't have one, do anything to get one: buy one. Borrow one! Steal one! That's the springboard that will get you over the hurdles."

Herlihy added in commiseration, that he needed more than I did, "I'm sorry you're feeling the loss of 'something vital.' I know how that is; I'm in the same pickle. But there's always plenty to laugh about, one of Jimmy's most important bequests. He was as you know compulsively entertaining and maybe when all is said and done that's what I miss most." In retrospect, I should have tried to maintain some connection to Herlihy—especially when I think of his horrid end, but after Jim was gone, I felt bereft.

Nowadays when I sit on a lawn swing on a lovely summer's day, a nagging thought remains with me: I see a twelve-year old boy with the dead body of his mother's boyfriend, but more than that—I see a child who is at a loss with his own and only most important friend. Novel, play, movie, it never exorcised the demon that lived inside James Kirkwood.

Writing a book about Jimmy Kirkwood has not exorcised *my* demon.

One of the last comments Jim made to me rings in my head. Not long before he died, he requested plaintively in a letter, "Keep teaching me." At first reading, I smiled, thinking it was a joke, and then after he died, I realized it was his last important message to me. In his last messages to me the juice was gone from his tone. In its stead was a kind of sadness as he tried to make me laugh, "You better keep on teaching me and make students buy the books." During his last year, he said this to me several times. There was something desperate in his need to know he'd not be forgotten. His comments made me laugh then, but now seem to me to be a plaintive cry. He threatened me repeatedly with that twinkle of delight: "You better keep on teaching my books or I'll get you."

When I last heard from James Leo Herlihy, he sent such warm regards, "It's so like Jimmy to say, 'Keep teaching me.' By the way I've found I can still have lively chats with Jimmy any time I want to. I'll bet you can too."

Yes, I still talk with James Kirkwood.

Well, Jim, you are probably exasperated with me for writing this book. Yes, I know. I hear your words now.

"Wait till I get my hands around your throat, I will make everything perfectly clear to you . . . you will be shot at sunrise, disemboweled on the Boston Common, etc., etc . . . and I will have a wild gypsy lady I know up there read your entrails."

Oh, Jim, though I still teach you, it's not the same anymore. Rather, it's you, Jim, you who teaches me every day. And I have learned so much since you went away. It changes nothing in my estimate of you.

Oh, now I can hear you laughing and teasing: *"Yeah, but how does that help ME? And what in bejesus took you so phuquing long to write the damn book?"*

You're always Too Much! After long thought, I am convinced now that you did find that pony amidst the horseshit around us . . . and for that I feel tremendous happiness for you.

"Well, Billy-boy-bub, in life one has to look for the goodies they hand out—you have to savor a sunset, a good set of tennis, an hour talking to a good friend, someone

you'd tell anything to—a hot fudge sundae. There will always be bad news, but I think we're here to get the through tough times, to survive."

Thank you for everything, dear Jim . . . Jimbo . . . Jimmy . . .

The last words you ever wrote to me reverberate: *"I send all sorts of embraces to my trusty spy and hope that you had a terrific time molesting the Easter Bunny. Love, your very own obedient author friend, xoxoxoxox, Jim."*

SOURCES

CHAPTER ONE

"Featured Author: J.D.Salinger," *Boston Globe*, July 8, 1980. Kirkwood, James. Interviews, conversations, letters, publicity materials, personal messages.

CHAPTER TWO

"12 year old son of Lila Lee Finds Body," *Chronicle Telegram*. Nov. 14, 1936, p 1.
"Author Objects to Murder Probe Quizzing," *Zanesville Signal*. Nov. 24, 1936, p. 14.
"Author, Wife Questioned on Strange Death," *Sheboygan Press*. Nov. 14, 1936. p.4.
"Death Mystery Surrounds Writer," *Kingston Daily Freeman*. Nov. 17, 1936, p 2.
"Death Scene on Author's Estate to be Acted Out," *Fresno Bee*. Nov. 14, 1936, p. A-2.
"House Guest's Suicide Draws Attention," *Mexia Weekly Herald*. Nov. 20, 1936. p. 2.
"Hunt In Vain for Slain Russell's Death Clothing," *Hammond Times*, Nov. 23, 1936, p. 4.
"Hunt Missing Gun in Taylor Inquiry." *New York Times*. May 8, 1937, p. 7.
"Investigate Slaying at Beach House of Gouverneur Morris. *Syracuse Herald*, Nov. 10, 1936, p. 1.
"Investigators Reconstruct Russell Death Scene," *Reno Evening Gazette*. Nov. 18, 193. p.8
"Jury Acts as Russell Death Baffles Police," *Hammond Times*, Nov. 20, 1936, p. 2.
"Los Angeles Police will Attempt to Determine if Reid Russell Committed Suicide or was Slain," *Kansas City Star*. Nov. 15, 1936, p A-4
"Mock Suicide to be Enacted," *Charleston Daily Mail*. Nov. 16, 1936, p.2.
"Morris to Bar Death Probers from Estate," *Oakland Tribune*. Nov. 24, 1936, p. 18,.
"Mrs. Gouverneur Morris Burned Notes Left By Friend found Shot on Her Lawn," *Syracuse Herald*. Nov. 15, 1936, p. 13.
"Murder or Suicide Answer Sought," *Brainerd Daily Dispatch*. Nov. 21, 1936, p. 1.
"Murder or Suicide Riddle in coast Death," *Williamsport Gazette and Bulletin*. Nov. 20, 1936, p 12.

"MurderTheory Explored in Mystery Death," *PortArthur News*. Nov. 17, 1936, p. 1.
"Mystery Death of Salesman Riddle for Police," *Newark Advocate*. Nov. 19, 1936, p. 1.
"Mystery Deepens in Reid Russell Death," *Dunkirk Evening Observer*. Nov. 23, 1936, p 2.
"Lila Lee and Beach Guests at Santa Cruz," *Oakland Tribune*. July 3, 1935. p D-3
"Original Report of Reid Suicide Stands." *Ironwood Daily Globe*. Nov. 20, 1936. p. 1.
"Plan Investigation of Russell's Private Life," *Oshkosh Northwestern*. Nov. 17, 1936, p.3.
"Playmakers Entertained at two parties," *Chronicle Telegram*. Feb. 20, 1939, p.6.
"Police Make Gun Test in Reid Russell Death," *New York Times*. Nov. 17, 1936, p. 7.
Kirkwood, James. *There Must Be a Pony*. Galley proof copy. 1960.
Kirkwood, James. Interviews, conversations, letters, publicity materials, personal messages.
Dennis, Jan. *A Walk Beside the Sea: a History of Manhattan Beach*. 1987.

CHAPTER THREE

"Author Denies Youth Shot in House," *Fresno Bee*. Nov. 14, 1936, p. 1
"Beach Killing Held Suicide." *Los Angeles Times*. Sept. 27, 1936, p B16
"Boy's Story Spurs Suicide Investigation," *Hammond Times*. Nov. 18, 1936, p 26.
"Continue Quiz in Russell Death," *Hammond Times*. Nov. 20, 1936, p 12.
"Crime Comes Back," *Charleston Daily Mail*. Nov. 21, 1936, p. 1.
"Day's News," *Stevens Point Daily Journal*. Nov. 21, 1936, p 10.
"Death is Called Murder in Disguise," *Charleston Gazette*. Nov. 20, 1936, p 26.
"Death Last Night," *Kingston Daily Freeman*. April 20, 1939, p. 8
"Death of Writer's Friend Held Suicide," *Oakland Tribune*. Dec. 12, 1936, p C-3.
"Finds Russell Death Gun Not Fired in Weeks," *Hammond Times*. Nov. 18, 1936, p. 2.
"Five Play Major Role in Probe of Mystery Death on Author's Estate," *Chronicle Telegram*. Nov. 17, 1936.
"Freedom by Decree," *Oakland Tribune*. July 2, 1935, p 18.
"Girl Rescues James Kirkwood," *New York Times*. July 3, 1938, p. 12.
"Gouverneur Morris Art Stolen," *New York Times*. Oct. 22, 1938, p. 34.
"Gouverneur Morris, Novelist." *New York Times*. Aug. 15, 1953, p. 15.
"Inquiry Asinine, Charges Morris." *Hammond Times*. Nov. 24, 1936, p. 7.
"Involved in Murder Case," *Edwardsville Intelligencer*. Nov. 17, 1936. p. 1.
"Lila Lee Sees Son after Three Year Absence," *Nevada State Journal*.
"Lila Lee to seek divorce," *Nevada State Journal*. May 17, 1935, p. 1

"Lila Lee Wed to Broker," *New York Times.* Aug. 31 1944, p. 15.

"Lila Lee Will be at Lake Pier," *Newark Advocate.* Aug. 2, 1938, p.11.

"Lila Lee, Actress, Granted Divorce." *Nevada State Journal.* July 2, 1935, p. 1.

"May Exhume Morris Lawn Death Victim," *Syracuse Herald.* Nov. 17, 1936, p. 5.

"Morris Denies Shot Fired Inside Home," *Hammond Times.* Nov. 16, 1936, p 1.

"Morris Lawn Shooting to be Reenacted," *Syracuse Herald.* Nov. 14, 1936, p. 2.

"Morris Quizzed in Death Case," *Oakland Tribune.* Nov. 15, 1936, p. 10.

"Morris to show bank book," *Oakland Tribune.* May 16, 1936. D-3.

"Mother Reopens Death Case," *Gettysburg Times.* Nov. 18, 1936, p3.

"Mystery Deepens in Youth's Death," *Times Herald.* Nov. 20, 1936, p. 1.

"Mystery in suicide Case," *Nevada State Journal.* Nov. 21, 1936, p. 1.

"Novelist and Wife Tell of Mystery," *Frederick Post.* Nov. 15, 1936, p.6

"Novelist Dies in New Mexico," *Modesto Bee.* Aug. 14, 1953, p. 8.

"Novelist is Annoyed over Inquiry," *Hammond Times.* Nov. 14, 1936, p. 2.

"Novelist to Appear in the Russell Case," *New York Times.* Nov. 14, 1936, p. 2.

"Obituary: Mrs. Gouverneur Morris," *New York Times.* April 20, 1939, p 23

"Police Reconstruct Mystery Killing On Gouverneur Morris Estate," *Syracuse Herald.* November 27, 1936, p. XX.

"Police Reconstruct Mystery Killing," *Syracuse Herald.* Nov. 17, 1936, p.1.

"Police Search for Bullet on Morris Estate," *Middletown Times Herald.* Nov. 16, 1936, p. 3.

"Probe Financial Affairs of Dead Motor Salesman," *Dunkirk Evening Observer.* Nov. 20, 1936, p. 8.

"Probe of Death Mystery Re-Opened: Lila Lee Questioned," *Nevada State Journal.* Nov. 24, 1936, p. 1.

"Query Stirs Mystery," *Los Angeles Times.* Nov. 19, 1936, p. 3.

"Reid Russell's Body May be Dug Up Again," *Helena Daily Independent.* Nov. 19, 1936, p. 2.

"Russell Death Garb Found," *Los Angeles Times.* Nov. 22, 1936, p. 11

"Russell Death Gun Not Fired in Weeks," *Hammond Times.* Nov. 18, 1936, p. 2.

"Russell Death Now seen as Love Slaying," *Syracuse Herald.* Nov. 18, 1936 p.13.

"Russell Mystery," *Helena Daily Independent.* Nov. 20, 1936, p. 4.

"Russell's Death to be Enacted," *New York Times.* Nov. 15, 1936, p.46.

"Screen Actress on way to Reno for Divorce," *Reno Evening Gazette.* May 17, 1935, p. 2.

"Search Estate for Death Slug," *Times Herald.* Nov. 16, 1936, p. 1.

"Second Mystery Death is Probed by Officials," *Charleston Gazette,* Nov. 19, 1936, p 5.

"Strange Death of Russell is Still Puzzling Police," *Helena Daily Independent.* Nov. 17, 1936, p. 6.

"Service for C.P. Von Herzen." *The News.* April 18, 1975. p. 3-A

"Strange Killing in California is Put Under probe," *Helena Daily Independent.* Nov.14, 1936, p.6.

"Study of body Fails to Help Russell Probe," *Oakland Tribune.* Nov. 29, 1936, p.2.

"Suicide Bet Explained by Author's Wife," *Syracuse Herald.* Nov.17, 1936, p. 12.

"Tells of Russell Party," *Daily Courier.* Nov. 27, 1936, p. 5.

"To Exhume Russell Body," *New York Times.* Nov. 17, 1936, p. 12.

"To Probe Private Affairs of Slain Man at Los Angeles." *Stevens Point Daily Journal.* Nov. 18, 1936, p. 2.

"Too Much Publicity Rapped in Death Probe," *Charleston Daily Mail.* Nov. 19, 1936, p. 18.

"Two Writers Sail for South Seas," *Oakland Tribune.* May 16, 1928, p. 40.

"Wager by Novelist's wife enters Death Probe," *Kansas City Star.* Nov.14, 1936, p. 1

"Wife of Writer Collapses," *Coshocton Tribune.* Nov. 18, 1936, p. 6

"Writer's Guest is Shot," *Kansas City Star.* Sept. 26, 1936, p. 3.

Dennis, Jan. *A Walk Beside the Sea: a History of Manhattan Beach.* 1987.

Fleming, E.J. *The Fixers :Eddie Mannix, Howard Strickling, and the MGM Publicity Machine.* 2005.

Kirkwood, James. Interviews, conversations, letters, publicity materials, personal messages with author.

Kirkwood, James. *There Must Be a Pony.* 1960.

Kirkwood, James. Archives, Howard Gottlieb Special Collection, Boston University.

CHAPTER FOUR

"Call Me Madam Opening," *Newport News.* June 30, 1953, p. 18.

"Clyde Plummer," *New York Times.* Sept. 17, 1947, p. 25.

"EHS Grad Has Made Good," *Chronicle Telegram.* Feb. 26, 1978. p. D-2.

"Hospital News," *Chronicle Telegram.* Aug. 26, 1958.

"James Kirkwood in Junior Miss," *New York Times.* Jan. 18, 1943, p. 18.

"James Kirkwood, Jr. Now in Movies," *Chronicle Telegram.* Aug. 28, 1942, p 2.

"Lila Lee Back in Movies after Rest." *Charleston Daily Star.* April 24, 1932, p. 6.

"Lila Lee Scores Again After Long Illness." *Zanesville Signal.* May 21, 1957, p.8.

"Lila Lee's Mother Dies," *New York Times.* Nov. 25, 1940, p. 21

"Thumping Hometown Welcome," *Chronicle Telegram.* Apr. 27, 1978, B-1.

Bishop, Jim. "Story that took 25 years to write," *Chronicle Telegram.* Feb. 5, 1960, p. 30.

Egan, Sean. Interview, discussion.

Gover, Jack. "Small Player," *Waterloo Sunday Courier.* Nov. 28, 1948, p 40

Kilgallen, Dorothy. "Broadway Bulletin Board," *Pottstown Mercury,* Apr. 24, 1948, p.6.

Kilgallen, Dorothy. "Gossip in Gotham," *Lowell Sun.* March 28, 1945. p. 37.

Kirkwood, James. Interviews, conversations, letters, publicity materials, personal messages.

Kirkwood, James. Archives, Howard Gottlieb Special Collection, Boston University.

Kirsch, Robert. "Tapping the Rich Salinger Vein," *Los Angeles Times,* Oct. 14, 1960, B5.

Kleiner, Dick. "Jekyll Hyde of Show Business," *Austin Daily Herald,* Jan. 11 1954, p. 24.

Othman, Frederick. "Kirkwood Tries Film Comeback," *Coshocton Times,* Sept. 14, 1941. p 8,.

Parsons, Louella. "Hollywood." *Middletown, N.Y., Times News.* Feb. 15, 1949, p. 16.

Winchell, Walter. "In New York," *Charleston Daily Mail.* Jan. 25, 1953, p.7.

CHAPTER FIVE

"Broadway Role," *New York Times.* June 11, 1962, p. 37.

"Teenage Costar for Myrna Loy," *Eagle Gazette.* June 11, 1962, p.3.

Brown, Jared. *Alan Pakula.* 2001.

Esterow, Milton. "News of the Rialto," *New York Times.* May 6, 1962, p. 143.

Glover, William. "Summer Theatre Season Opens," *Show Tim.,* May 27, 1962, p. 11

Heimer, Mel. "New York," *Lancaster Eagle Gazette.* July 19, 1962, p8.

Herlihy, James Leo. Correspondence with author.

Hopper, Hedda. "Lucy Well Again, Reading Scripts," *Los Angeles Times.* Aug. 25, 1961, p. B5

Kandel, Myron. "Starry Summer Trail," *New York Times.* June 17, 1962, p. 85.

Keating, John. "Broadway at Work," *New York Times.* June 10, 1962, p. 111.

Kerr, Walter. "UTBU Sad Waste of Nervous Energy," *New York Times.* Jan. 6, 1966, p. E11

Kilgallen, Dorothy. "Around New York," *Mansfield News Journal.* Oct. 23, 1961. p. 11.

Kirkwood, James. Interviews, conversations, letters, publicity materials, personal messages.

Kirkwood, James. "Author's Notes," *Legends.* Samuel French, Inc. 1987.

Kirkwood, James. Archives, Howard Gottlieb Special Collection, Boston University.

Lane, Lydia. "Don't Cry for Youth," *Oakland Tribune.* Aug. 19, 1962, S-5.

Loy, Myrna and James Kotsilibas. *Myrna Loy.*

Loy, Myrna. Archives, Howard Gottlieb Special Collection, Boston University.

Scheuer, Philip. "They All Like Myrna on Stage," *Los Angeles Times.* Dec. 5, 1966, p. D29.

Schumach, Murray. "Child of Hollywood." *New York Times.* Sept. 11, 1960, BR53.

Springer, John. "Myrna Loy: Great Movie Stars." *Screen Stories.* Dec., 1962. pp. 48-49.

Zolotow, Sam. "Broadway Bound Connelly Play to Open," *New York Times,* May 16, 1962, p. 34.
Zolotow, Sam. "Myrna Loy Plans to star on Stage," *New York Times,* Sept. 28, 1961, p. 50.

CHAPTER SIX

"Director of Video Dramas Signed," *New York Times.* July 22, 1963, p 18.
Carroll, Margaret. "Macabre Teen Memories Still Alive," *Chronicle Telegram.* Apr. 12, 1977, p D-1.
Connolly, Mike. "Notes from Hollywood." *Pasadena Star News,* Sept. 3, 1964, p 9
Driscoll, Marjorie. "Death of a Schoolmaster," *Los Angeles Times.* Dec. 8, 1968, p. Q63
Erino, Gary. "2nd Novel Draws Critics Applause," *Chronicle Telegram.* Dec. 18, 1968, p. B-1
Herlihy, James Leo. Correspondence with author.
Herlihy, James Leo. Archives, Howard Gottlieb Special Collection, Boston University.
Kirkwood, James. Interviews, conversations, letters, publicity materials, personal messages.
Kirkwood, James. *American Grotesque.* 1970.
Kirkwood, James. Archives, Howard Gottlieb Special Collection, Boston University.
Russo, William. "James Kirkwood." *In Touch.* Feb., 1978.
Soanes, Wood. "Curtain Calls," *Oakland Tribune,* Nov. 29, 1948, p D-15.
Thomas, Bob. "Unlikely Prospect in Big Film Success," *Lima News.* May 9, 1957, B-6.
Wilson, Earl. "It Happened Last Night," *Reno Evening Gazette,* March 26, 1963, p. 2.
Wilson, Earl. "Men are Scared to Death," *Lima News,* July 27, 1962, p. 3.
Wilson, Earl. "Ohio on Broadway," *Lima News.* April 3, 1962, p.8.

CHAPTER SEVEN

"Autobiographical Novelist," *Weekend Times.* Dec. 9, 1972. p 23.
"Novelist Does Film on Mother," *New York Times,* Aug. 25, 1974, p. 87
Curie, Glenne. "Rap with chorus Line Author." *Derry Herald.* March 3, 1978, section 2.
Guthmann, Edward. "Back on the Line," *In Touch.* Oct. 10, 1989.
Hannibal, Jack. Correspondence with author.
Kelly, Kevin. "Aunt Peg as a Drug Pusher . . . ." *Boston Globe.* May 4, 1980 Section: Arts/Film.

Kelly, Kevin. *One Singular Sensation: the Michael Bennett Story.*

Kirkwood, James. *American Grotesque.*

Kirkwood, James. Interviews, conversations, letters, publicity materials, personal messages.

Kirkwood, James. Archives, Howard Gottlieb Special Collection, Boston University.

Kirkwood, James. "Changing Muses in Midstream," *Playbill.* pp. 5-10.

Mandelbaum, Ken. *A Chorus Line and the Musicals of Michael Bennett.*

Martin, Betty. "Film rights for Good Times/Bad Times," *Los Angeles Times.* Aug. 22, 1968, p G21.

Raidy, William. "Actor Writes a Court Saga," *Herald American,* Dec. 27, 1970. p 3.

Russo, William. "PS Your Cat is Dead," *Theatre Review.* p. 363.

Seiler, Michael. "Joan Hackett, Noted for Film and TV Roles, Dies." *Los Angeles Times.*

Viagas, Robert, Baayork Lee and Thommie Walsh. *On the Line: the Creation of A Chorus Line.*

Wang, Li-Ling. "John Stix, Julliard." *Julliard News.* Oct. 5, 2004. p. 1

Wilson, Earl. "3 Burglaries Equal One Broadway Hit," *Daily Intelligencer.* June 10, 1978, p. 18.

CHAPTER EIGHT

"Heart to Heart with Liz & R.J." *People Weekly.* pp. 106-111.

"NBC Wins," *Post Standard.* Oct. 9, 1986, p. B-4.

"Up Front," *People Weekly.* pp. 24-27.

Baker, Kathryn. "Wagner Brings Kirkwood Novel to Small Screen," *Chronicle Telegram.* Oct. 5, 1986, D-4.

Herlihy, James Leo. Archives, Howard Gottlieb Special Collection, Boston University.

Jewell, Shannon. "Channing and Martin are Stars of Legendary C-T." *Chronicle Telegram.* April 2, 1986.

Jewell, Shannon. "Kirkwood Down on Hollywood." *Chronicle Telegram.* March 14, 1982, p 12-C.

Jewell, Shannon. "Stars Come Out," *Chronicle Telegram.* July 3, 1992. p. 28.

Jewell, Shannon. "TV News." *Chronicle Telegram.* June 10, 1989, C-4.

Kirkwood, James. *Diary of a Mad Playwright.* 1989.

Kirkwood, James. Interviews, conversations, letters, publicity materials, personal messages.

Kirkwood, James. Archives, Howard Gottlieb Special Collection, Boston University.

Levy, Ellen. "Movie update," *Intelligencer Record,* Oct. 5, 1986.

Roebuck, Karen. *Los Angeles Times.* Nov 9, 1986. p. 1

Wagner, Robert. Interview with Author.

Walsh, Gordon. "Pony Can't Get out of Starting Gate," *Daily Herald*. Oct. 3, 1986, p. 6-1.

CHAPTER NINE

Kirkwood, James. Interviews, conversations, letters, publicity materials, personal messages.
Kirkwood, James. Archives, Howard Gottlieb Special Collection, Boston University.

CPSIA information can be obtained at www.ICGtesting.com
Printed in the USA
LVOW040227090112

262966LV00002B/5/A